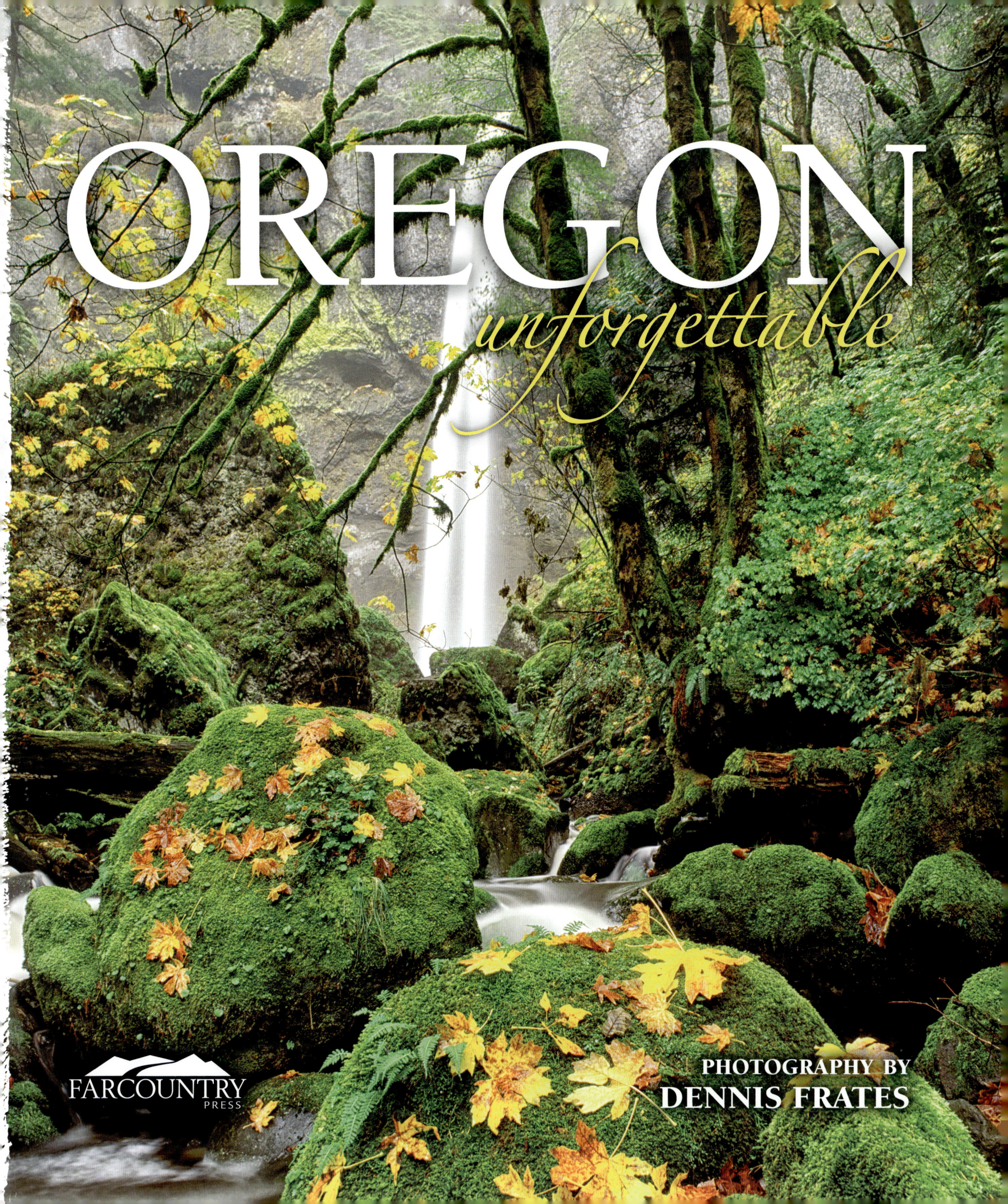
OREGON
unforgettable

PHOTOGRAPHY BY
DENNIS FRATES

FARCOUNTRY PRESS

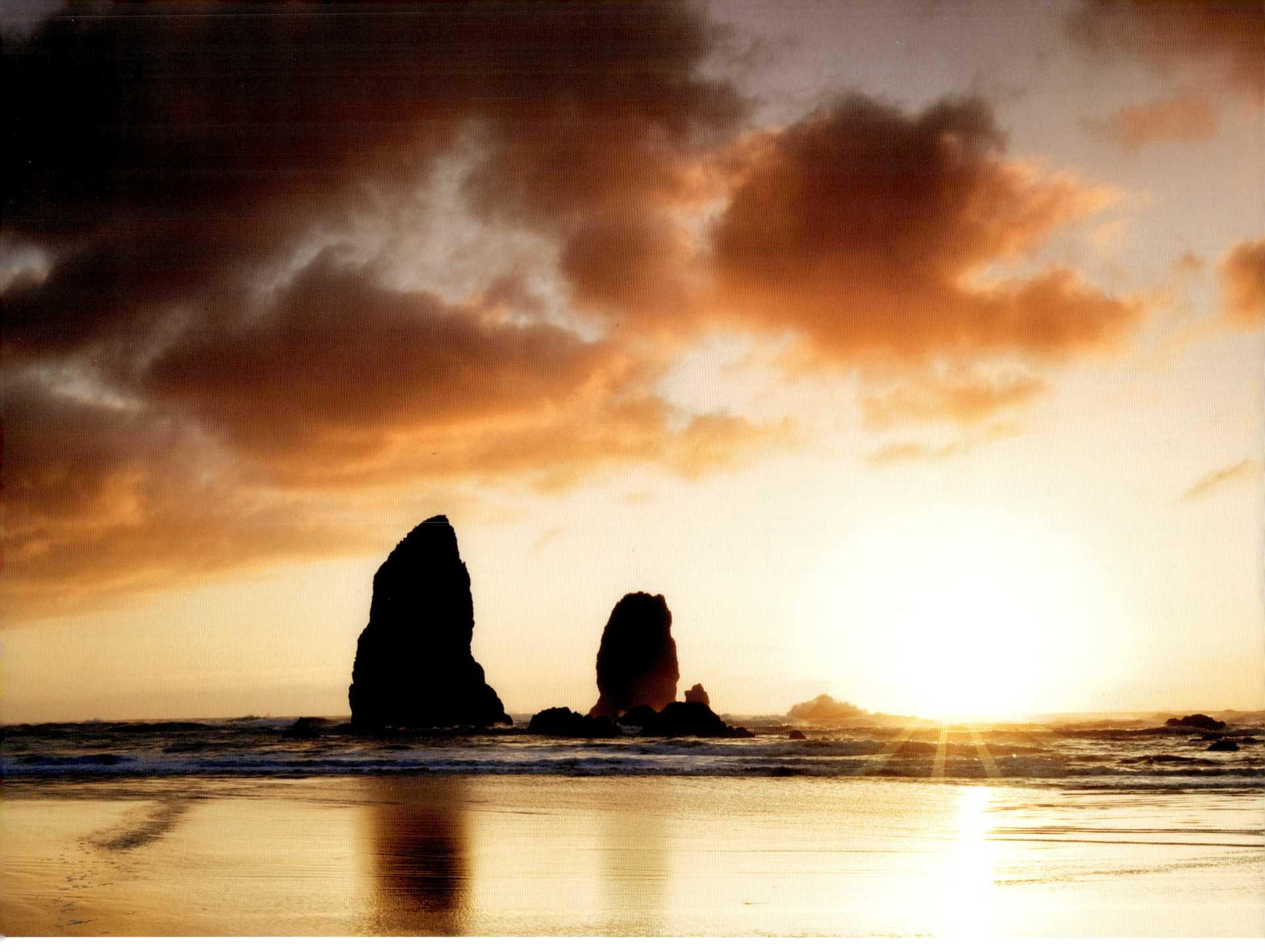

Above: The 235-foot-tall Haystack Rock stands sentry at Cannon Beach on Oregon's northern coast. At low tide, visitors explore the teeming tide pools and watch the nesting birds at this federal- and state-protected sanctuary.

Right: Girls inspect the ocean's treasures at low tide. From the Columbia River to the California border, the Oregon coastline offers tide pools, rocky headlands, giant dunes, and plenty of sandy strands for beachcombing.

Title page: Plunging more than 200 feet from basalt rock cliffs, Elowah Falls is one of the tallest waterfalls in the Columbia River Gorge National Scenic Area.

ISBN 10: 1-56037-563-9 (Mt. Hood version)
ISBN 13: 978-1-56037-563-0 (Mt. Hood version)
ISBN 10: 1-56037-586-8 (Beach version)
ISBN 13: 978-1-56037-586-9 (Beach version)

© 2013 by Farcountry Press
Photography © 2013 by Dennis Frates

All rights reserved. This book may not be reproduced in whole or in part by any means (with the exception of short quotes for the purpose of review) without the permission of the publisher.

For more information about our books, write Farcountry Press, P.O. Box 5630, Helena, MT 59604; call (800) 821-3874; or visit www.farcountrypress.com.

Created, produced, and designed in the United States.
Printed in China.

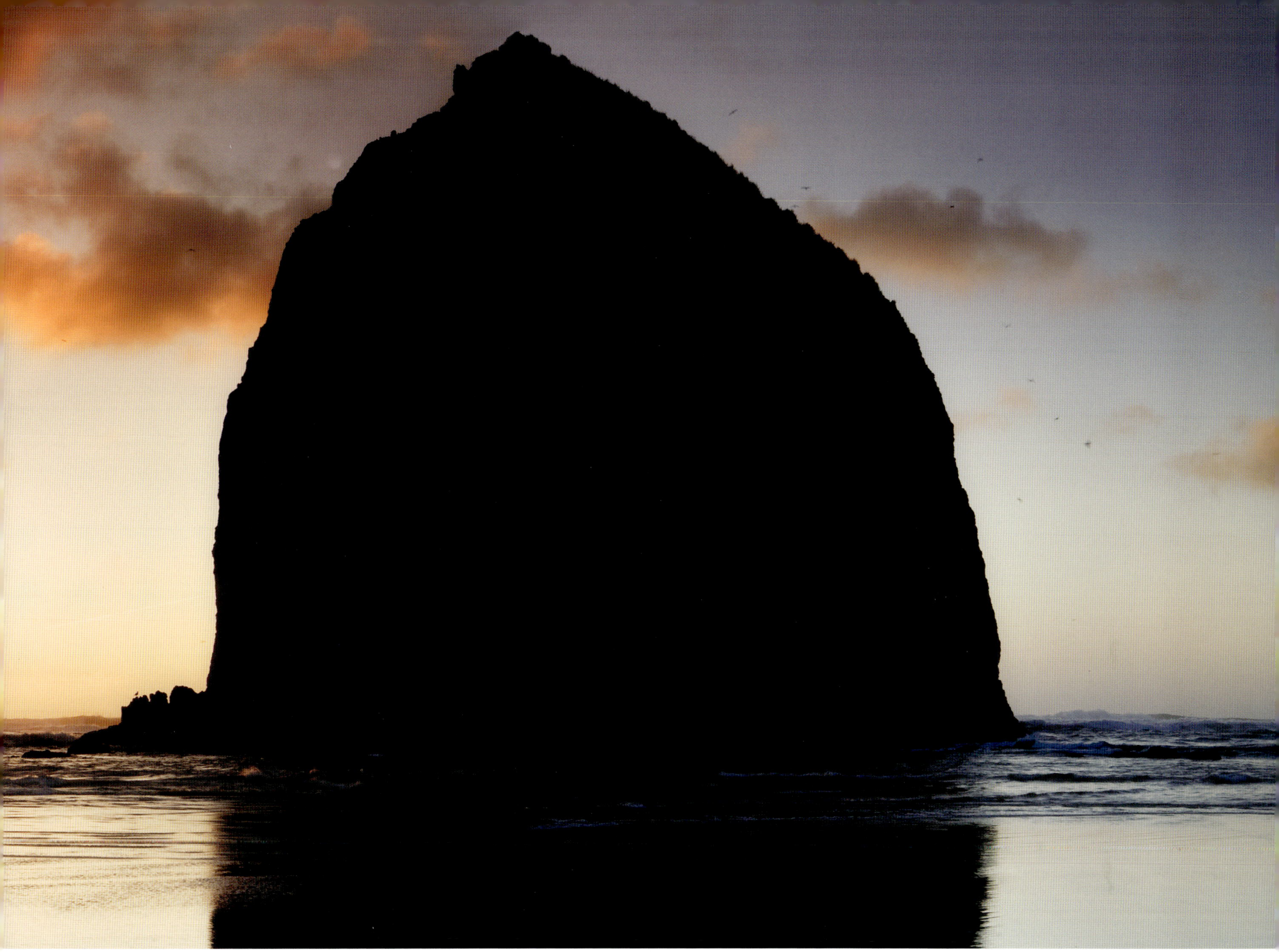

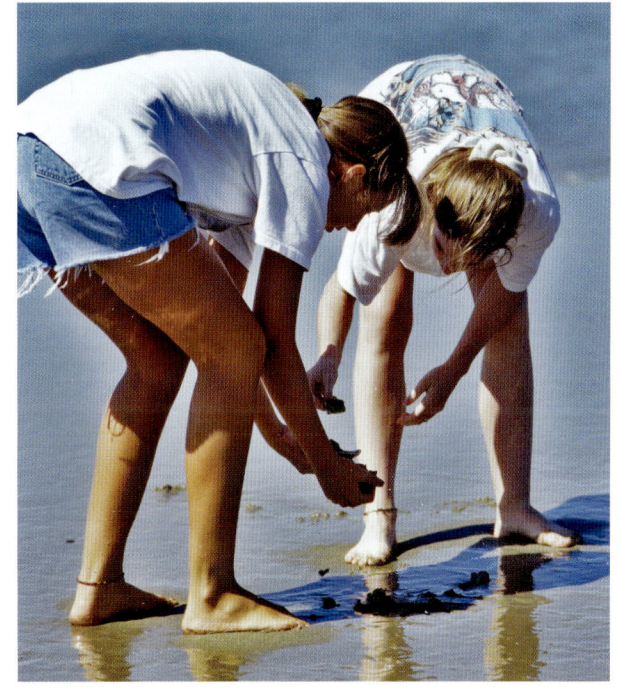

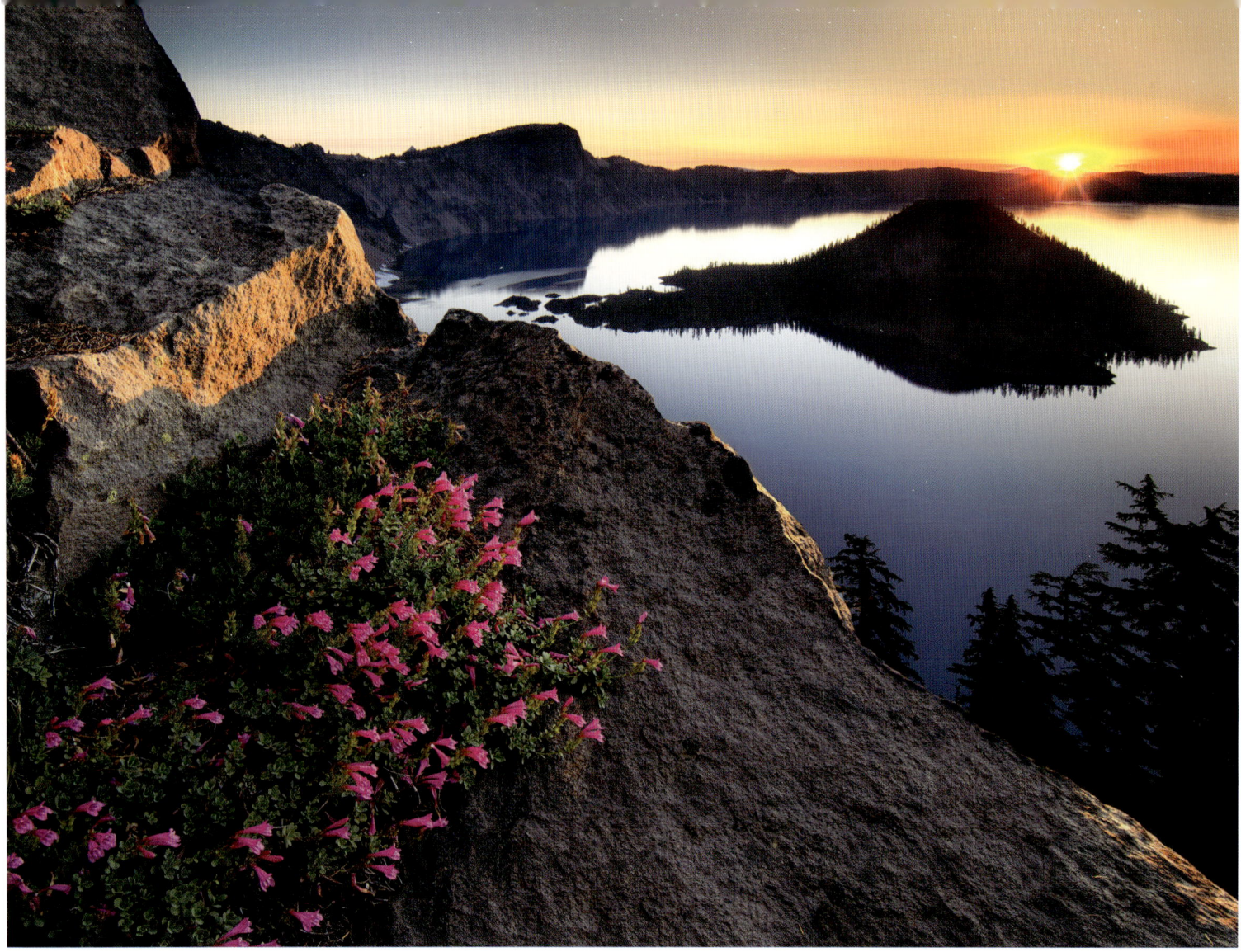

Above: Dawn breaks over the native penstemon and vertical lava flow patterns on the rim walls of Crater Lake in the southern Cascade Mountains.

Facing page: The brilliant reds and oranges of vine maple and pale blue of elderberry fruit signal the arrival of autumn in Oregon.

FOREWORD *by Dennis Frates*

I WAS FIRST DRAWN TO OREGON'S OUTDOORS as a fly fisherman, fishing some of the best, most scenic waters anywhere. About thirty years ago, I became intensely interested in photography and decided I would sell my images to help fund my fishing trips. I soon had a dilemma. I would be casting my fly to some hungry trout while an incredible sunrise or sunset lured me toward my camera. Twenty-eight years later, after traveling extensively to photograph the very best scenery, the inspiration I feel when photographing has never abated. I simply love what I do.

The photographs in this book are among my best work, and many have been sold as fine art prints. A fine art photograph should be visually stunning and capable of encouraging a deep emotional connection with the viewer, the way an inspiring piece of music stirs the listener's soul. Through composition and color, I strive for my images to sing to the viewer just like a beautiful aria.

It is no small feat to create a photograph that serenades the senses. I prefer to work during the first and last light of the day and during strange weather events, of which Oregon has many. I often visit the same location many times until I get just the right image.

The emotionally powerful scenes in this book speak to me as I hope they will to subsequent viewers. While creating the image, I get so excited that I shake. I start babbling about how great the scene is, even if no one is listening. I am so absorbed in this process that I have on occasion accidently cut or bruised myself on a rock or a piece of equipment and not even been aware of it. In photographing the drama of nature, my goal is for you to experience some of this same thrill when viewing my photographs—minus the cuts and bruises, of course.

There's so much to explore in this beautiful state. Oregon's coasts, deserts, and mountains offer a medley of outdoor recreational options and sights not seen in many other states—a true treasure. It is unsurprising that Oregonians are so inextricably linked to the outdoors. Thousands of volunteers show their appreciation each year by picking up trash along their beaches. The natural beauty of the coast is shared with all; thanks to some visionary legislation, all 363 miles of Oregon's coastline are open to the public. I have photographed countless times along the coast, and because of the extraordinary public access, I always seem to find something new in my viewfinder.

If solitude is what you seek, eastern Oregon has much to offer. In the Alvord Desert, Steens Mountain rises to a crescendo above a rugged, ancient lakebed. In the northeast, the Wallowa Mountains provide incredible vistas with stunning landscapes to tour. They are like nothing else in the state. These areas are among my favorite to photograph because they are so wild and isolated.

Oregon's legendary mountains are mostly volcanic in origin, and the snow-covered peaks and associated lakes, streams, and forests provide some of the most breathtaking scenery the United States has to offer. Crater Lake, in the southern Cascade Mountains, is our only national park. It is the crown jewel of the Cascades, but the central and northern Cascades are equally impressive. A trip to Oregon's mountains would not be complete without driving Cascade Lakes Scenic Byway to view Mt. Bachelor or waltzing up to Mt. Hood, only a short day trip from Portland when you want to get away from it all.

I am lucky to have gotten to know this great state, Oregon. I hope that my photographs will sing to you all the hymns and sonatas that this state has to offer. Let the symphony begin.

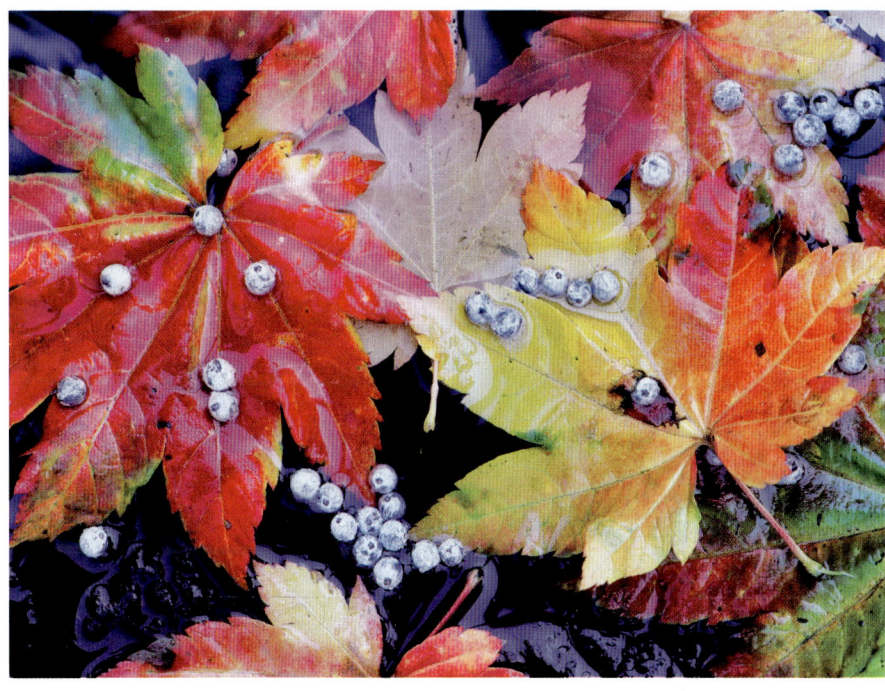

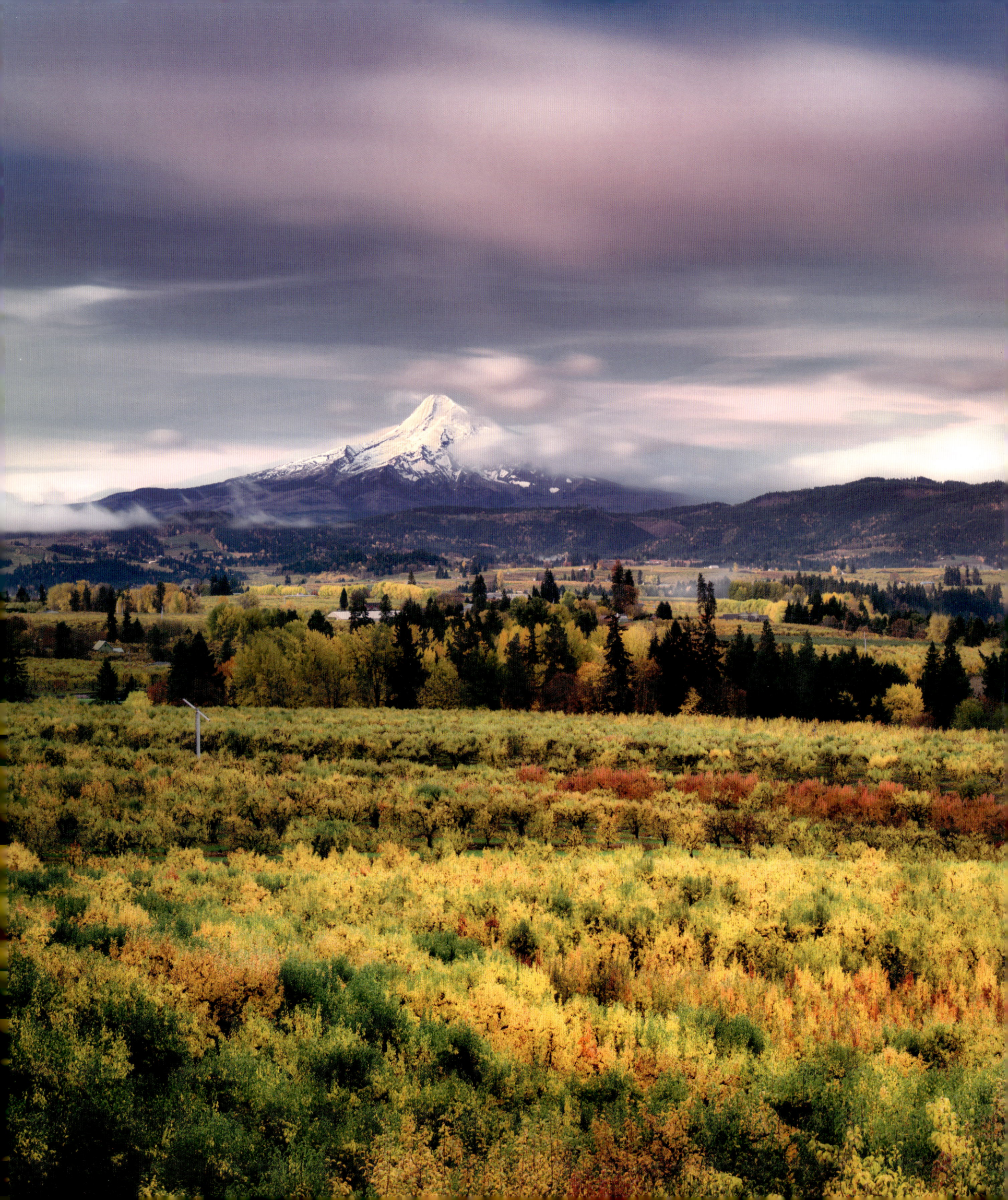

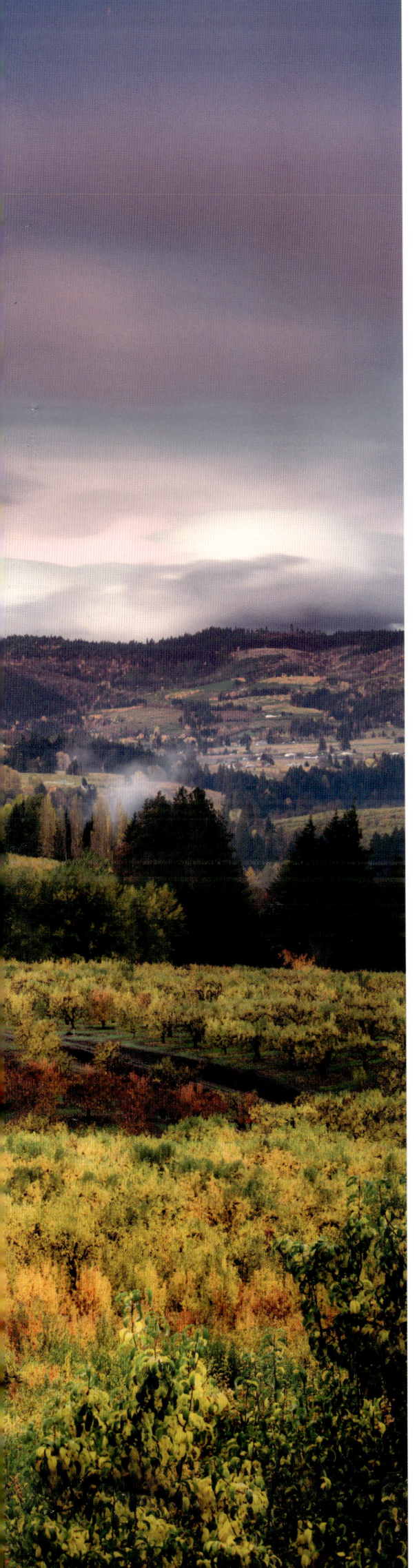

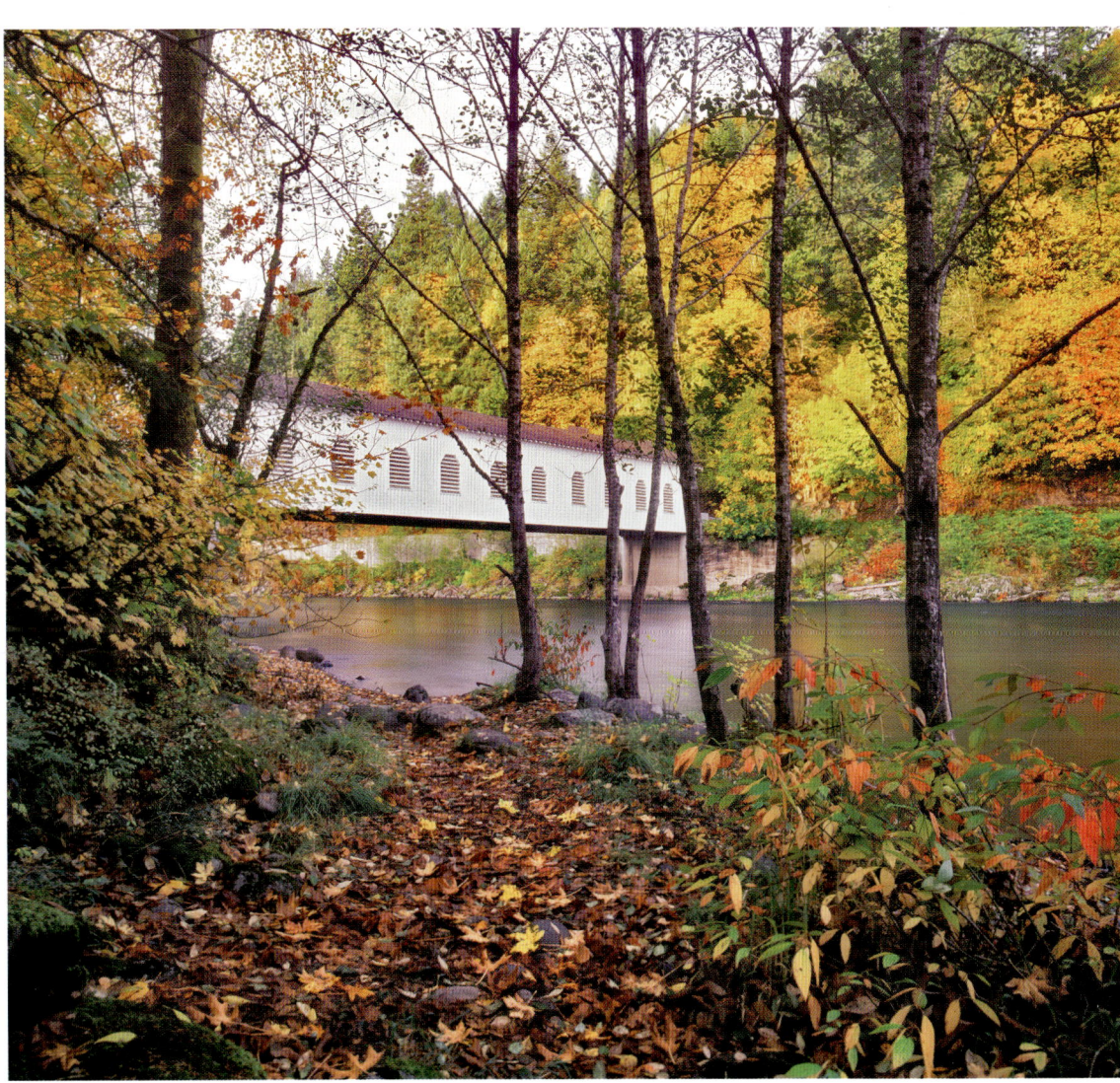

Above: One of the most beloved covered bridges in Oregon, the Goodpasture Bridge stretches 165 feet over the McKenzie River. The span is the longest of its kind still in daily use in the state.

Left: Below the flanks of Mt. Hood, the fertile Hood River Valley provides some of the state's finest growing conditions for cherries, apples, and pears. A 35-mile scenic drive known as the "Fruit Loop" meanders past orchards, vineyards, lavender fields, and berry farms where visitors can sample the bounty and bring home their favorites. The route is a favorite for cyclists and drivers alike when fall foliage washes the valley in gold and crimson.

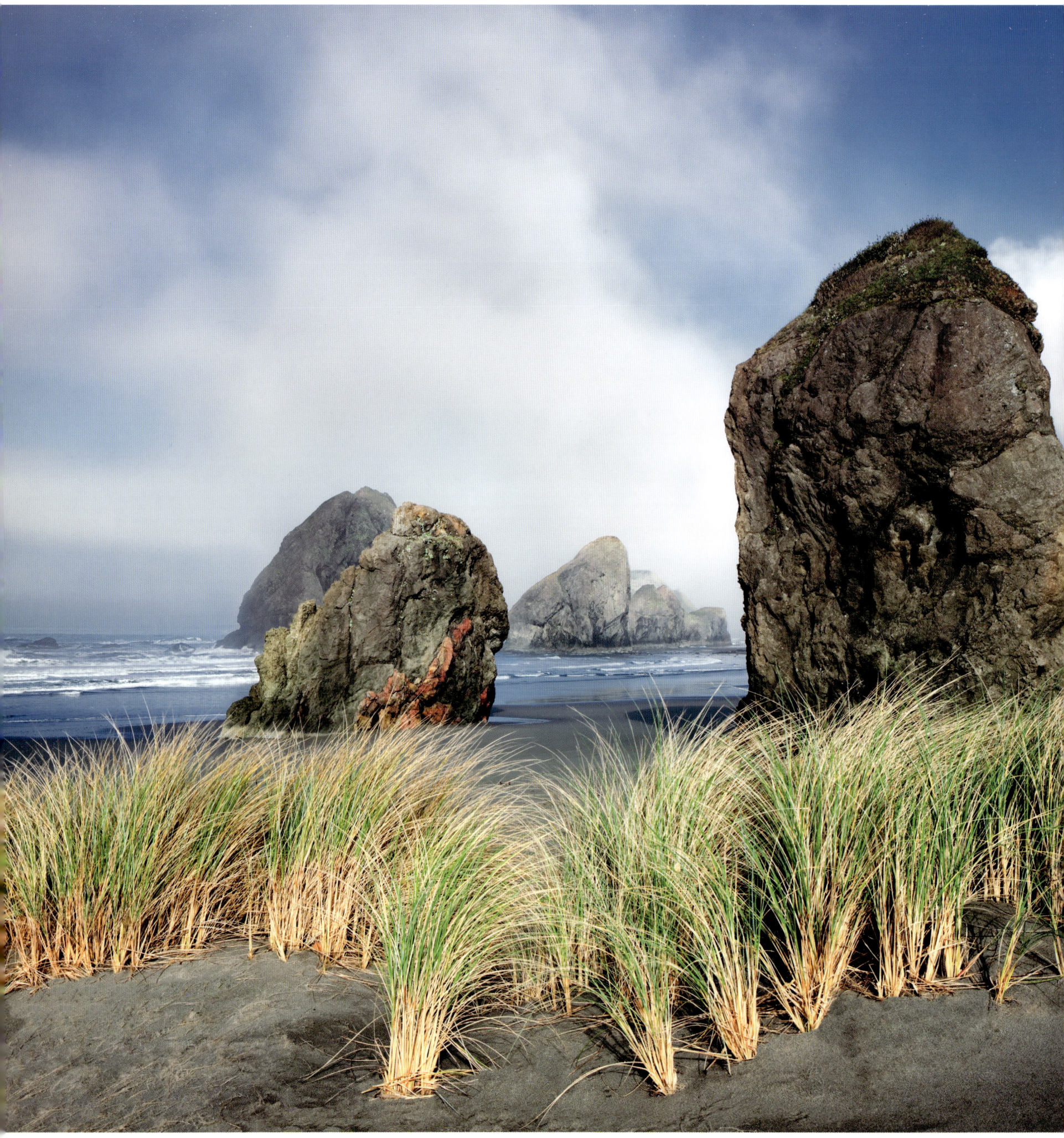

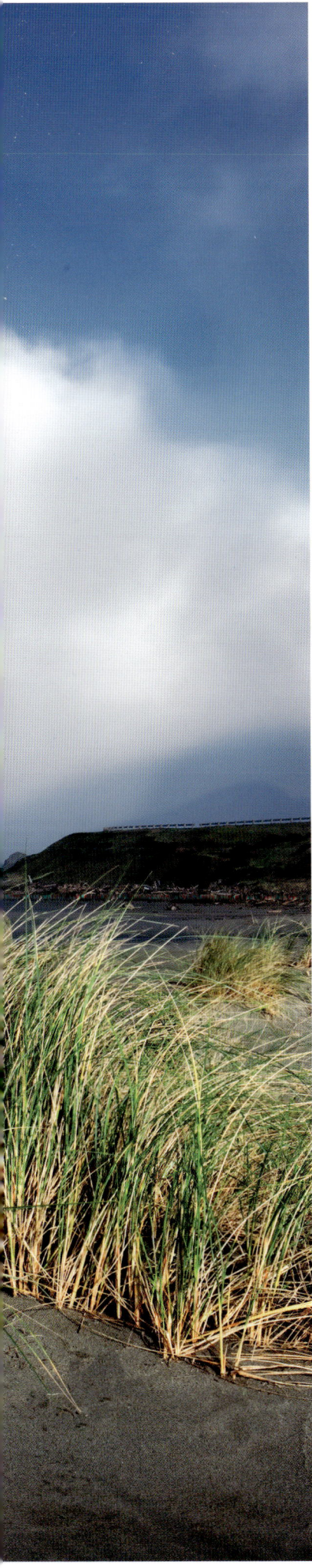

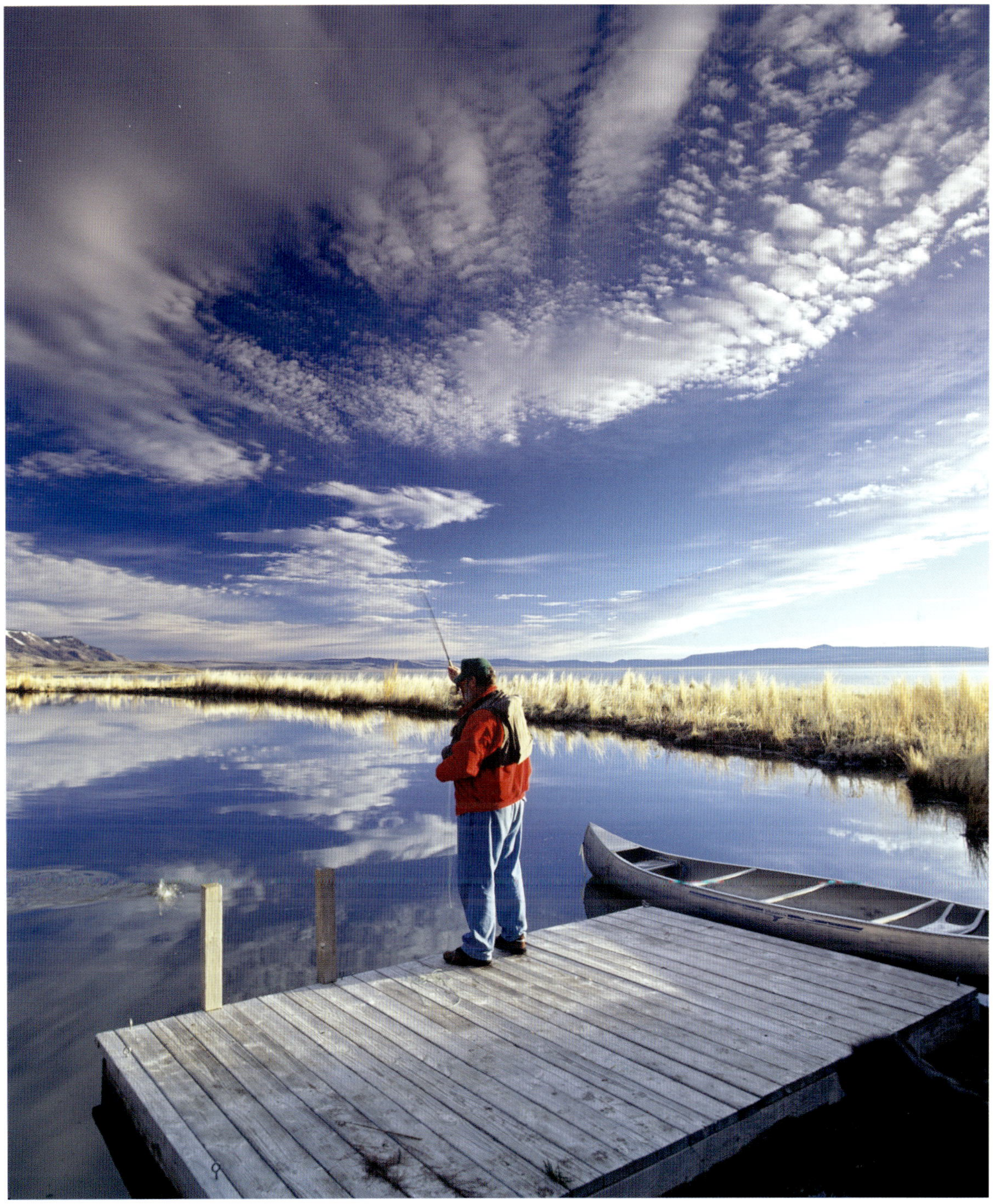

Above: A fly fisherman readies his rod and casts his luck in hopes of bringing home a prize catch from Summer Lake. The lakes and rivers of Oregon are a destination for sport fishermen of all kinds.

Left: Beach grass and volcanic sea stacks stand watch over the misty shore at Cape Sebastian State Scenic Corridor. The beach grasses of the Oregon coast serve an important ecological purpose, stabilizing the sand dunes that protect roads and towns from the Pacific Ocean's mighty storms.

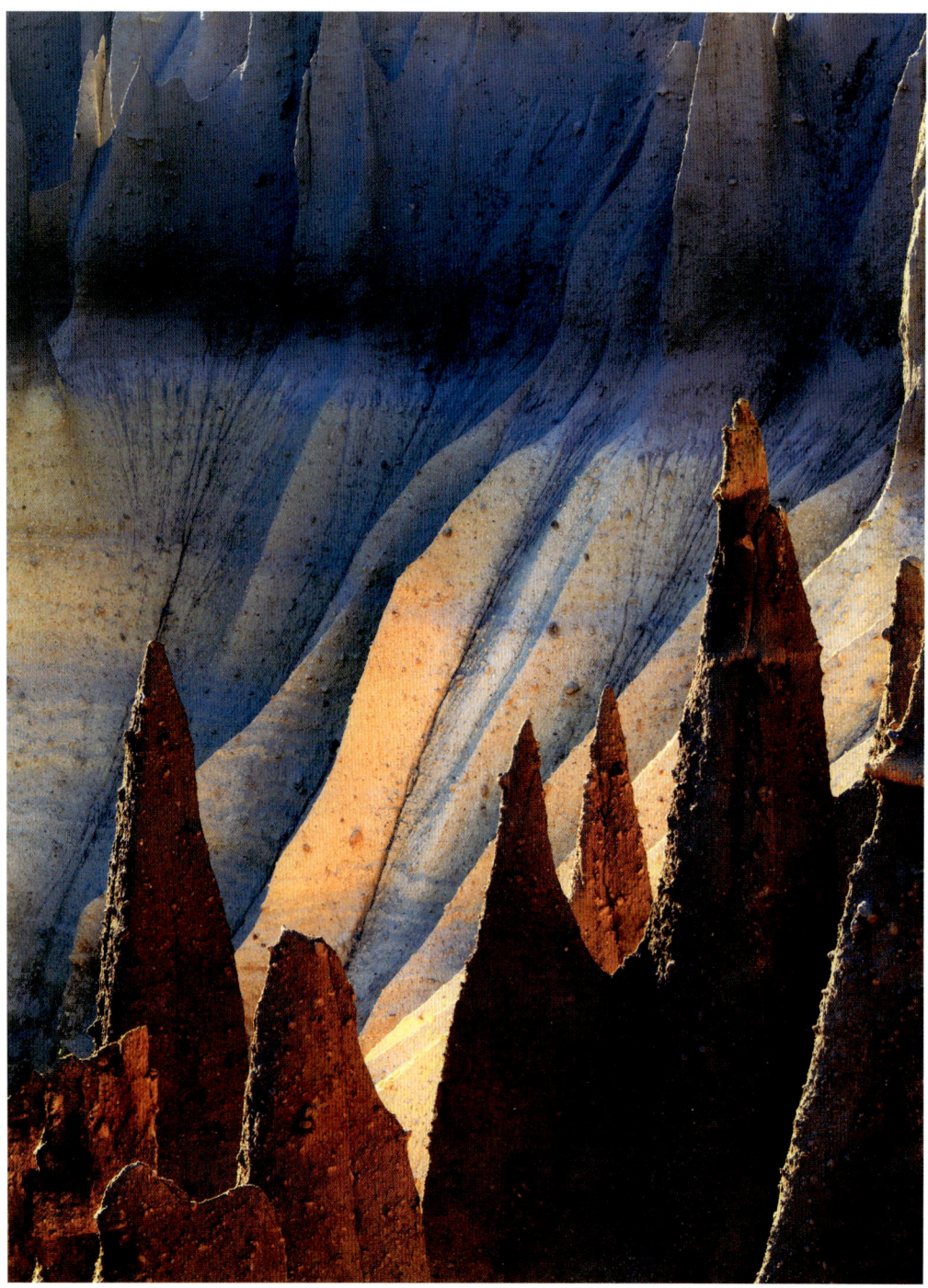

Above: The needle-like formations known as The Pinnacles project from the Sand Creek Canyon floor at Crater Lake National Park. An easy 0.6-mile hike along the rim of Pinnacle Valley provides views of the spires carved by wind and rain.

Right: Crater Lake sits inside the caldera of a collapsed volcano formed after the eruption of Mt. Mazama about 8,000 years ago. Visitors to Crater Lake National Park can view the crystal blue waters of America's deepest lake from scenic overlooks along the 33-mile Rim Drive. Boat tours to Wizard Island run during the summer months.

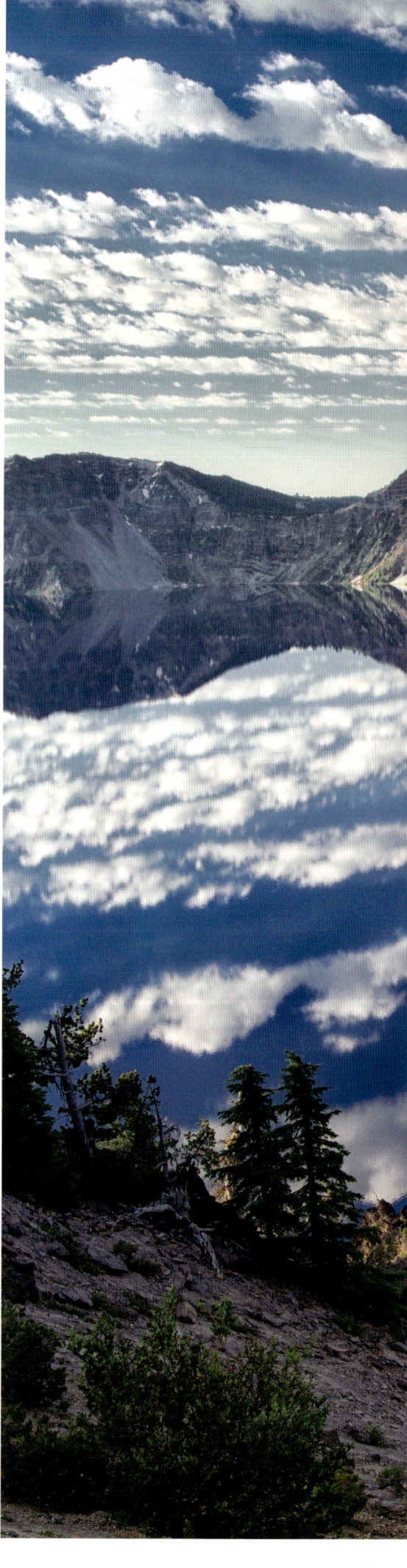

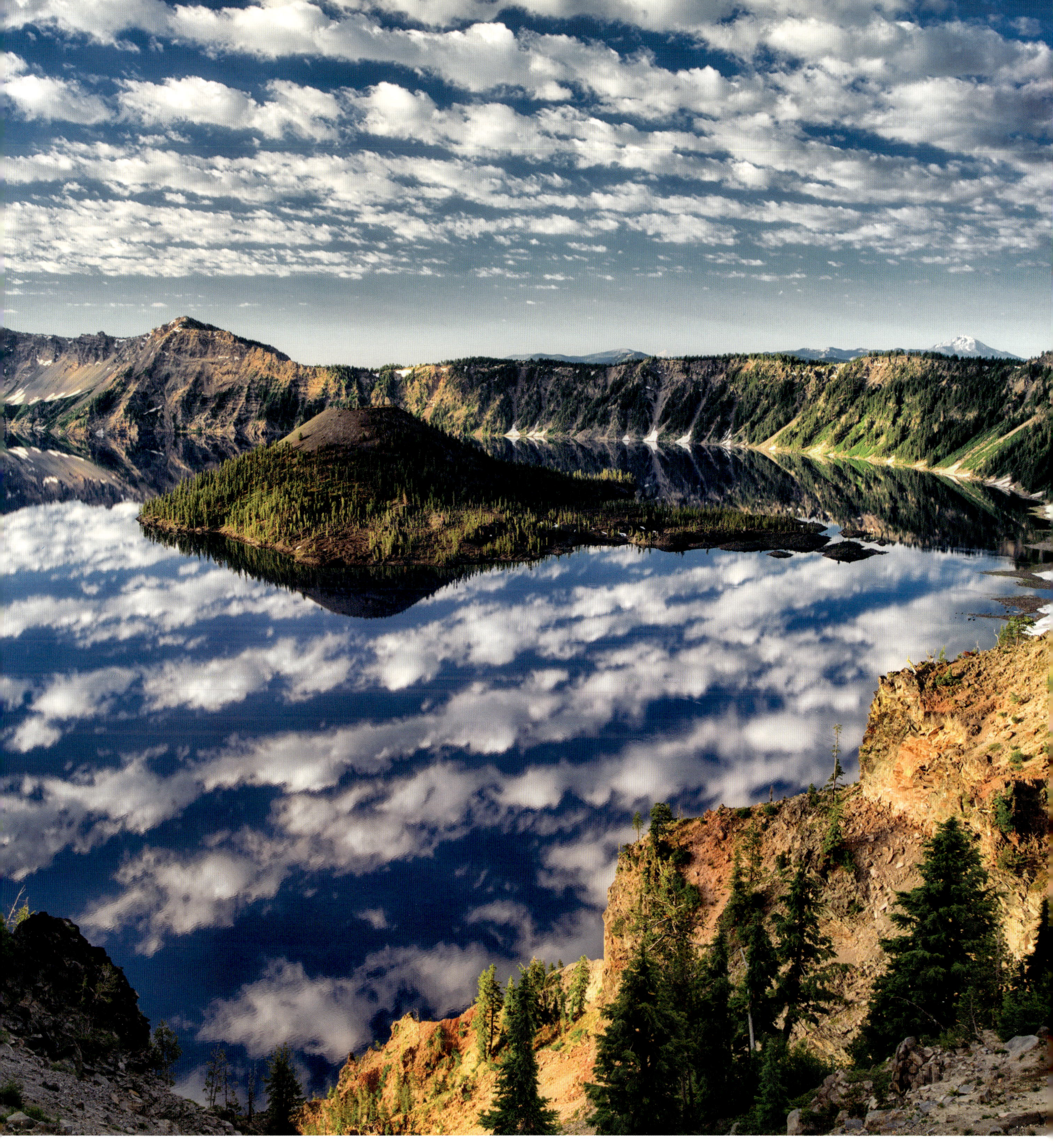

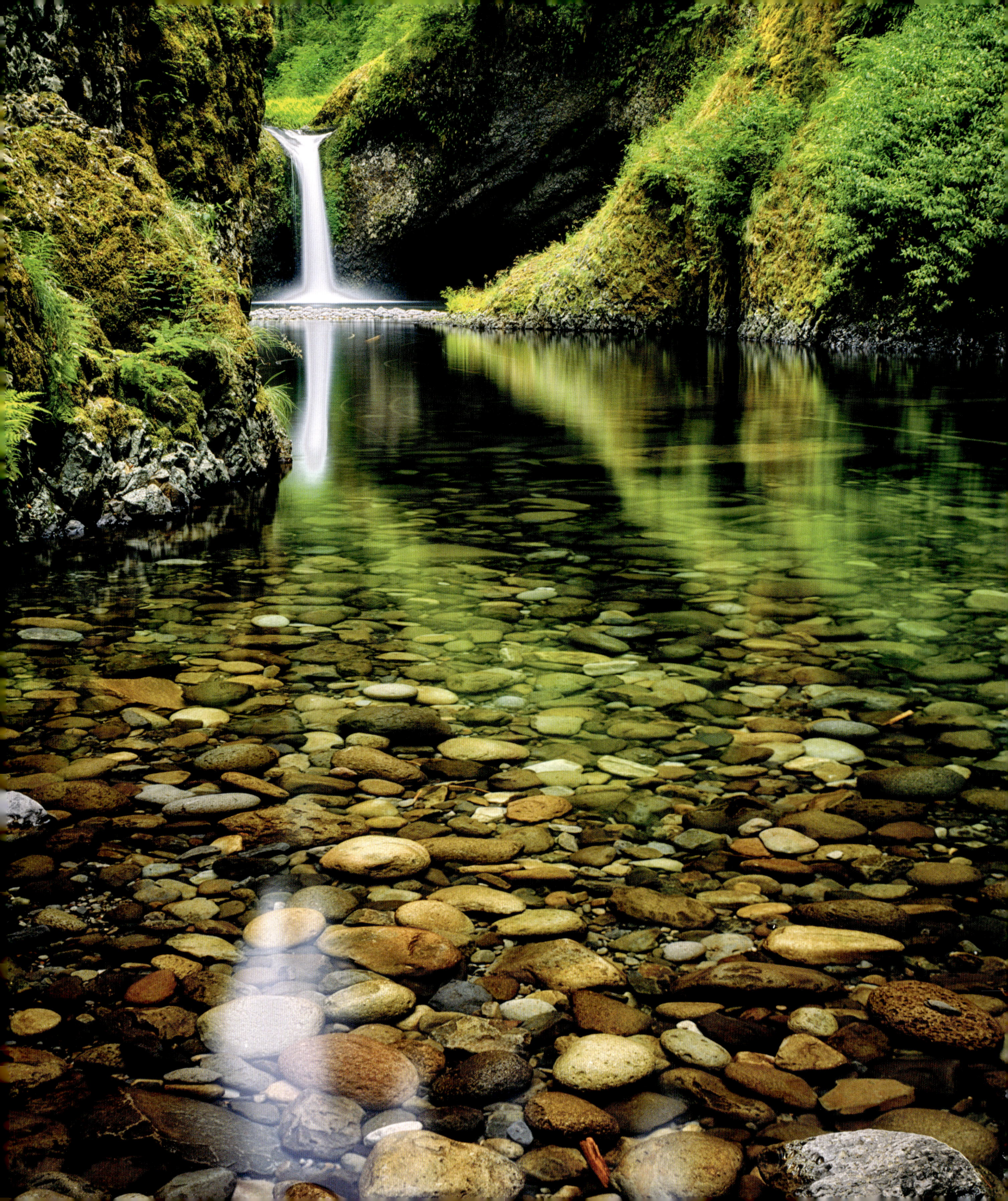

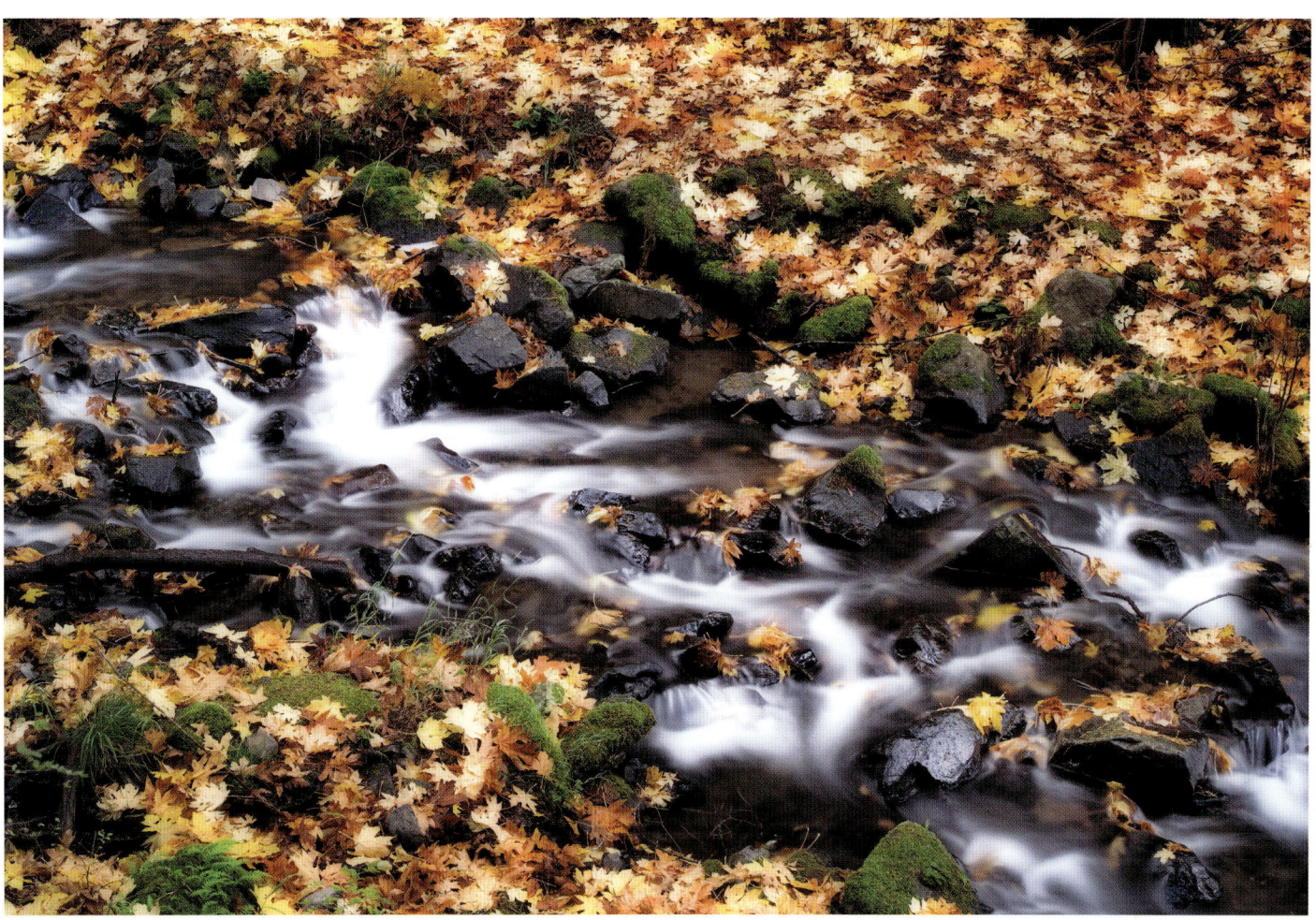

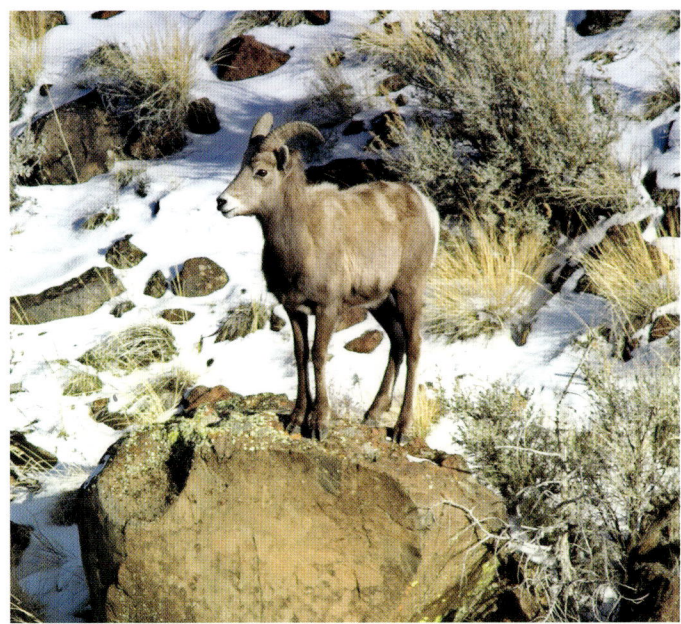

Above: Tucked into the basalt cliffs of the Columbia River Gorge National Scenic Area, Starvation Creek and its falls are among the many natural treasures scattered along the border of Oregon and Washington. Two theories endure about the origin of the name of this state park. One claims a group of pioneers nearly starved here. The other story holds that two trains stalled in the heavy snows of the winter of 1884-1885, forcing people from a nearby town to pack in provisions for the passengers.

Left: Bighorn sheep—along with pronghorn and mule deer—thrive in the Hart Mountain National Antelope Refuge in southeastern Oregon. The 278,000-acre refuge is one of the largest wildlife habitats free of domestic livestock in the high-desert West.

Far left: Punchbowl Falls in the Columbia River Gorge is one of the most scenic waterfalls in the state. It is a popular swimming and hiking destination on hot summer days.

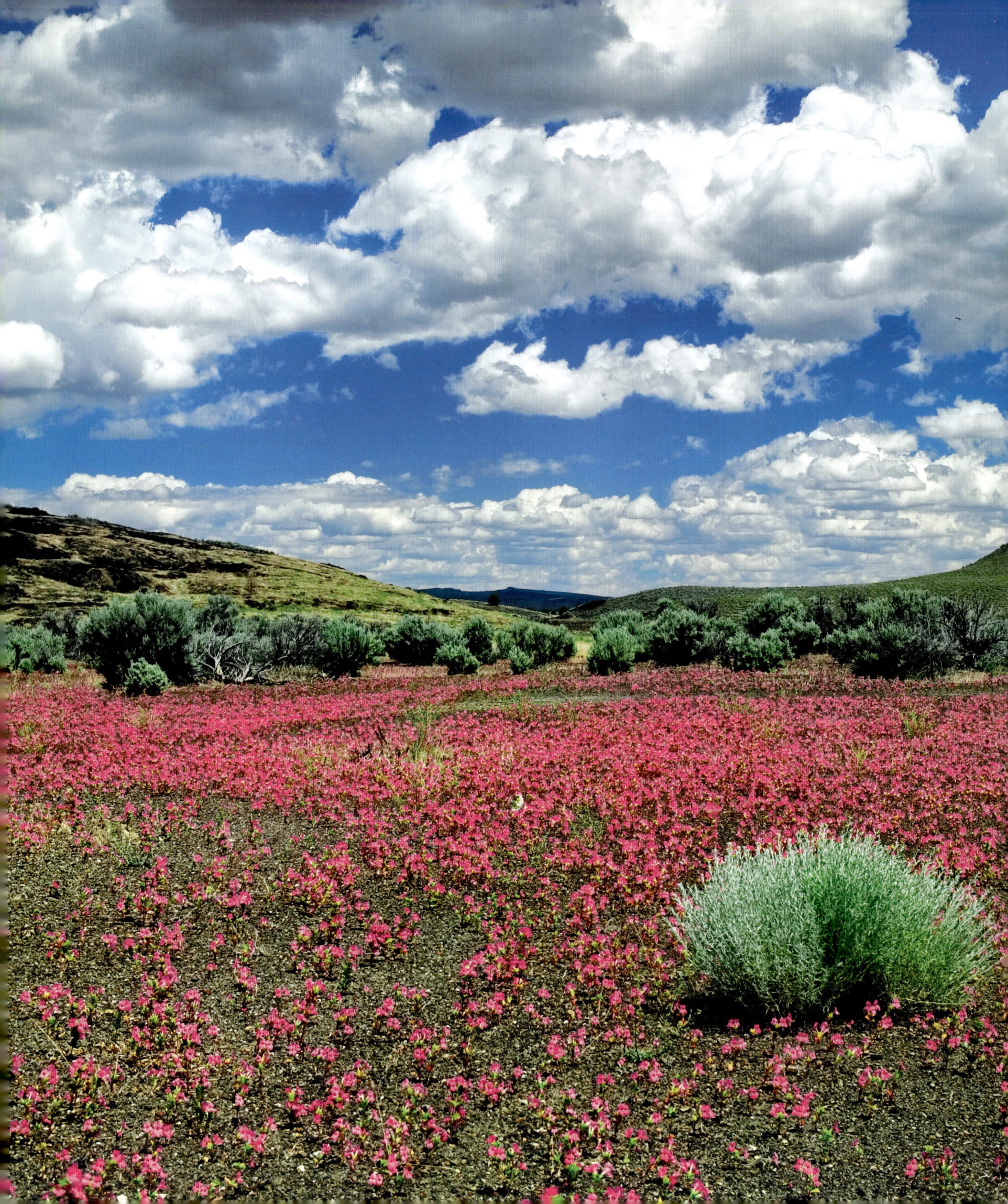

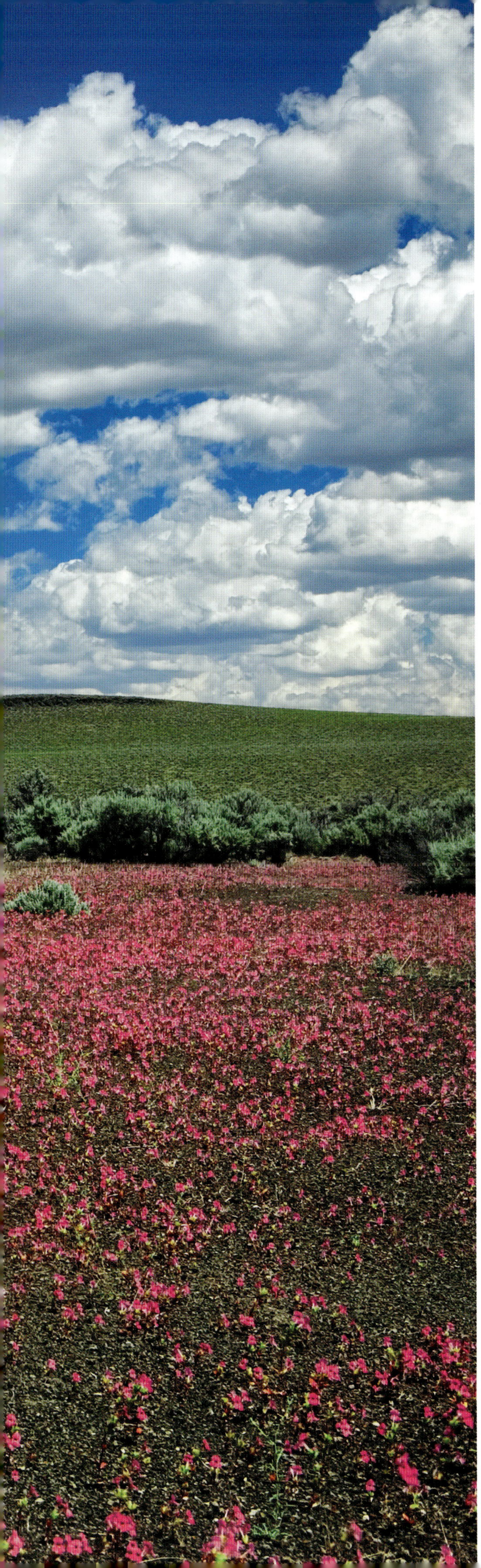

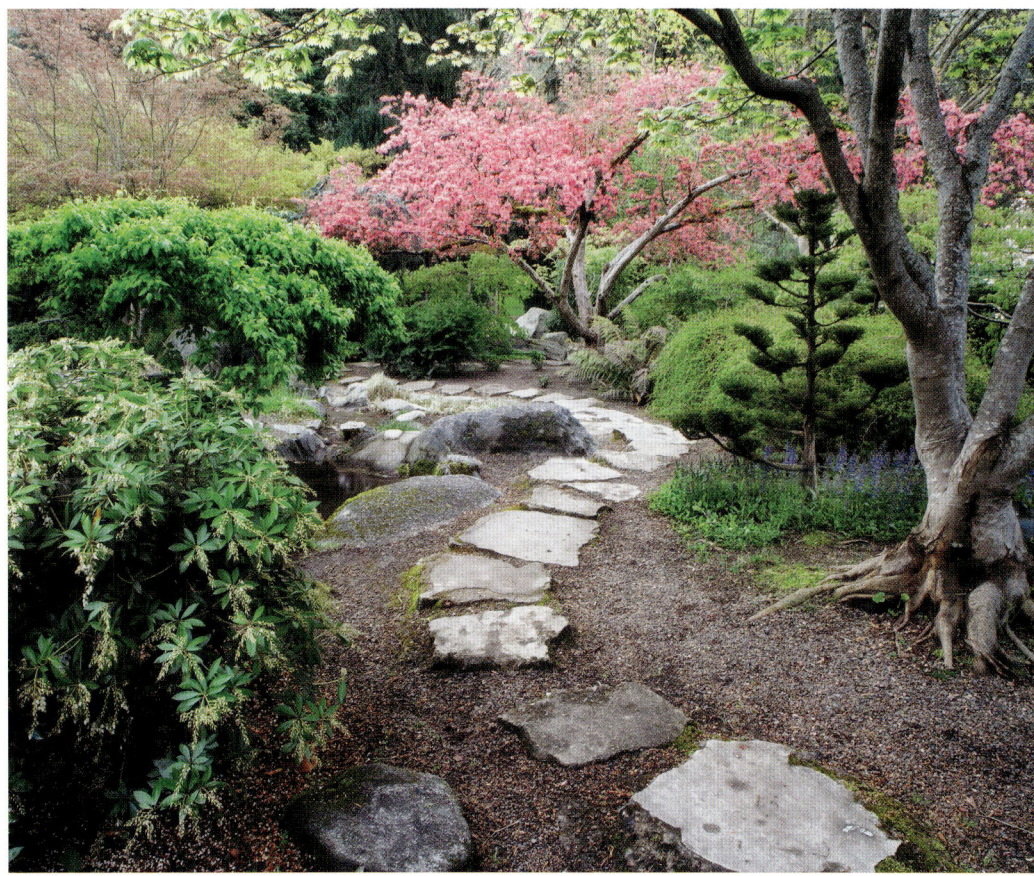

Above: Flowering cherry trees signal the onset of spring in Ashland's Lithia Park. The 93-acre urban oasis includes duck ponds, fountains, and a Japanese garden.

Left: From a distance, dwarf monkey flowers appear as a carpet of pink, but upon closer inspection, these wildflower blossoms resemble little faces peering from the greenery.

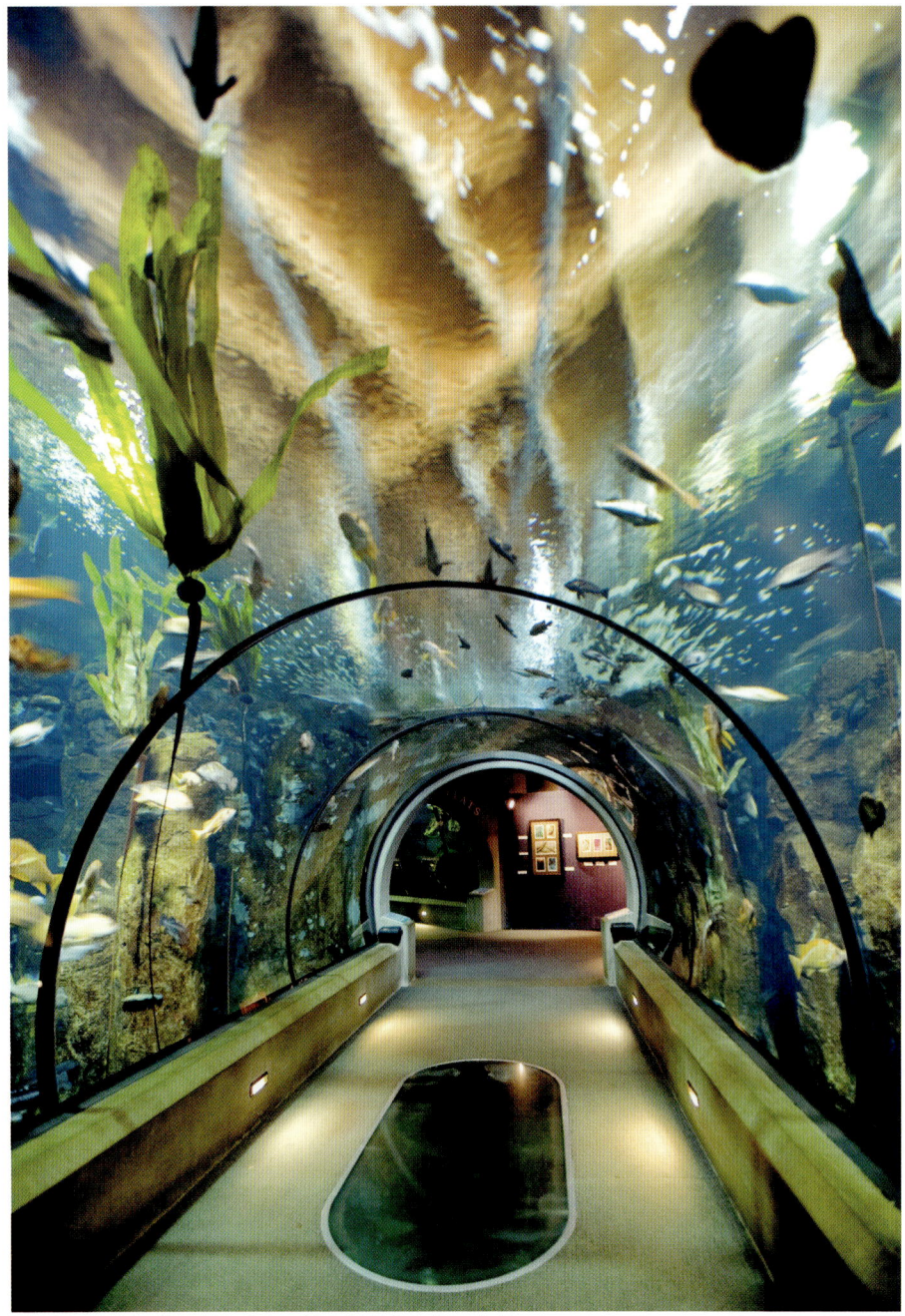

Above: Visitors can immerse themselves in the watery worlds of three Pacific Ocean ecosystems at the Oregon Coast Aquarium in Newport. A 200-foot underwater walkway gives visitors a close-up view of nearly 3,500 marine animals.

Right: Near the community of Otter Rock, the Pacific Ocean's restless surf slams into the collapsed sea cave known as Devils Punchbowl, creating a churning, foaming concoction. Designated a state natural area, the rock formation is a popular stop for whale watchers and tide pool explorers.

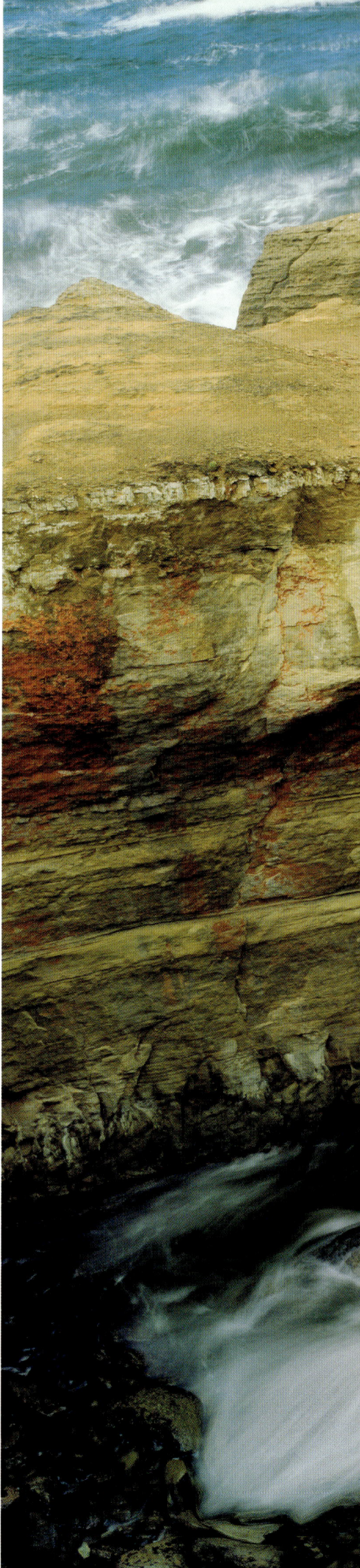

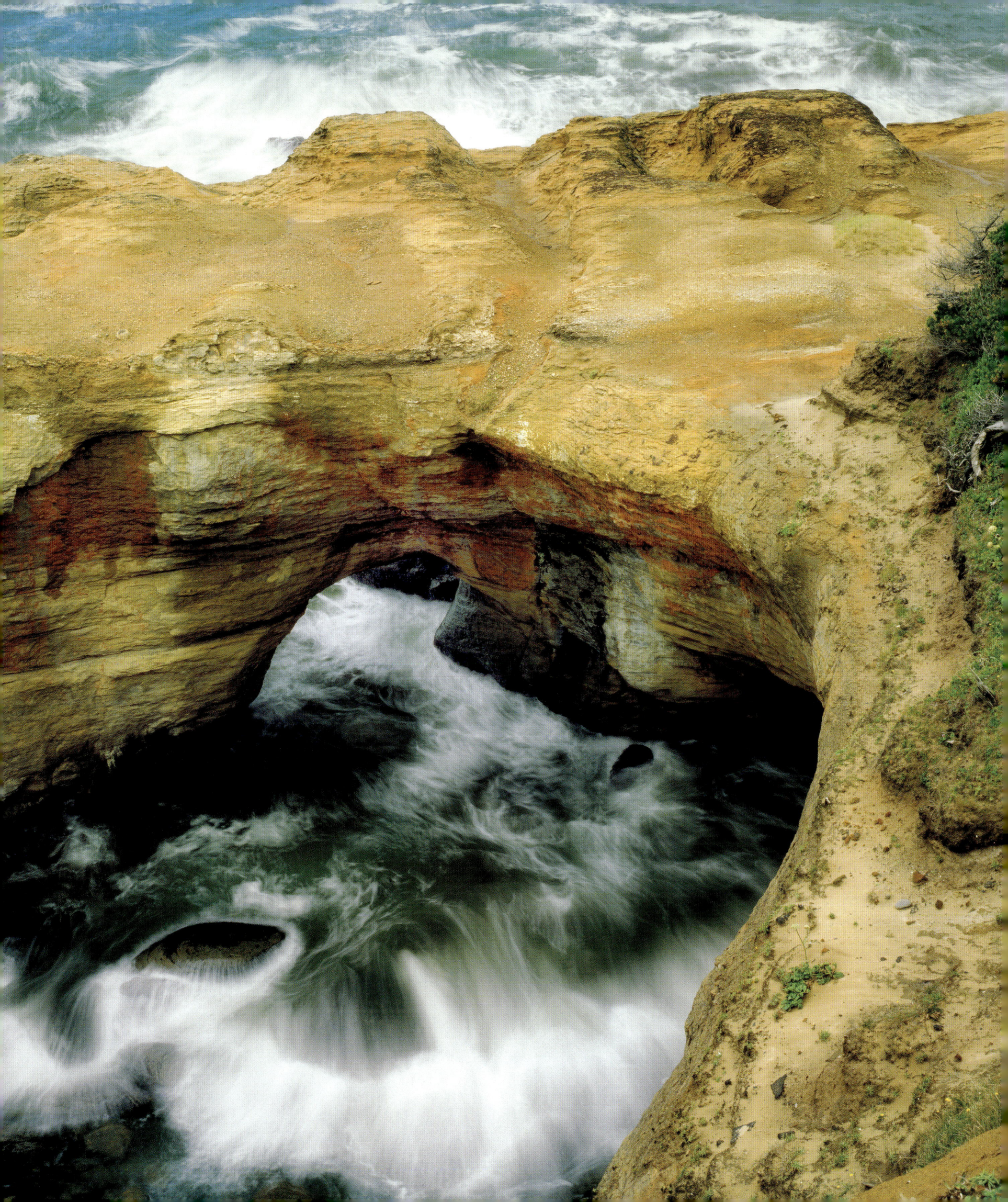

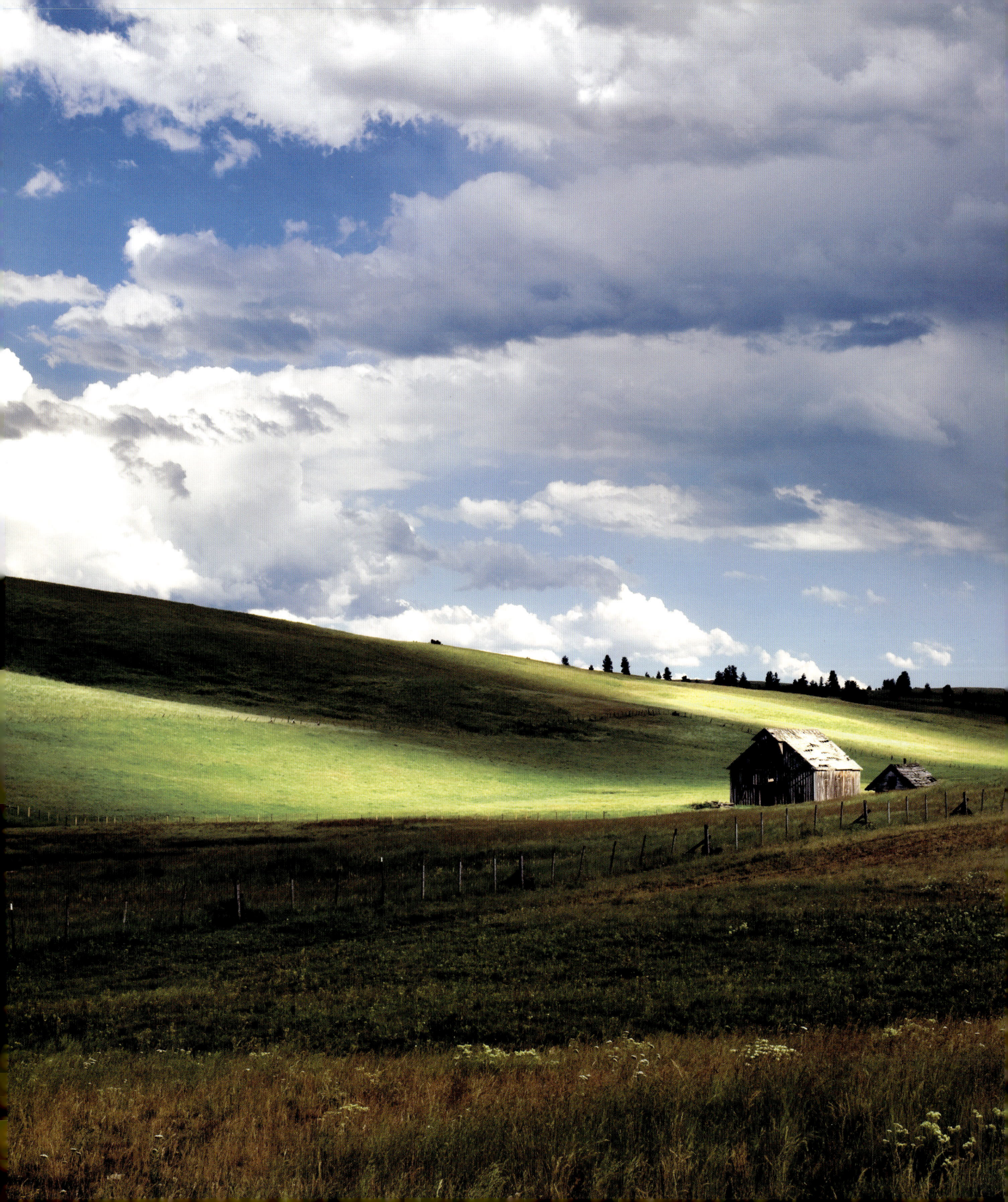

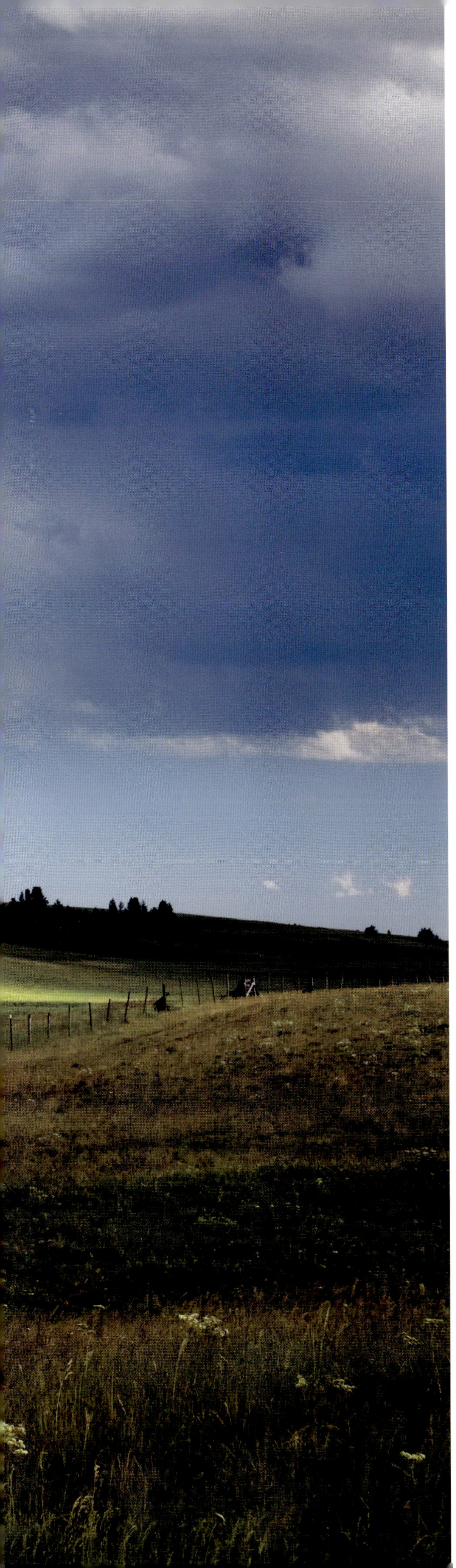

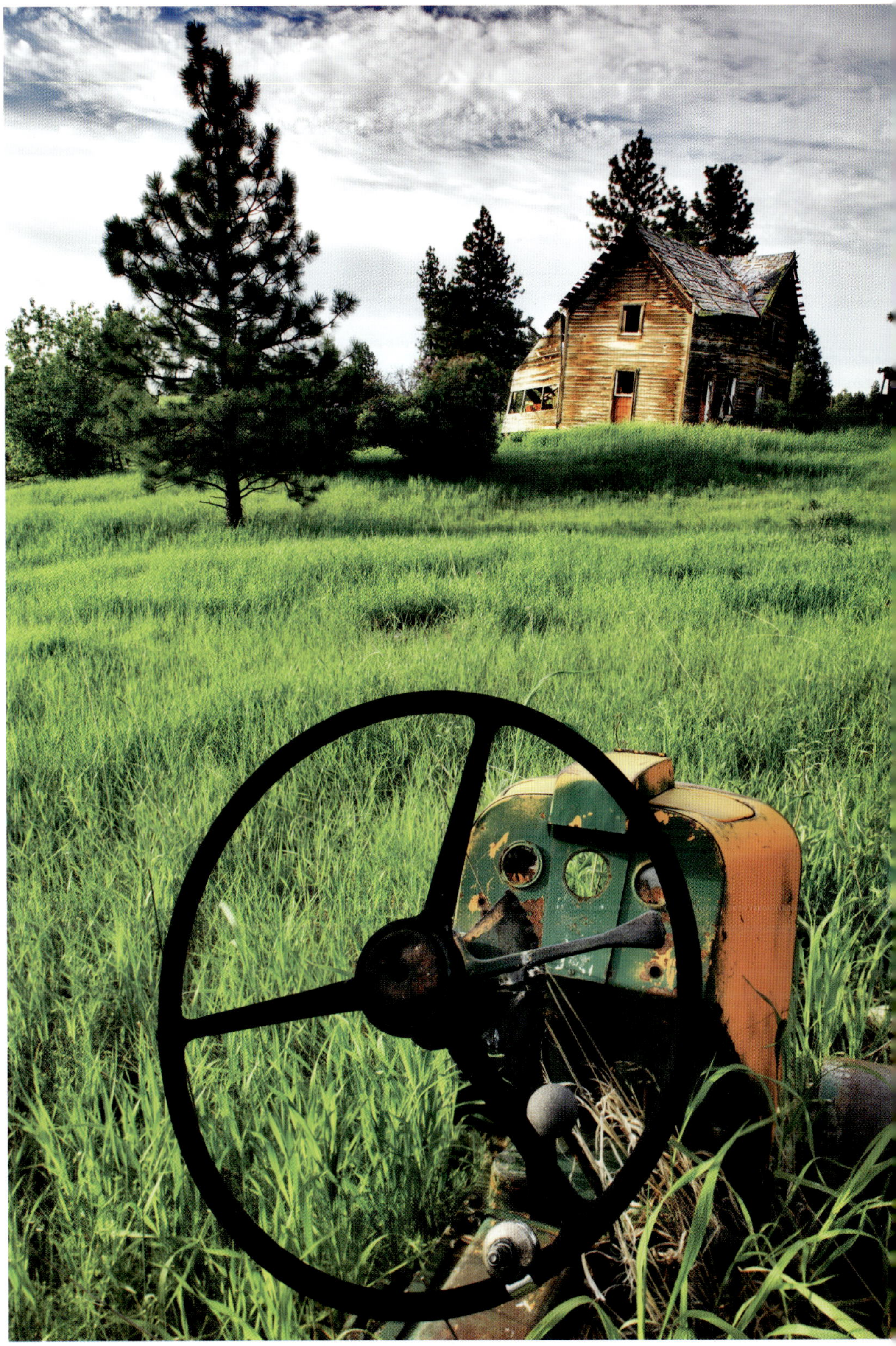

Above: An old tractor and abandoned house stand as evidence of better days when ranching and farming families held down their ancestral homesteads near the ghost town of Flora. In total, 62,926 homesteads were claimed in the state under the 1862 Homestead Act.

Left: Thunderheads threaten rain on the Zumwalt Prairie in Wallowa County, home of one of the Pacific Northwest's largest intact bunchgrass prairies. The prairie serves as habitat for the Columbian sharp-tailed grouse, ferruginous hawks, and various grassland songbirds.

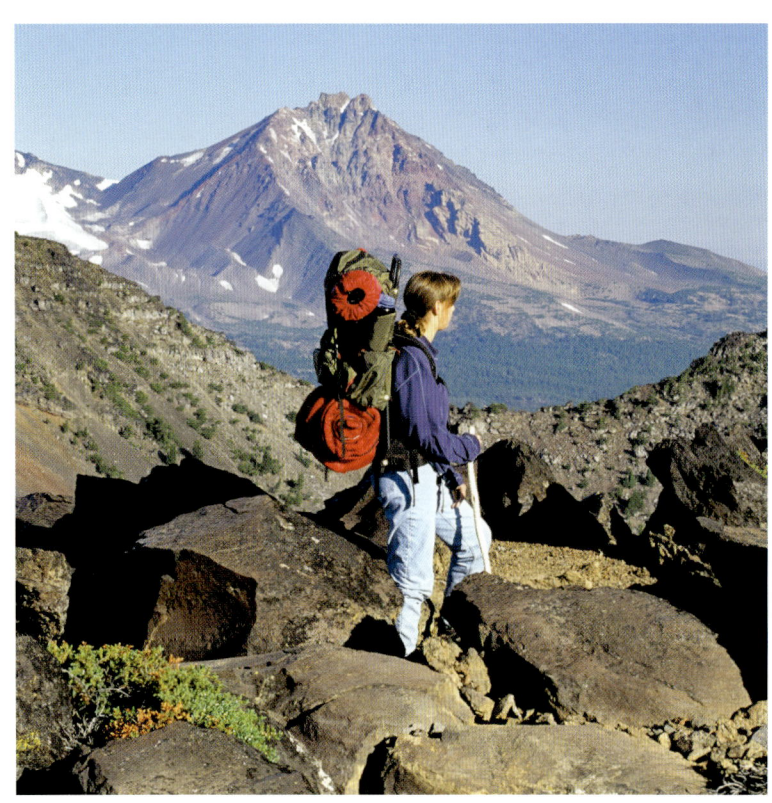
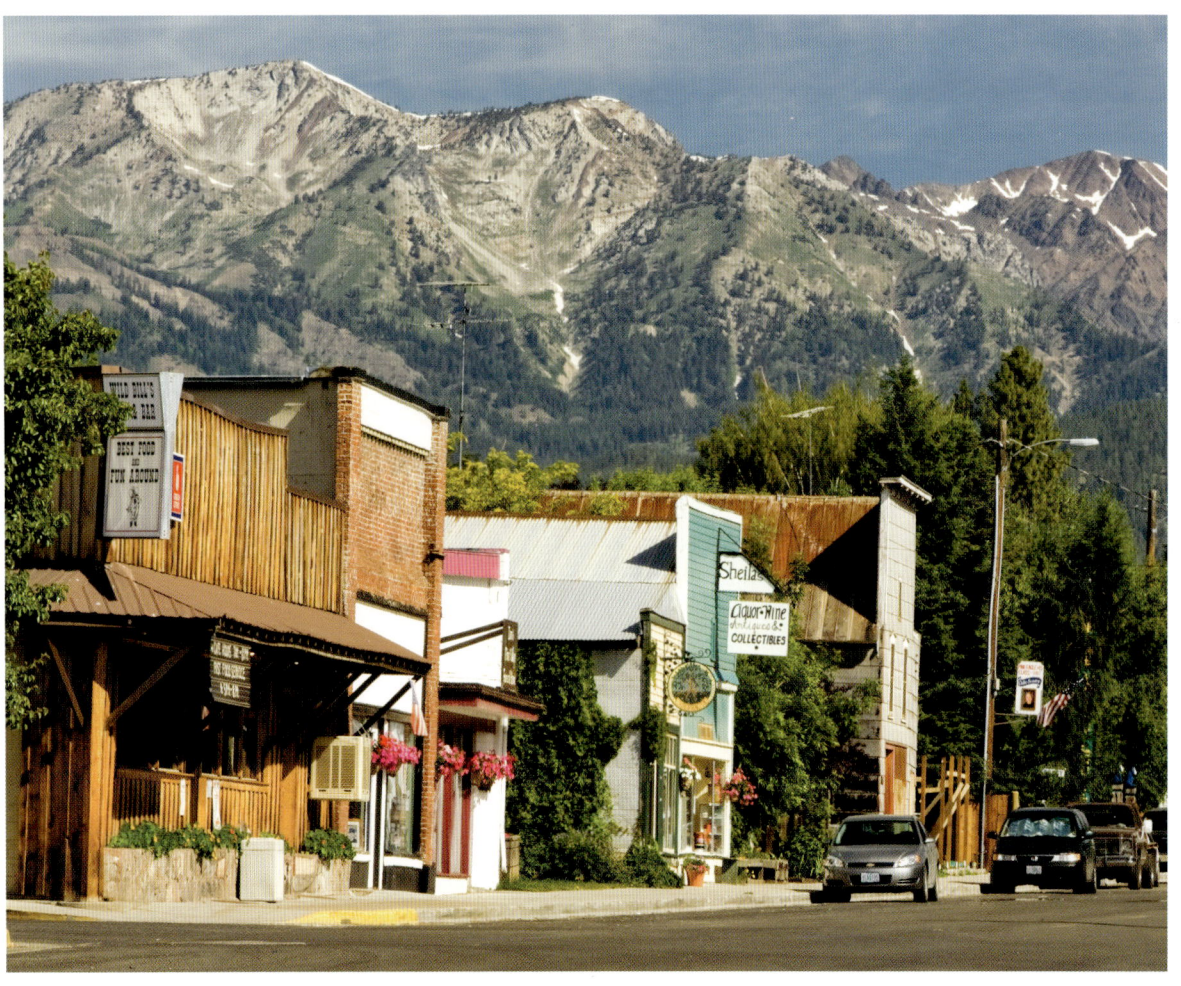
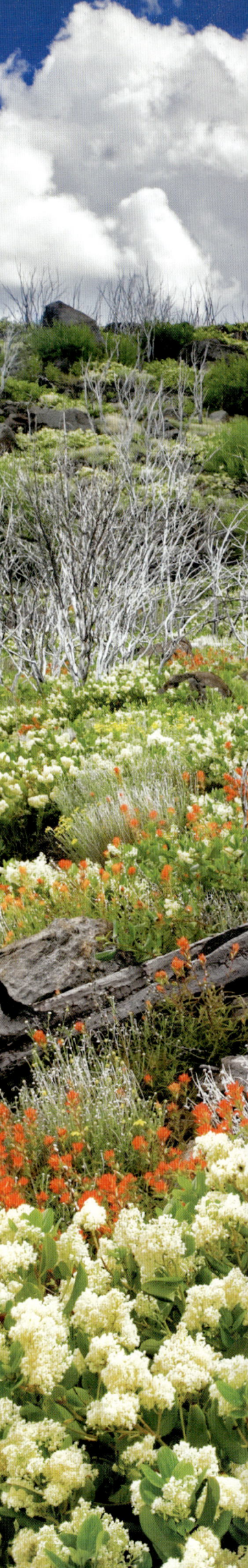

Right: The 2.5-mile uphill trek to Tam McArthur Rim in the Three Sisters Wilderness rewards hikers with views of Broken Top Mountain and the valley below.

Far right: Snowbrush ceanothus and fiery-red paintbrush thrive among the stems of Manzanita bushes scorched by wildfire in the Fremont-Winema National Forest of Oregon's southern Cascades. While a fire may kill an individual manzanita bush, the intense heat triggers the germination of the plant's dormant seeds so that manzanita may thrive there once again.

Below: Flanked by the Wallowa Mountains, the town of Halfway hosts the Hells Canyon Scenic Byway. The town and byway are a popular gateway to wilderness and river recreation.

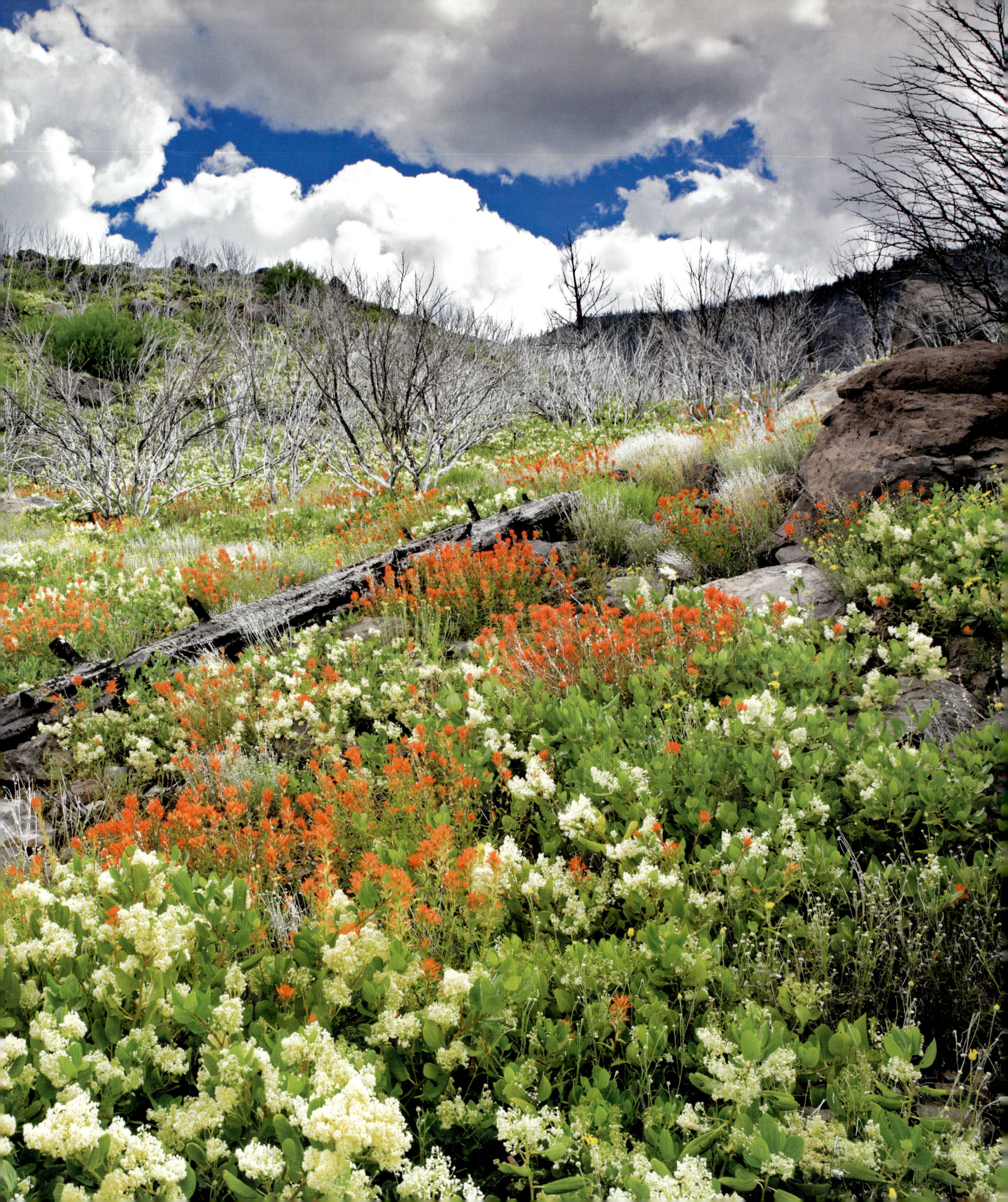

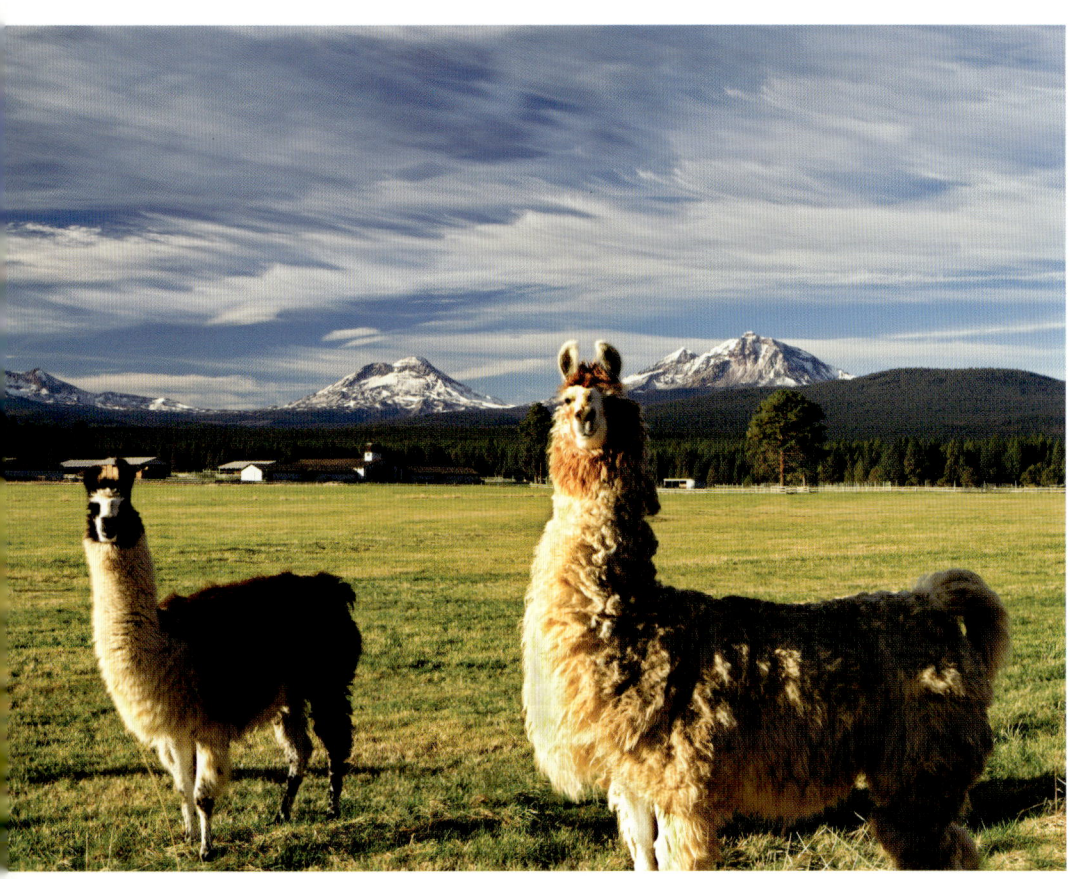

Above: Sure-footed llamas are hard-working companions when packing supplies along the trails of the Three Sisters Mountains.

Right: Cherry orchards lit in autumnal amber gild the banks of the river in the Columbia River Gorge National Scenic Area.

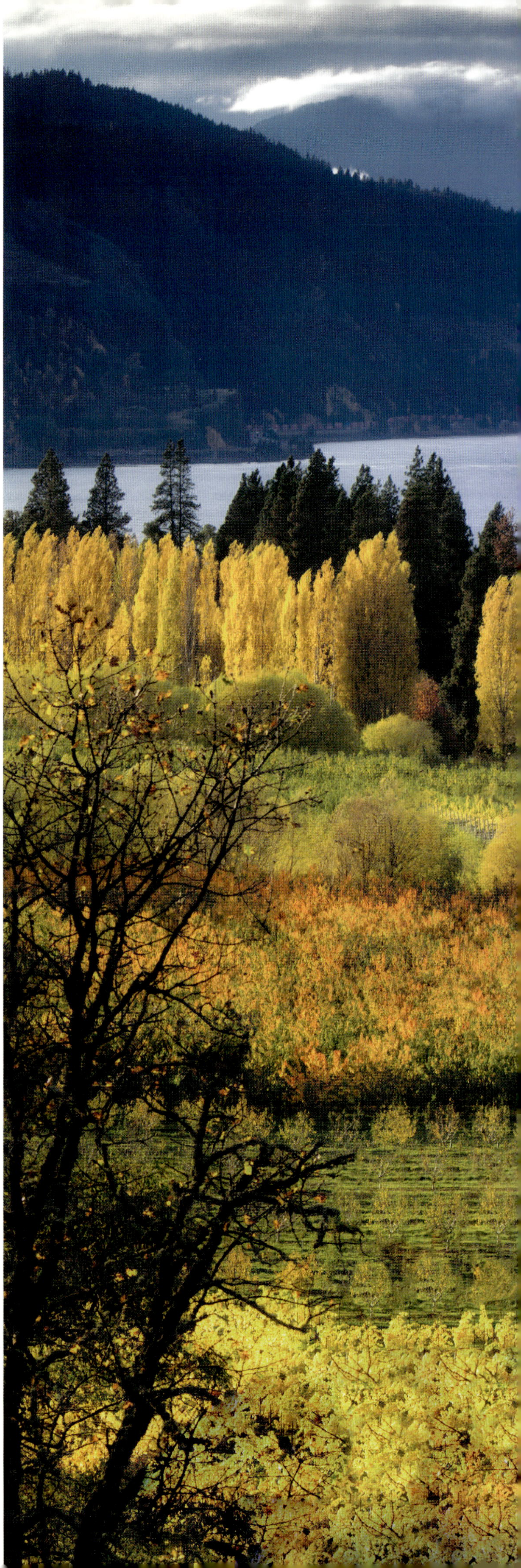

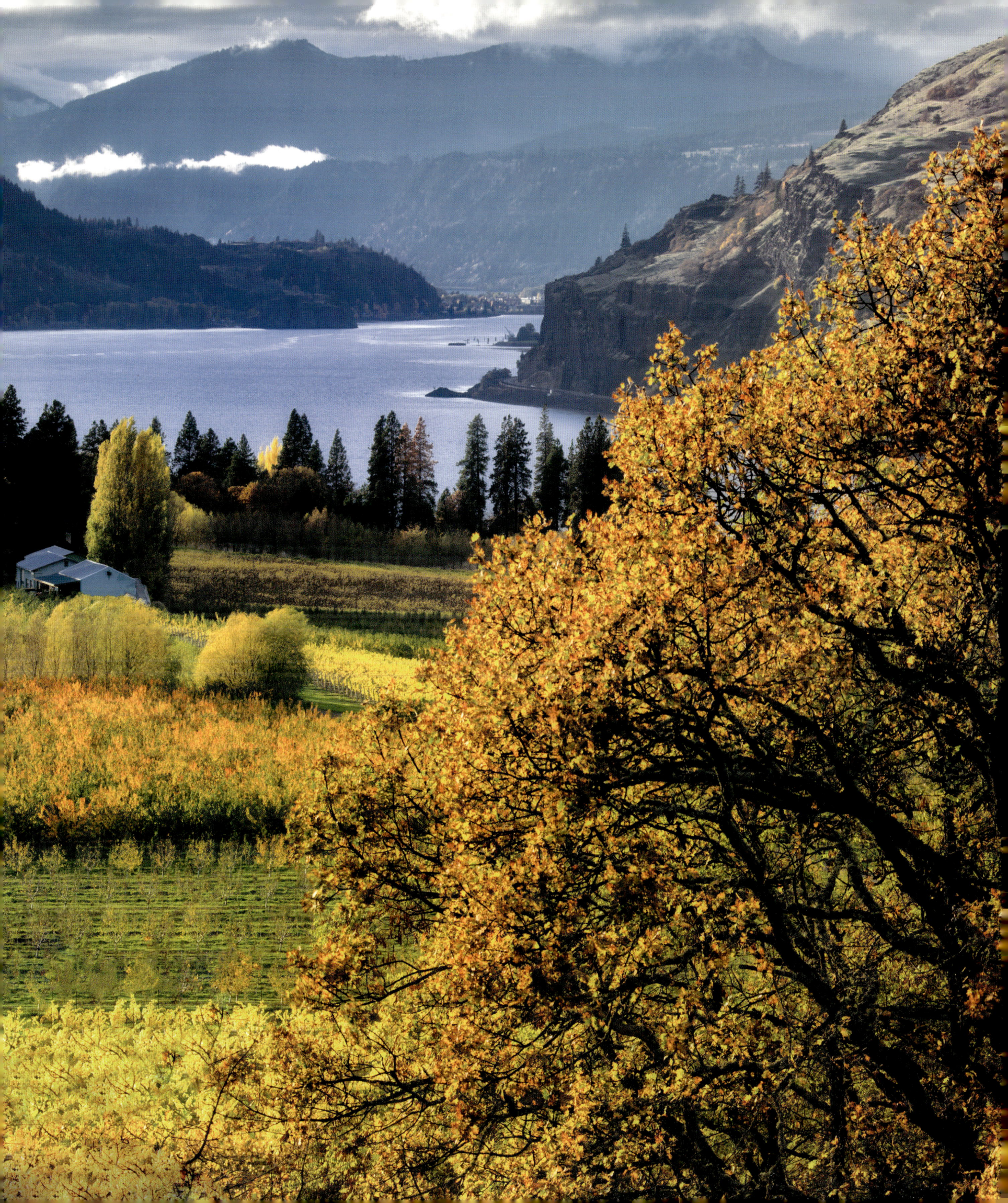

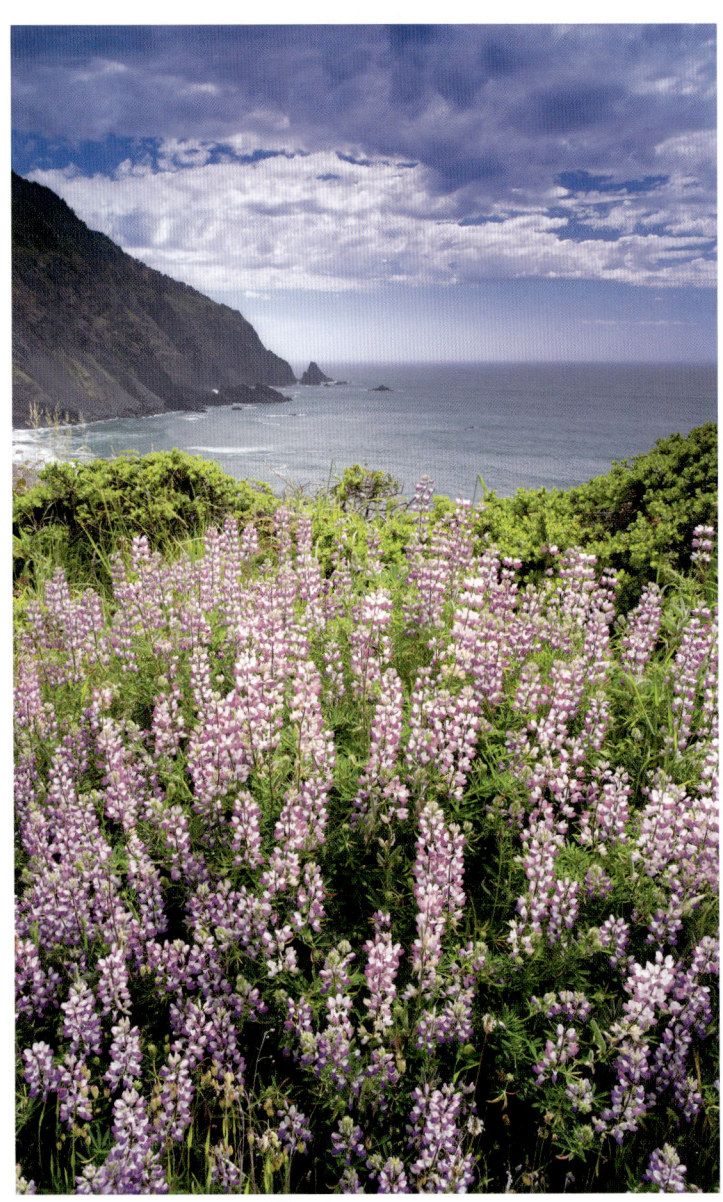

Above: The three-mile hike to the summit of 1,756-foot Humbug Mountain weaves through swaths of spring wildflowers, including these spiky blooms of blue-purple lupine.

Right: The flashing beacon of Yaquina Head, the tallest lighthouse in Oregon, has directed mariners along the rocky coast near Newport since 1873. An excellent example of late 19th-century lighthouses, it is one of the most visited on the West Coast.

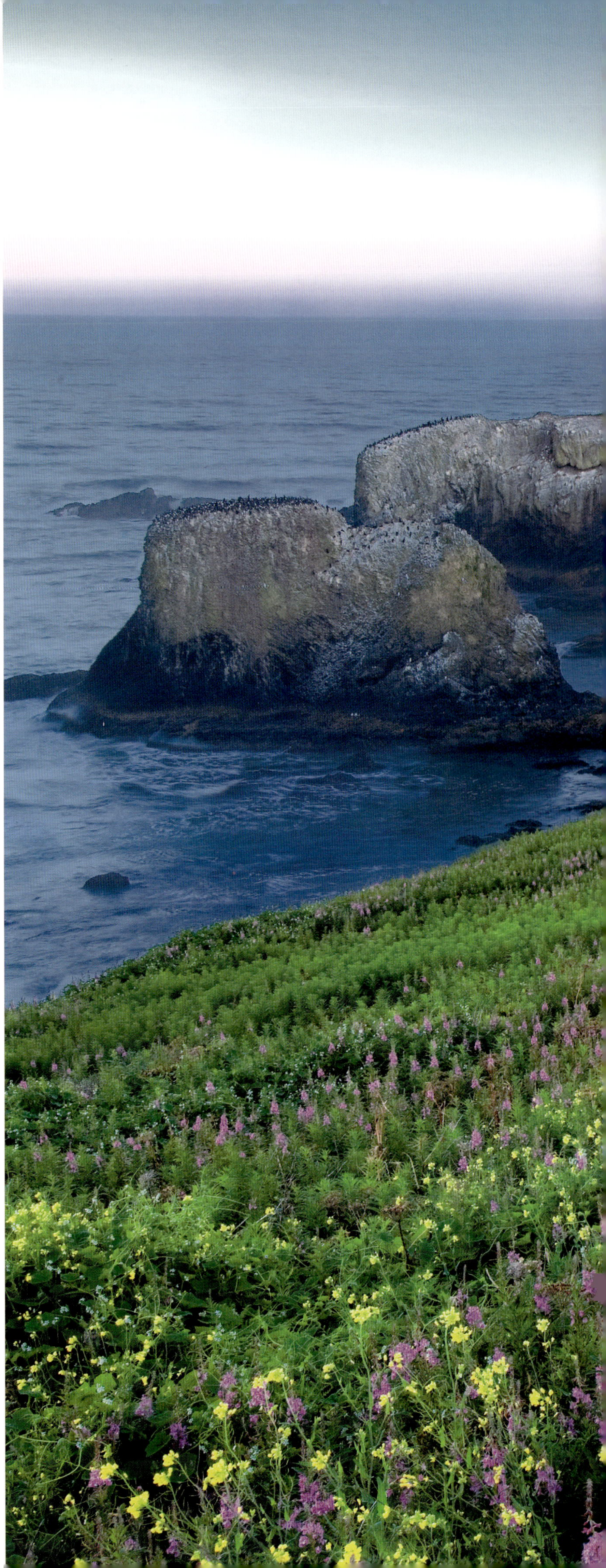

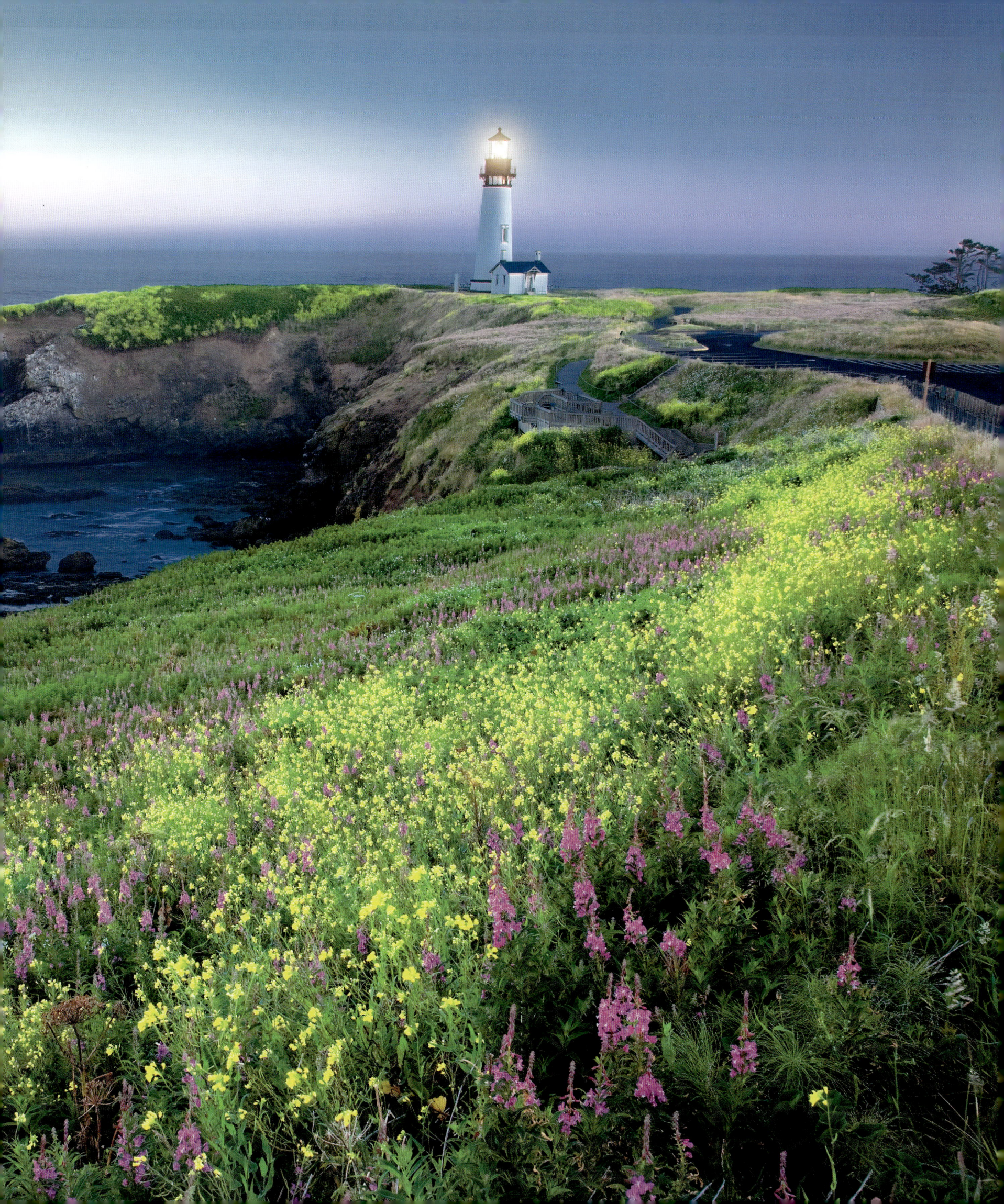

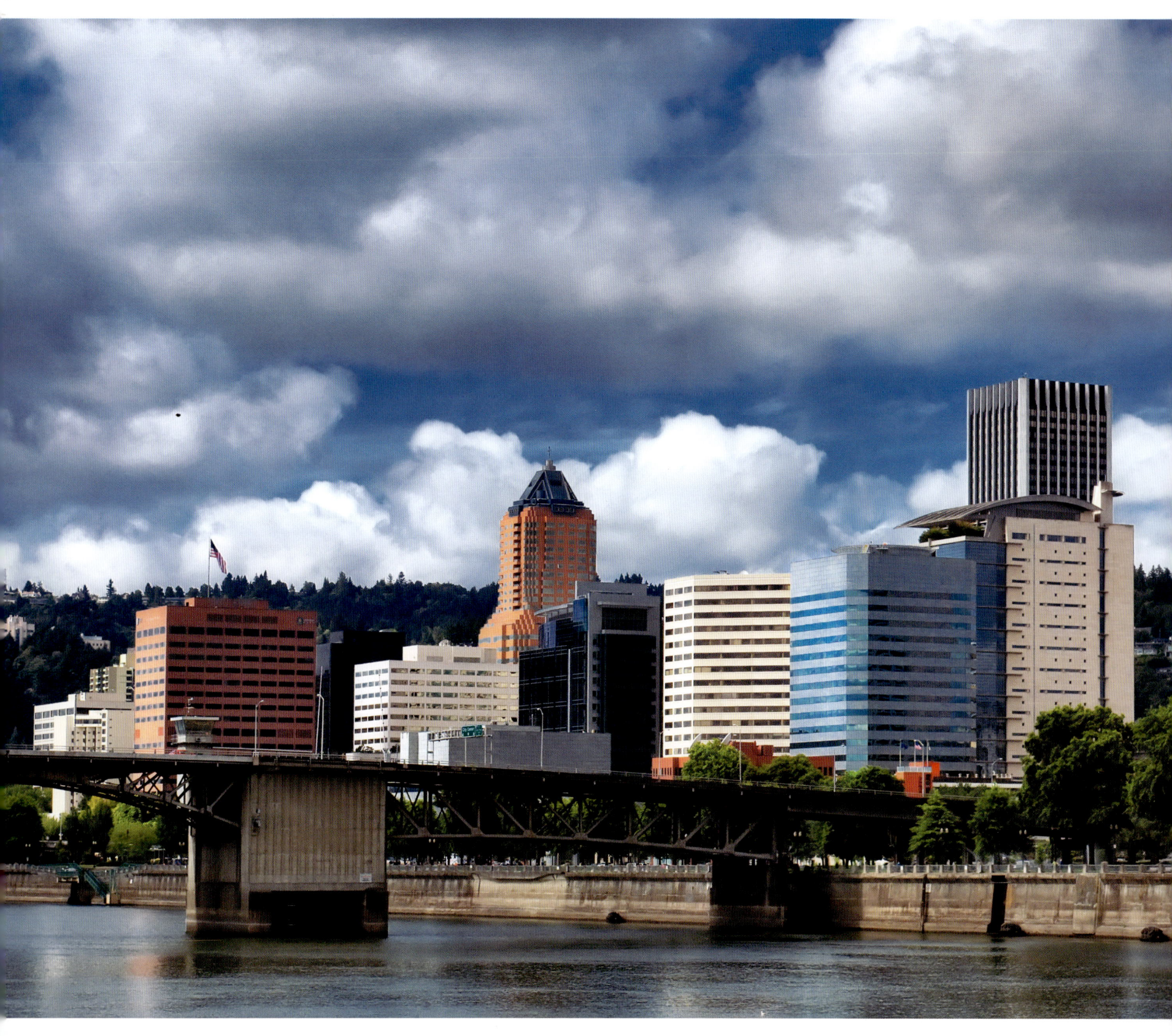

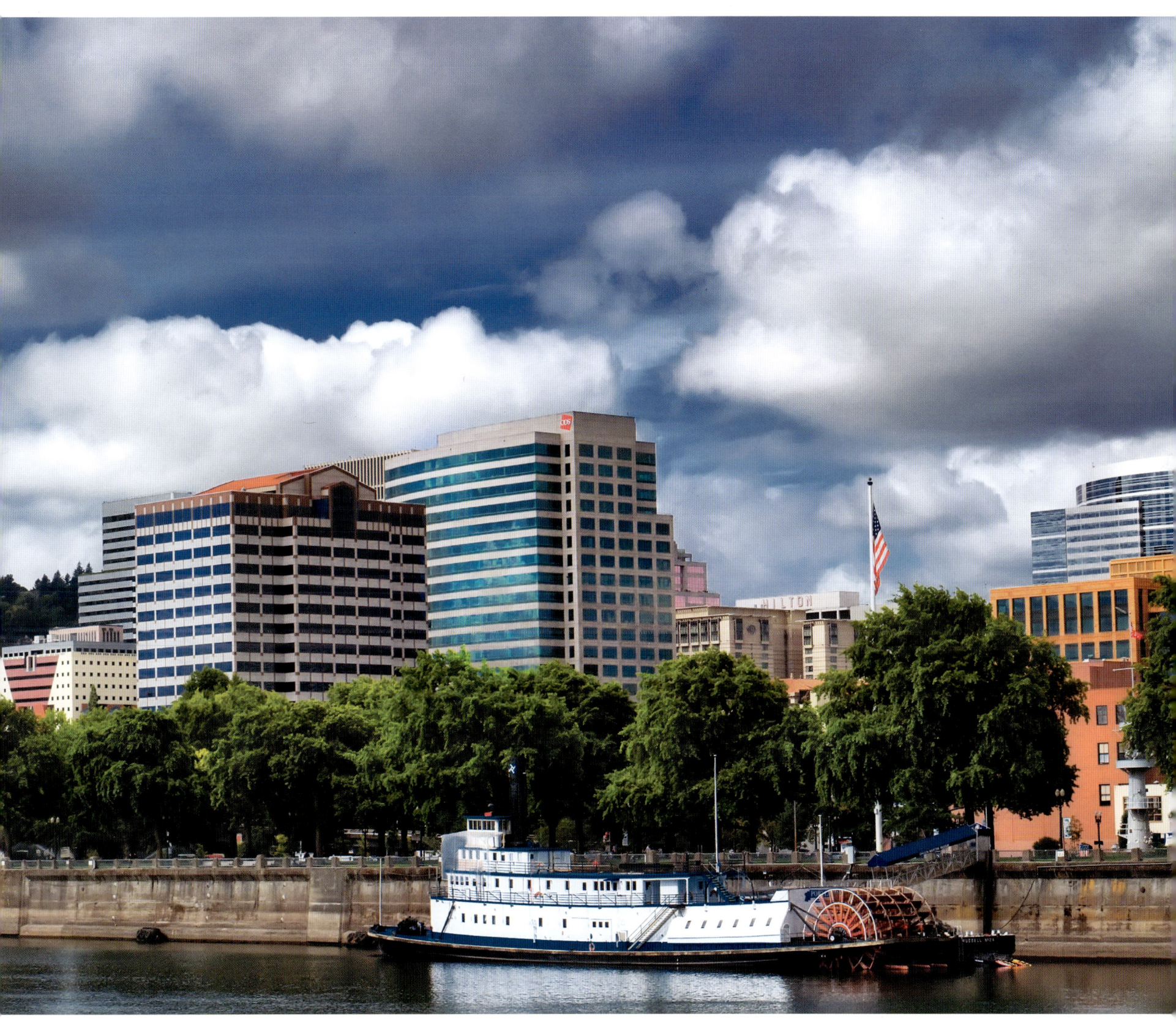

Portland, Oregon's largest city, sits just south of the confluence of the Willamette and Columbia rivers. The City of Roses draws nature enthusiasts, foodies, and wine and beer aficionados to its unique and varied neighborhoods. Half of the state's 3.9 million citizens reside in the metro area.

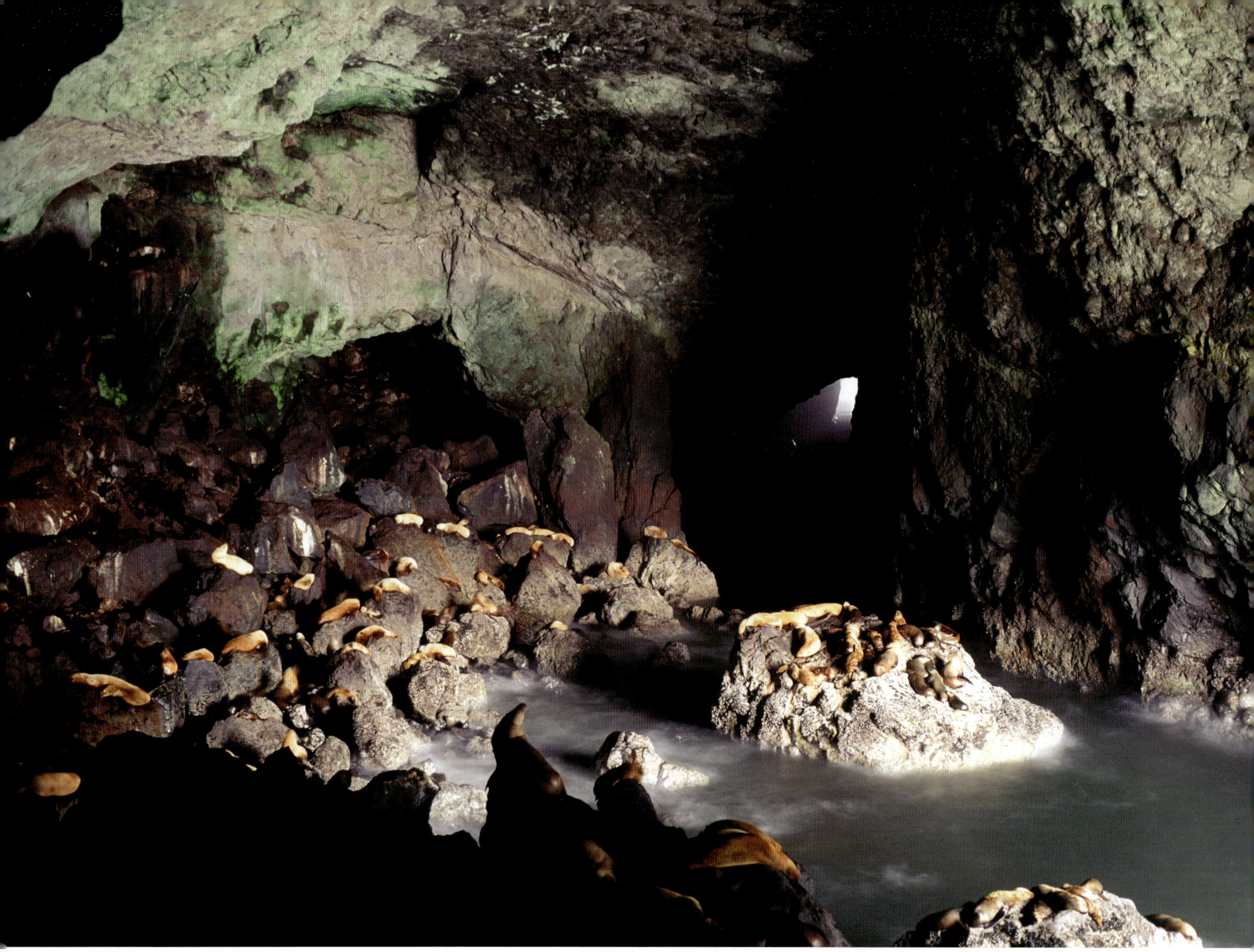

Above: Herds of up to 200 Steller sea lions make their home at the Sea Lion Caves, which claims the title of world's largest sea cave. In May and June, the caves, located north of Florence, offer an intimate look at the marine mammals in their natural habitat as they bear and nurse their pups.

Right: From December 1805 to March 1806, the famed Corps of Discovery led by Meriwether Lewis and William Clark camped on the north coast of what would later become the state of Oregon. Fort Clatsop, near Astoria, features a replica of the log shelter the explorers built to shield them from the weather. Learn the stories of the famed explorers' adventure from the park's costumed rangers.

Facing page: At 620 feet, Multnomah Falls is the tallest and most photographed of the 70 waterfalls in the Columbia River Gorge National Scenic Area. A trail leads visitors to the observation bridge between the upper and lower falls and one mile further to the top of the falls.

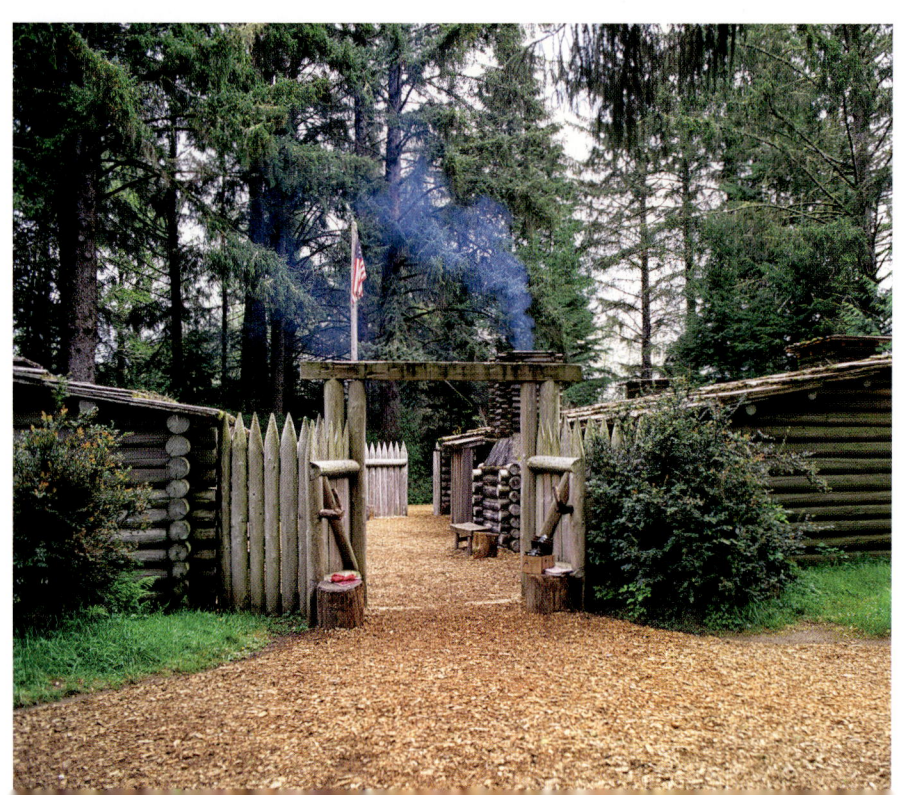

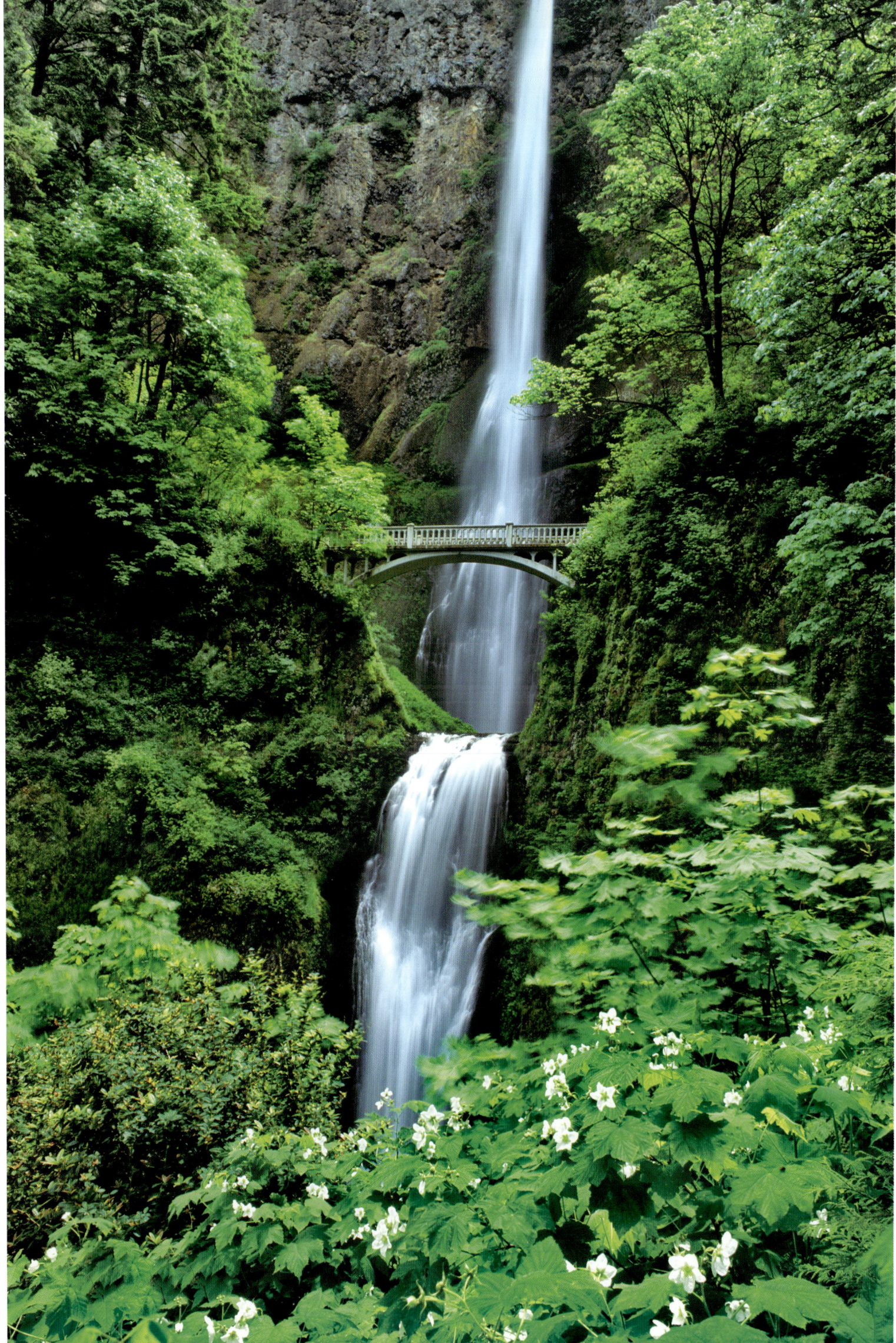

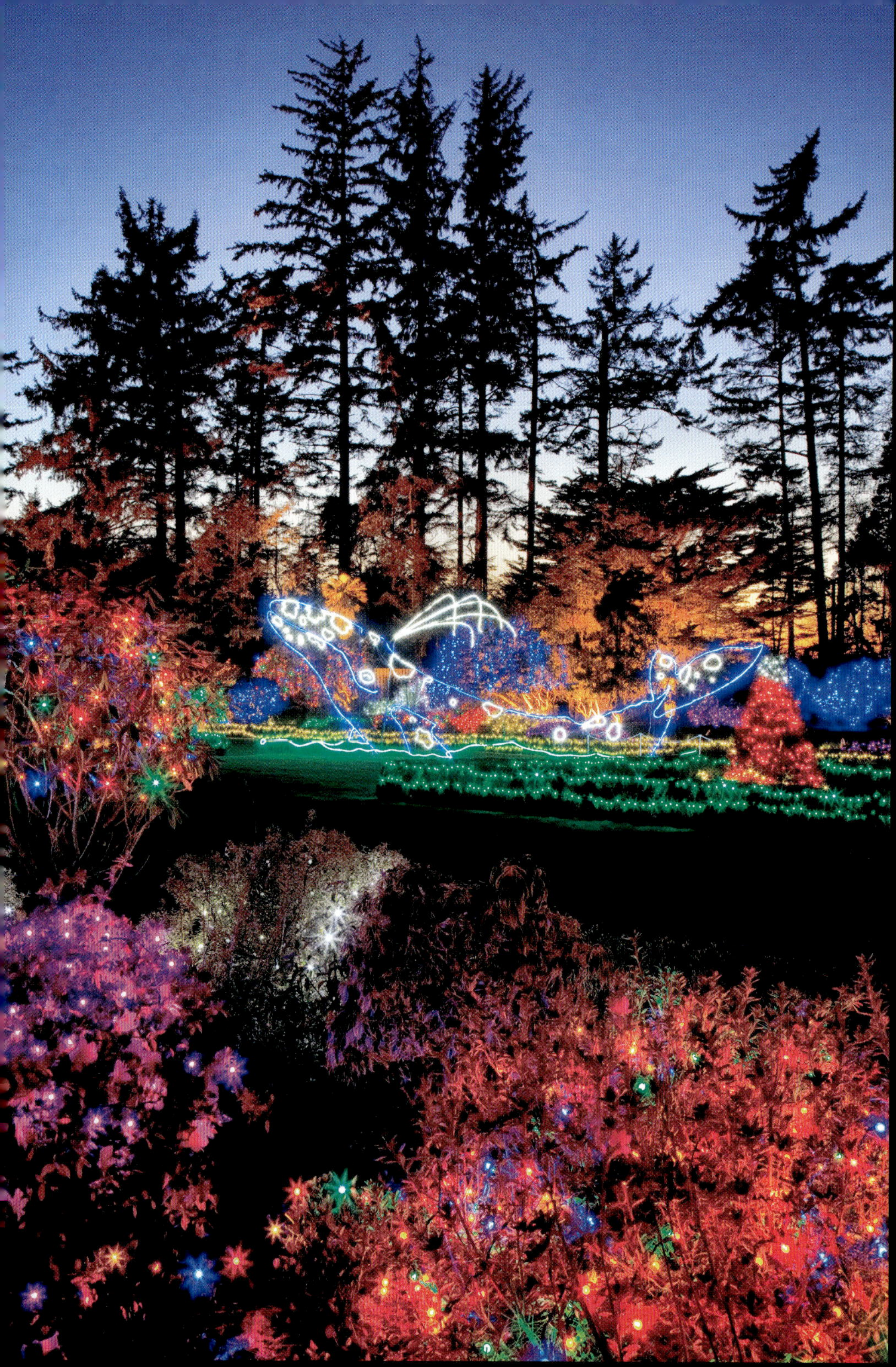

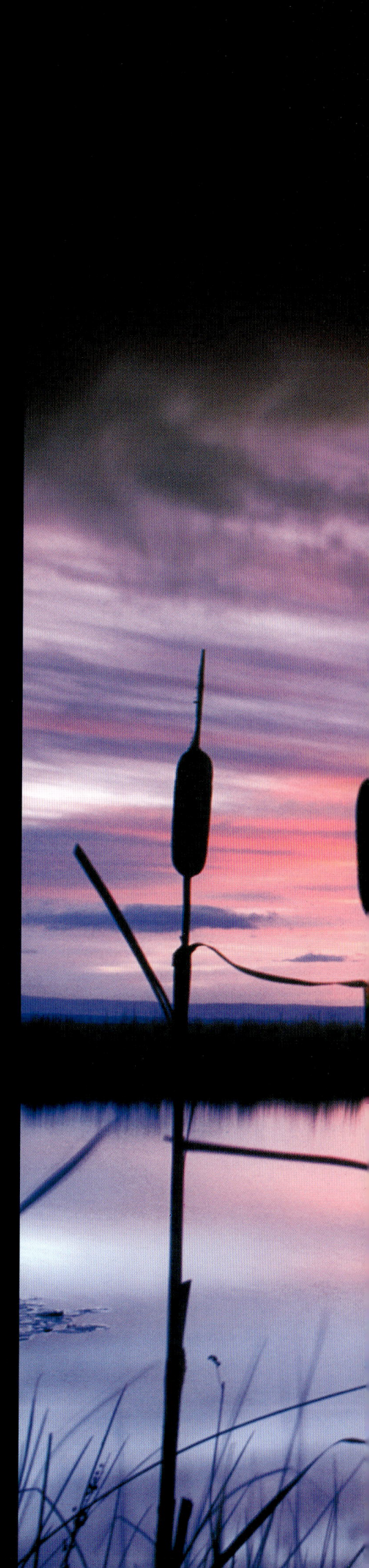

Above: A life-size spouting whale twinkles in the night during the annual holiday light display at Shore Acres State Park. Featuring more than 300,000 lights, the display draws visitors to the former private estate, which boasts seven acres of botanical gardens and plants from around the world.

Right: The 18,941-acre Summer Lake Wildlife Area is a tranquil stop for hundreds of thousands of waterfowl traveling along the Pacific Flyway during their spring and fall migrations.

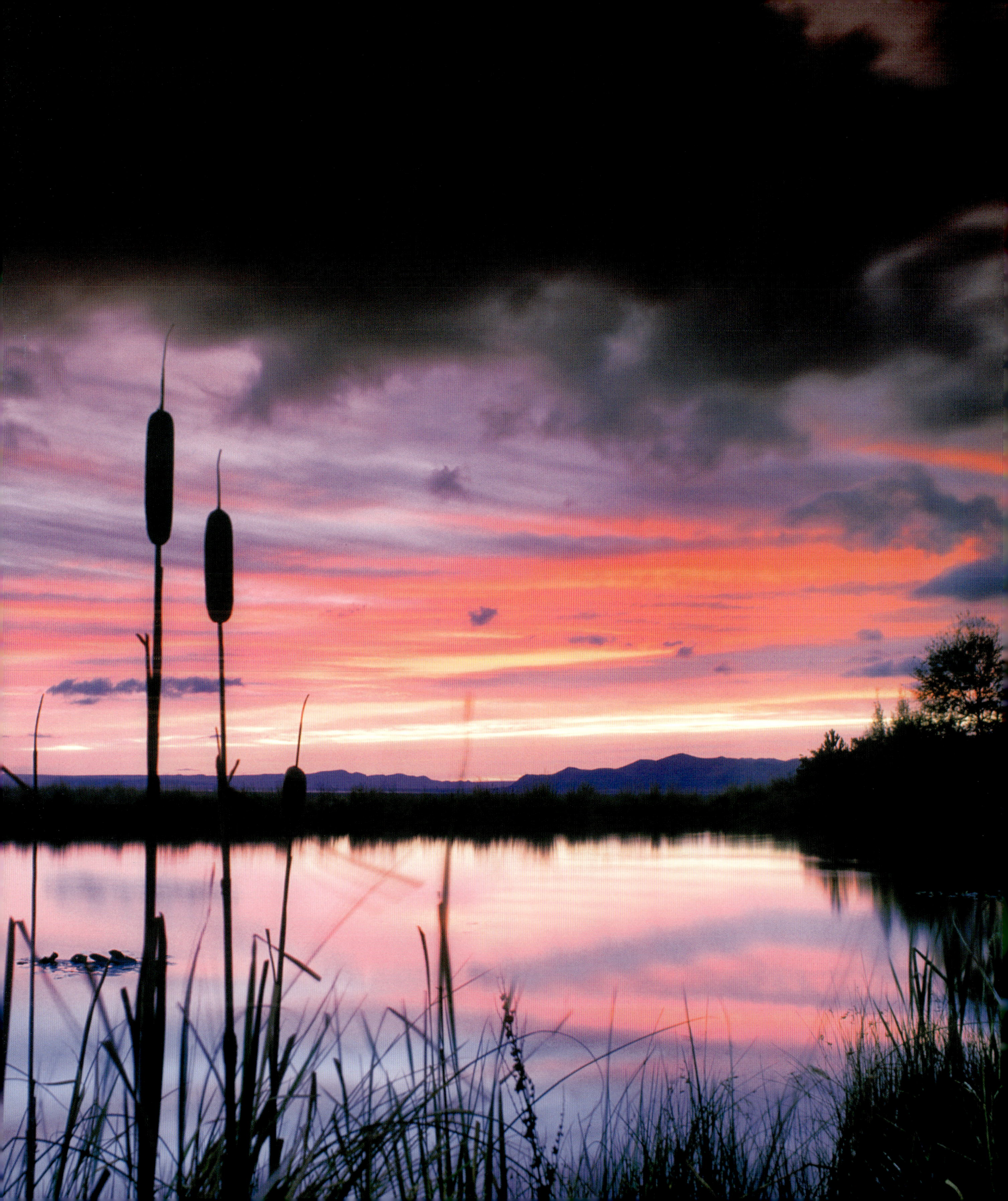

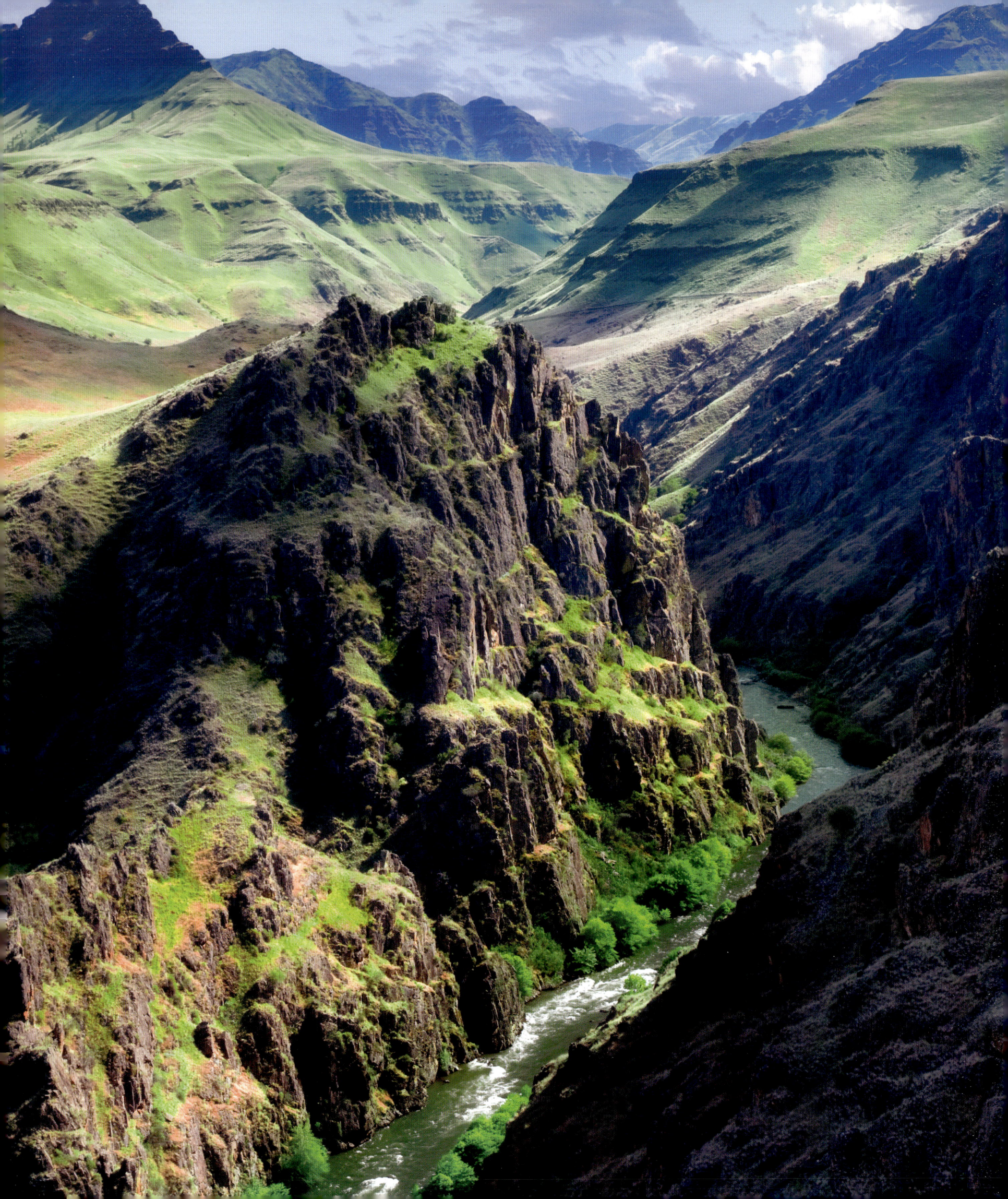

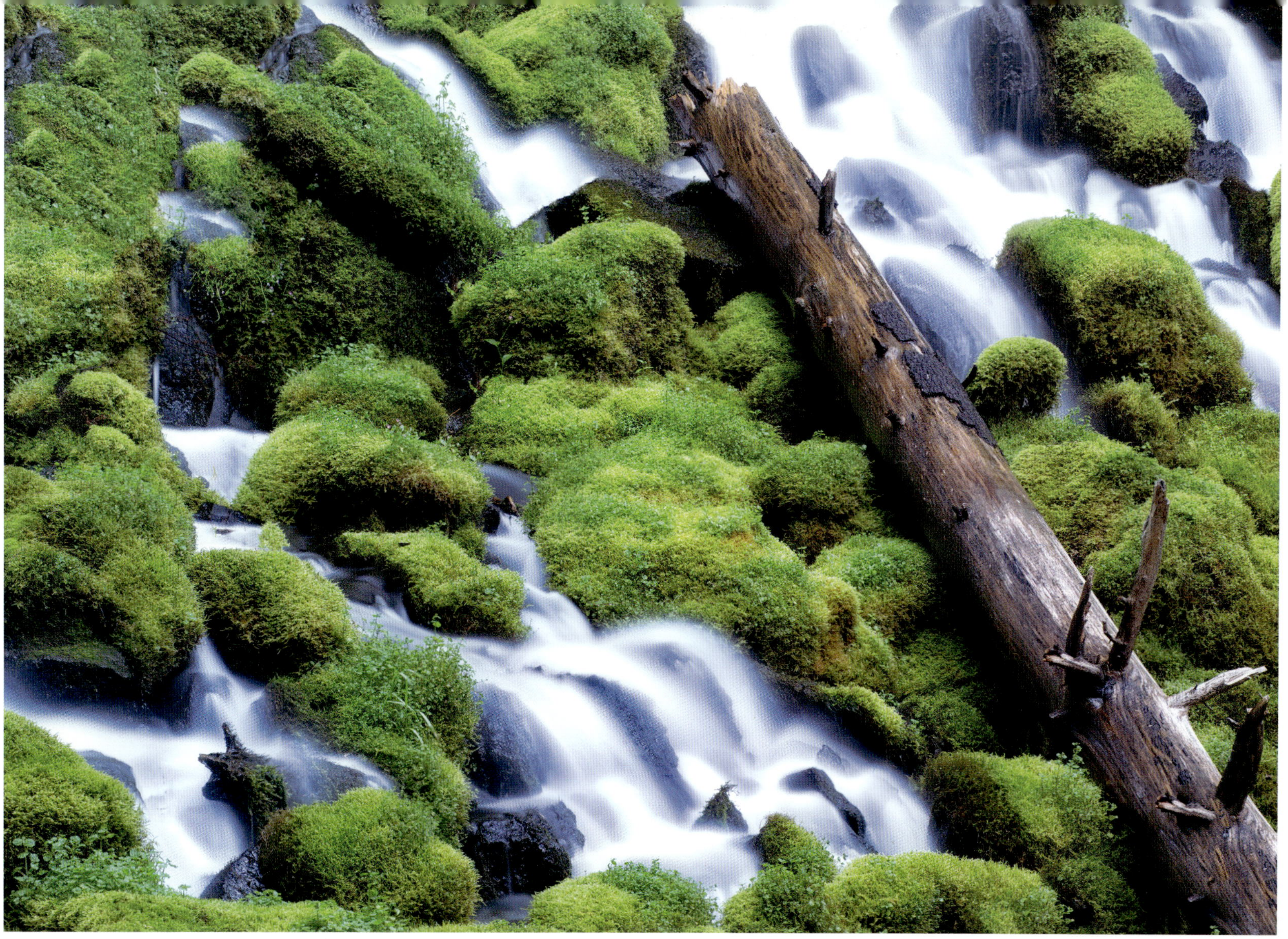

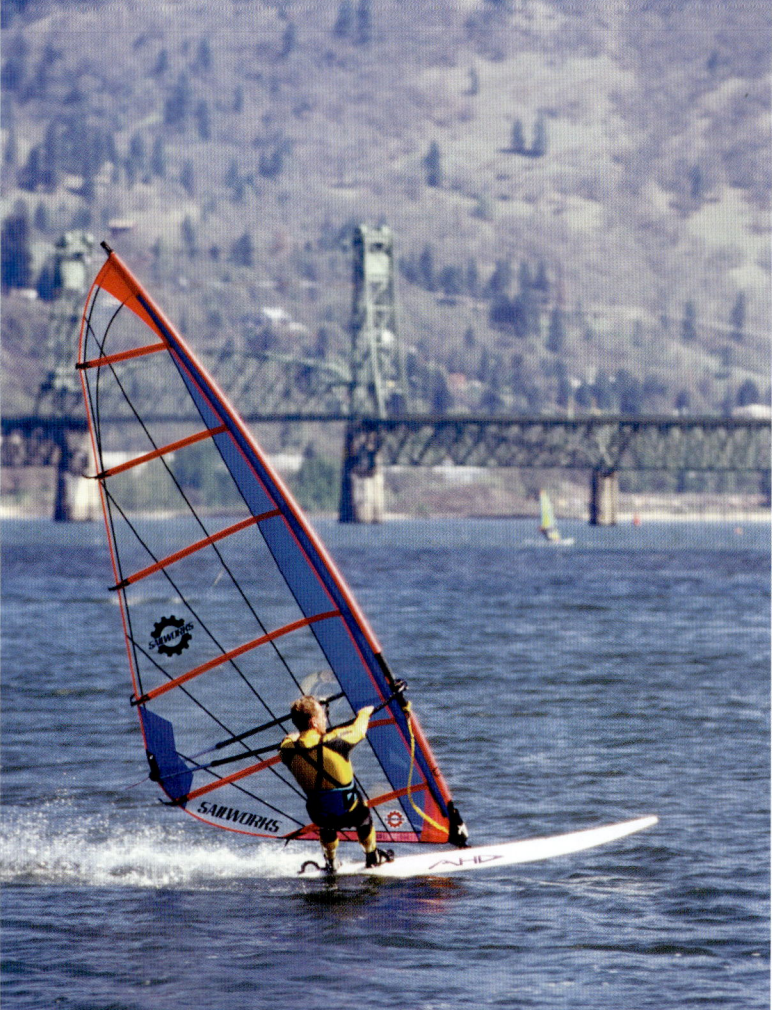

Above: Clearwater Falls tumbles over moss-cloaked rocks and logs in the Umpqua National Forest.

Left: Strong winds and stunning scenery draw windsurfers from around the world to the Columbia River Gorge. In the background, Hood River Bridge's 0.8-mile span carries automobiles from Hood River, Oregon, to White Salmon, Washington. The bridge features a vertical lift span to make room for Columbia River ship traffic.

Far left: The Imnaha River flows through lands that sheltered Chief Joseph and other members of the Nez Perce tribe. The river drops over 7,000 feet in elevation along its 77-mile route.

Right: Wild turkeys are free as a bird at the Wildlife Safari in Winston. The birds make their home at the preserve along with elephants, giraffes, rhinos, and other animals from Africa, Asia, and the Americas.

Far right: A crown of cherry blossoms encircles State Capitol State Park in Salem each spring. Above the urban green space, the gilded Oregon Pioneer statue atop the capitol represents the heroic spirit of the state's early settlers.

Below: Quiet beauty and simple living abound in small towns like Joseph in eastern Oregon. Surprises wait around every corner, though; local artists have contributed almost a dozen bronze sculptures to the streets of downtown Joseph.

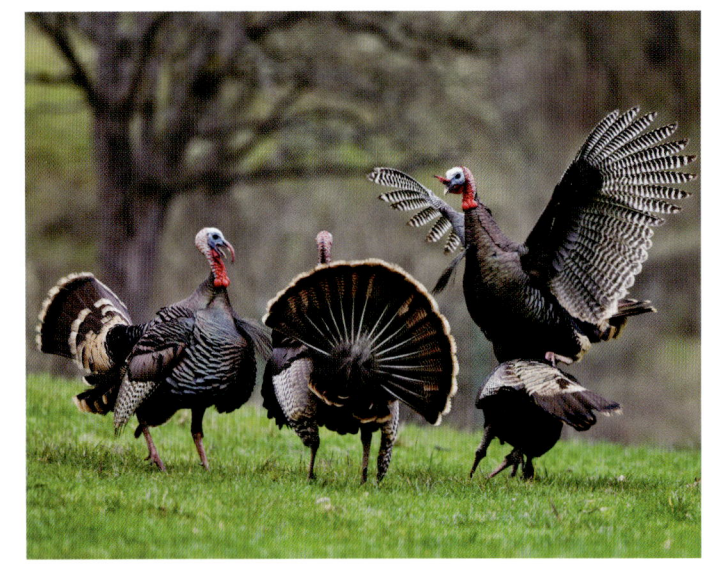

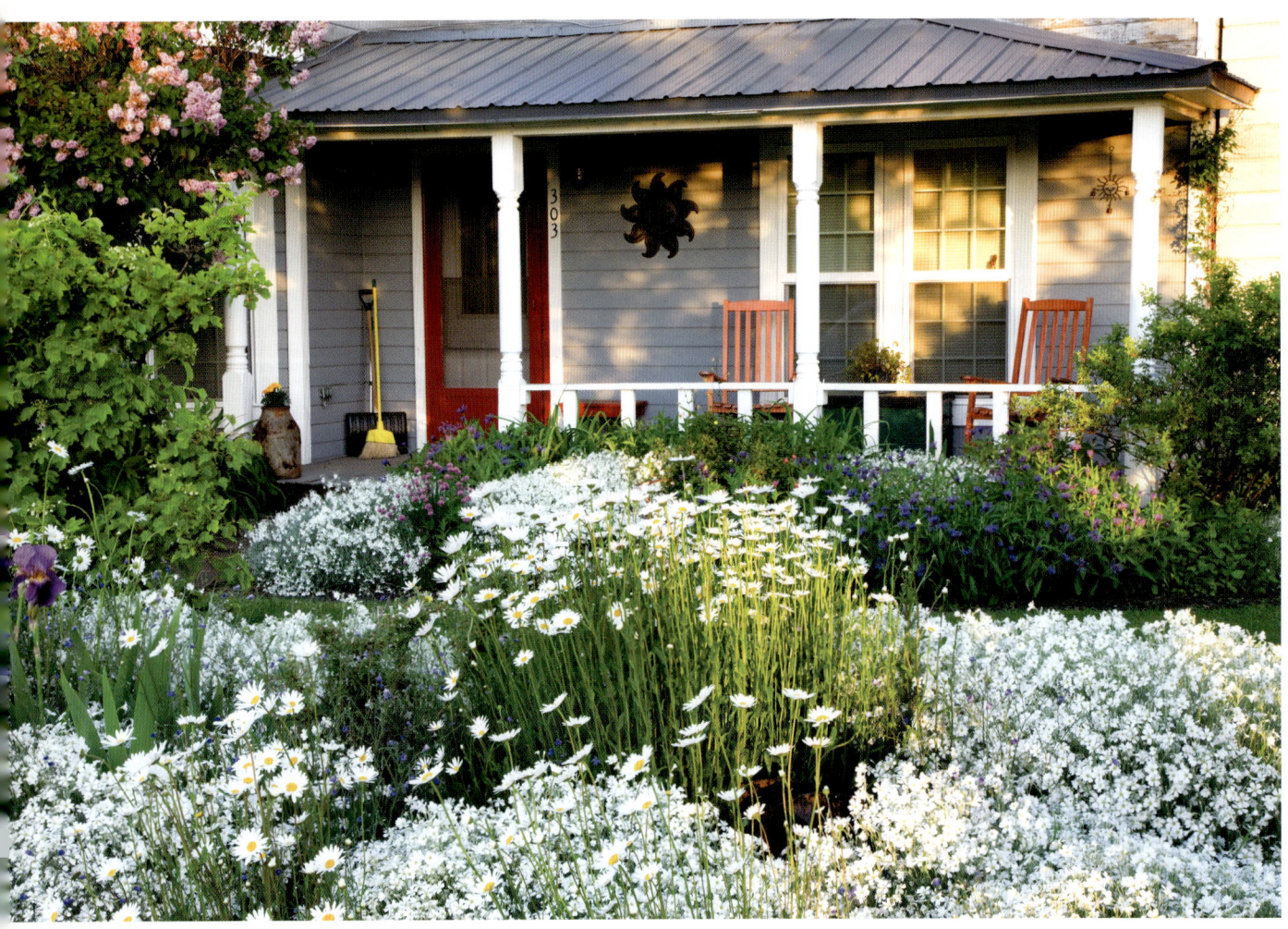

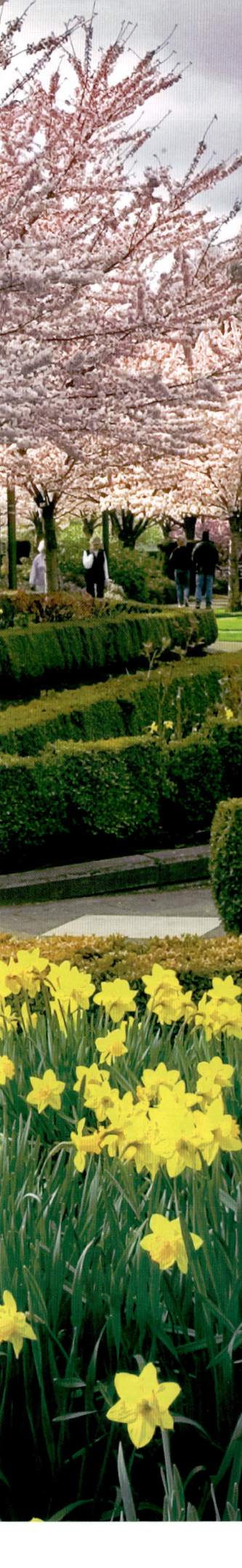

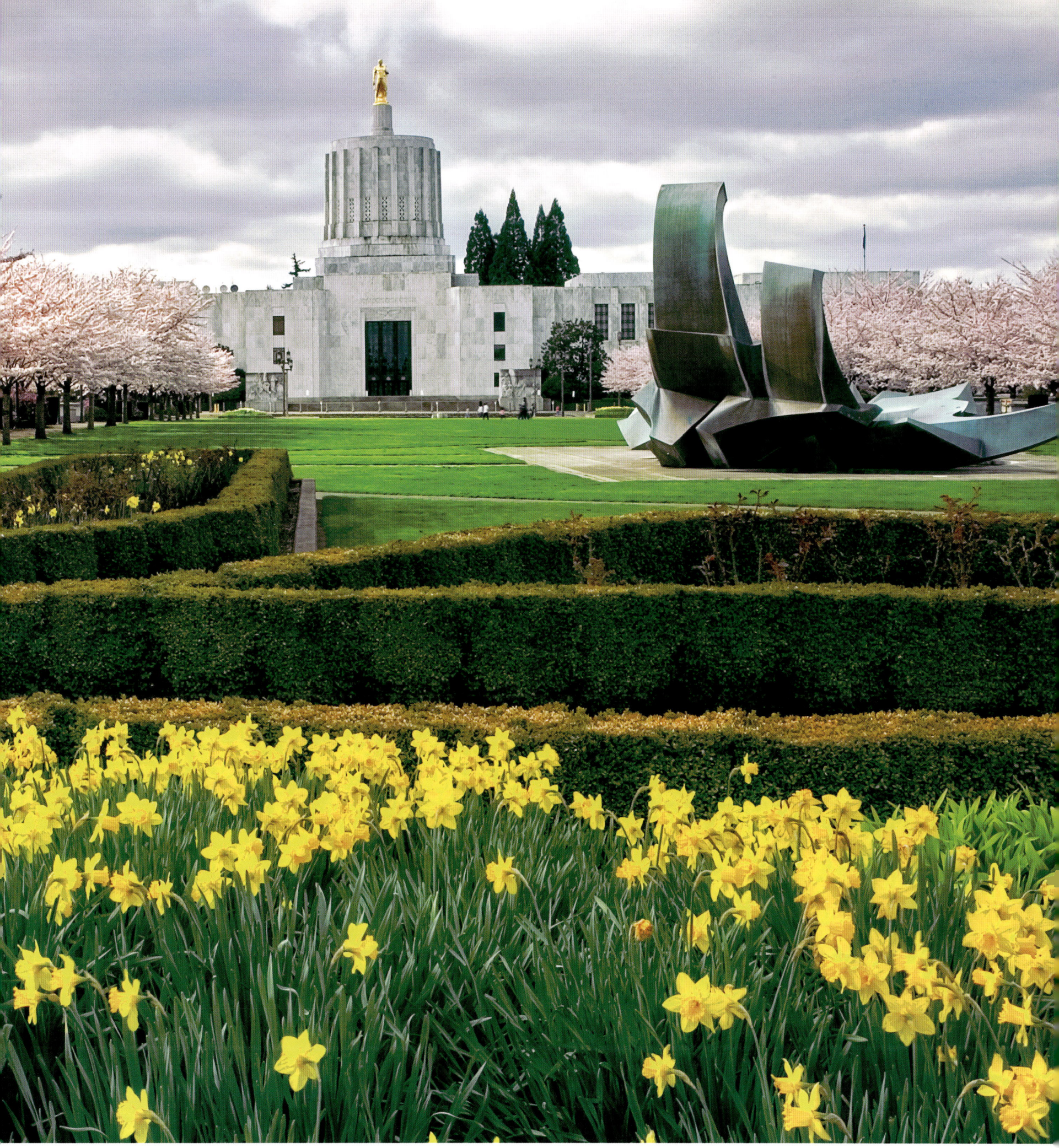

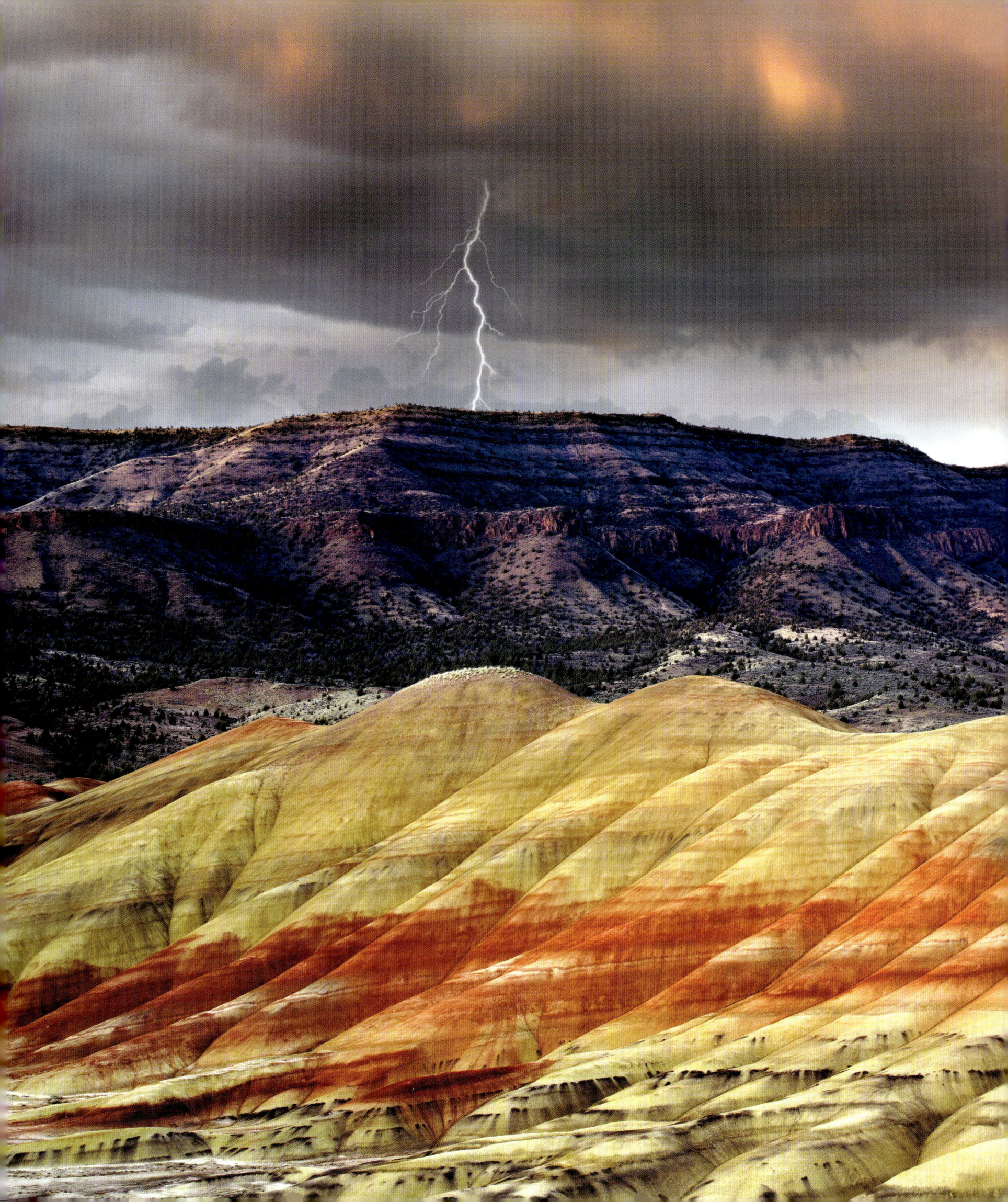

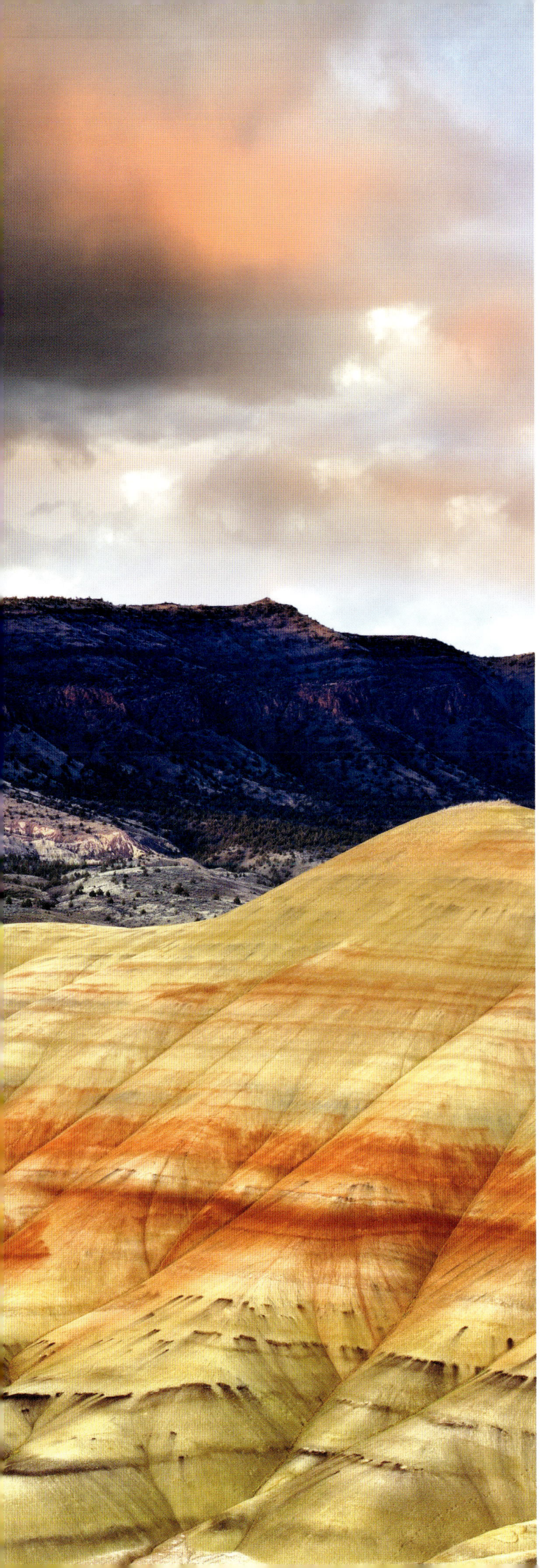

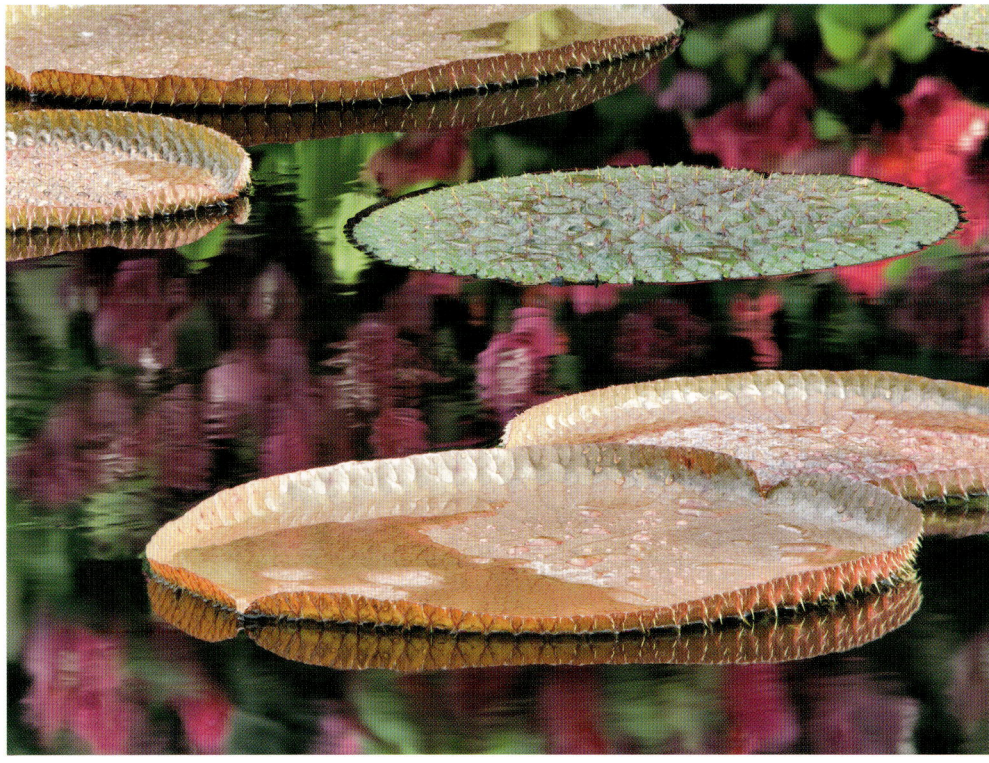

Above: Water lilies thrive in the quiet waters of ponds, lake margins, and slow-running streams, where roots burrow into the muddy bottom and foliage soaks up sunshine on the water's surface.

Left: Lightning strikes the Painted Hills of the John Day Fossil Beds National Monument at sunset. One of three distinct sections of the monument, the Painted Hills are known for their unique black, tan, and red striations of volcanic ash. Scientists have identified plant and animal fossils on the monument dating from 5 to 44 million years ago.

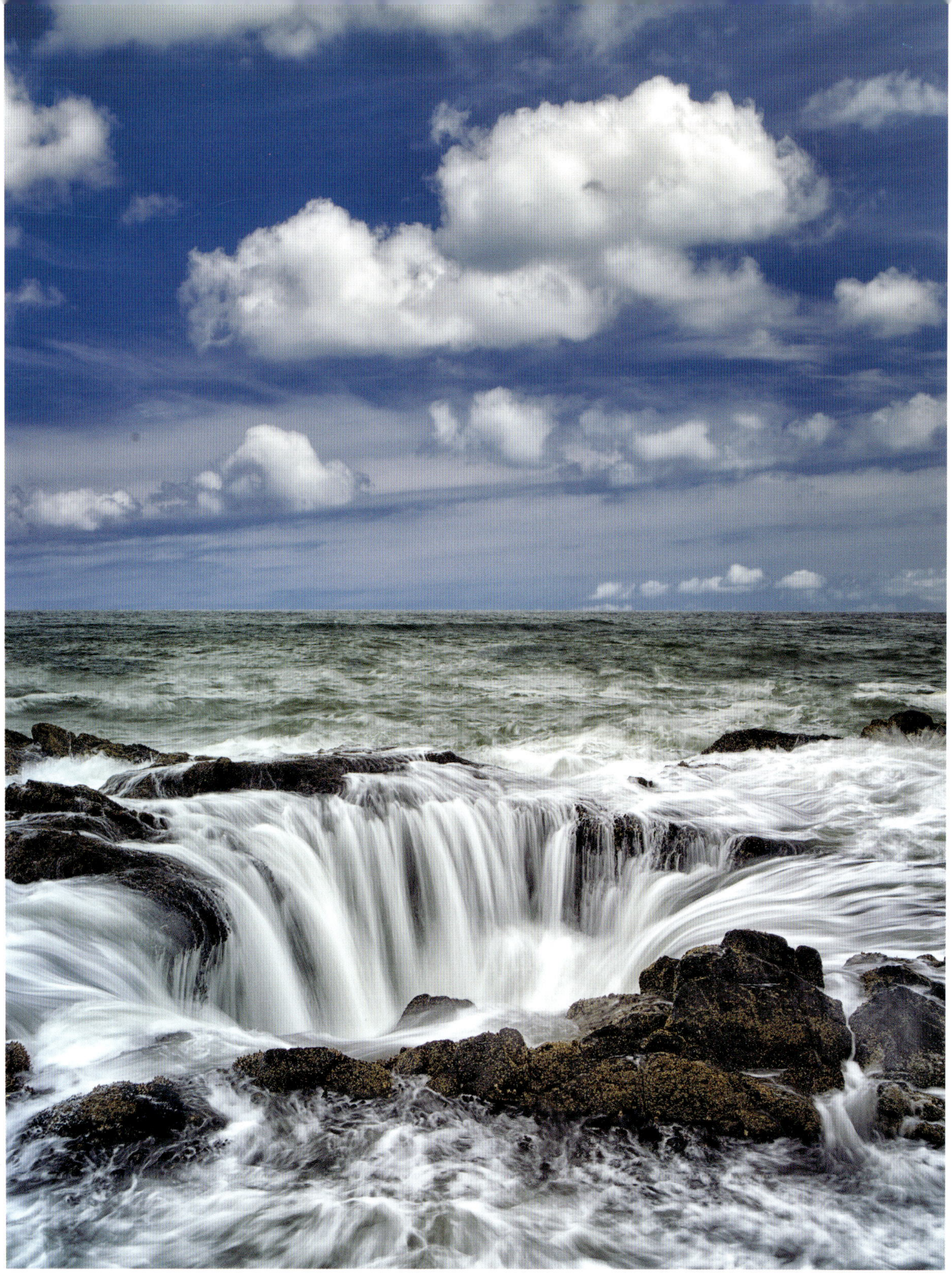

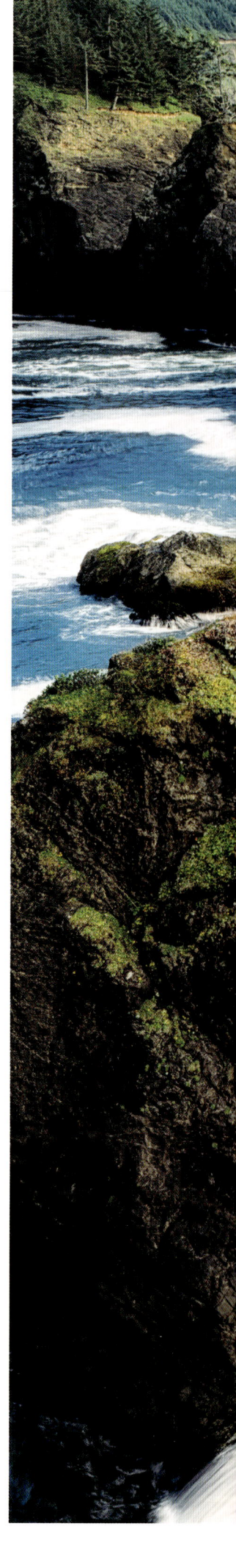

Above: Seawater drains into a bowl carved from the rocky shoreline at Thor's Well in the Cape Perpetua Scenic Area near Yachats. The formation developed when the roof of a sea cave collapsed, and with each tidal surge, water is forced into the opening, sending plumes of ocean spray skyward.

Right: Secluded beaches and forested sea stacks dot the rugged coastline at Samuel H. Boardman State Scenic Corridor on the Oregon Coast's southern tip.

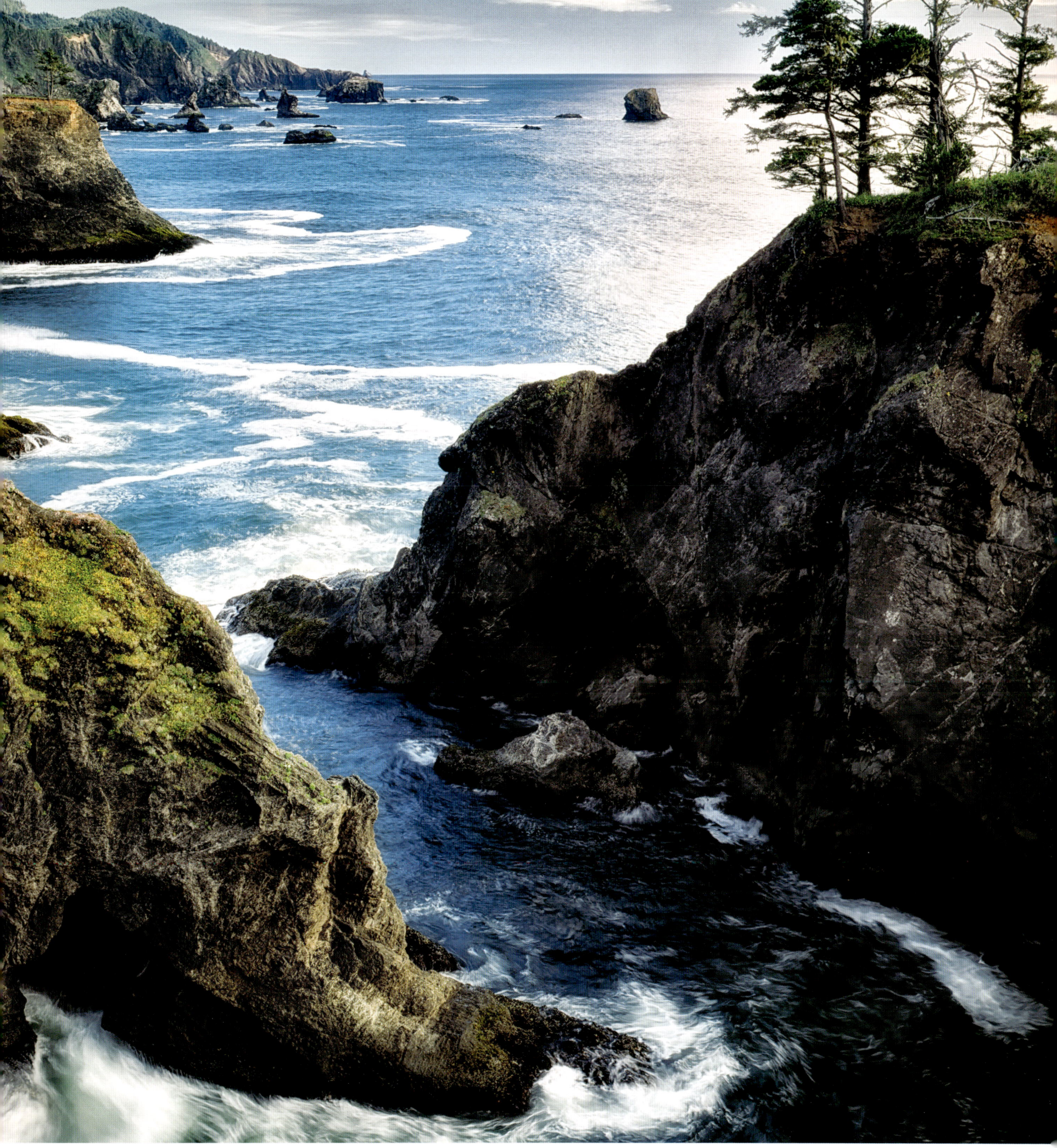

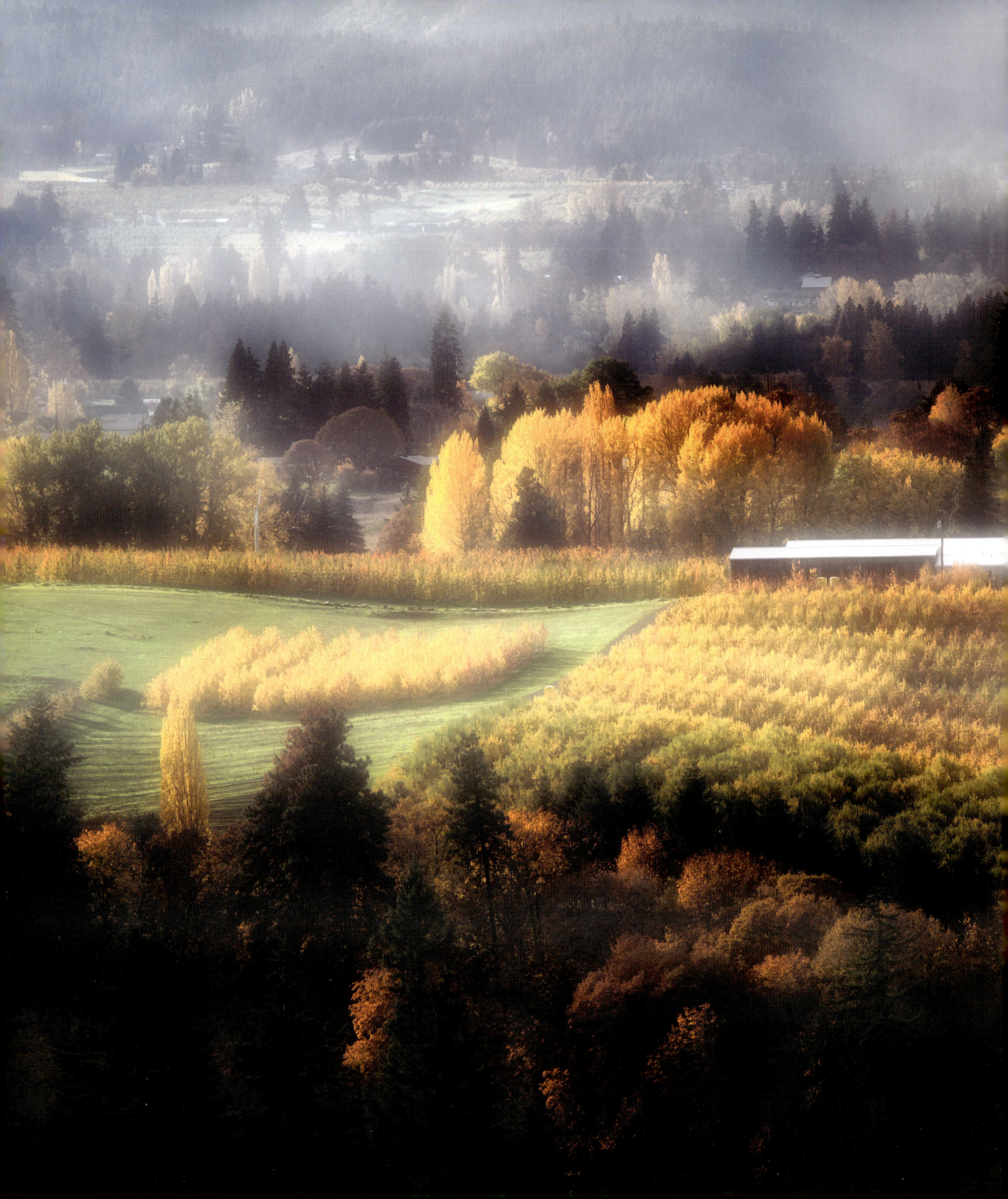

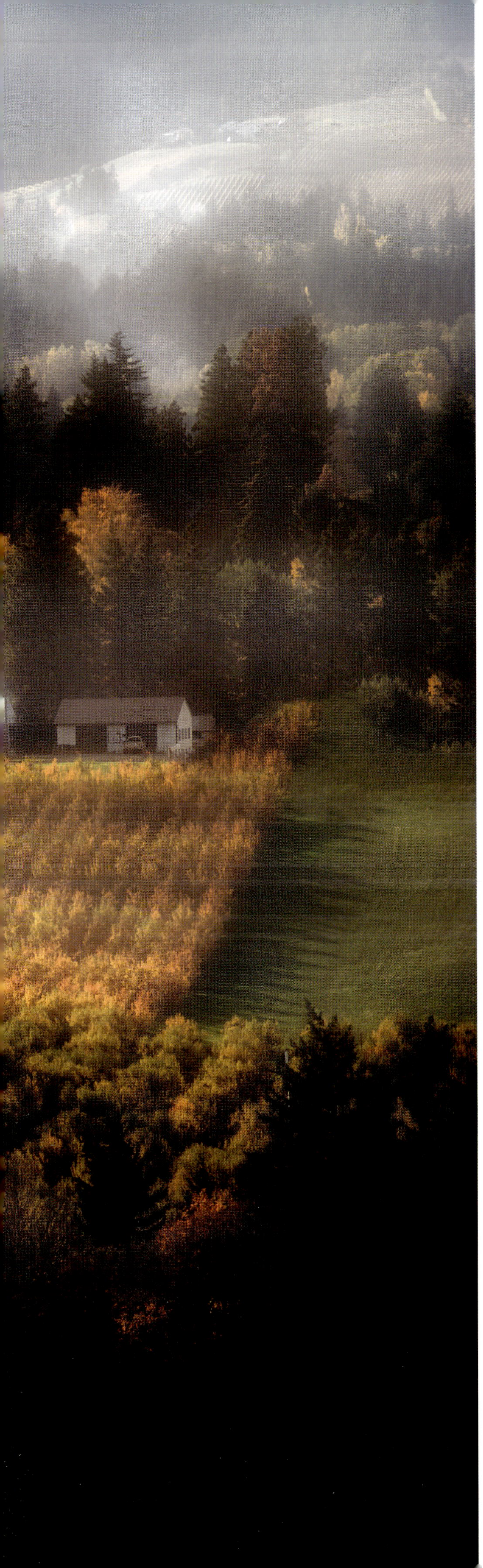

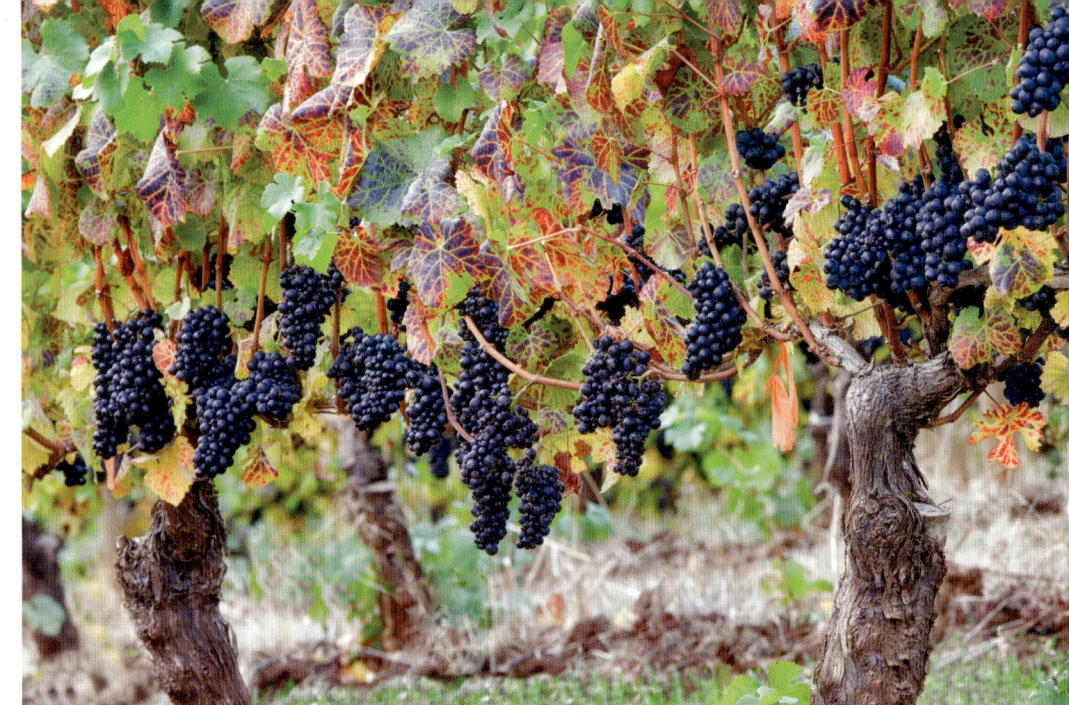

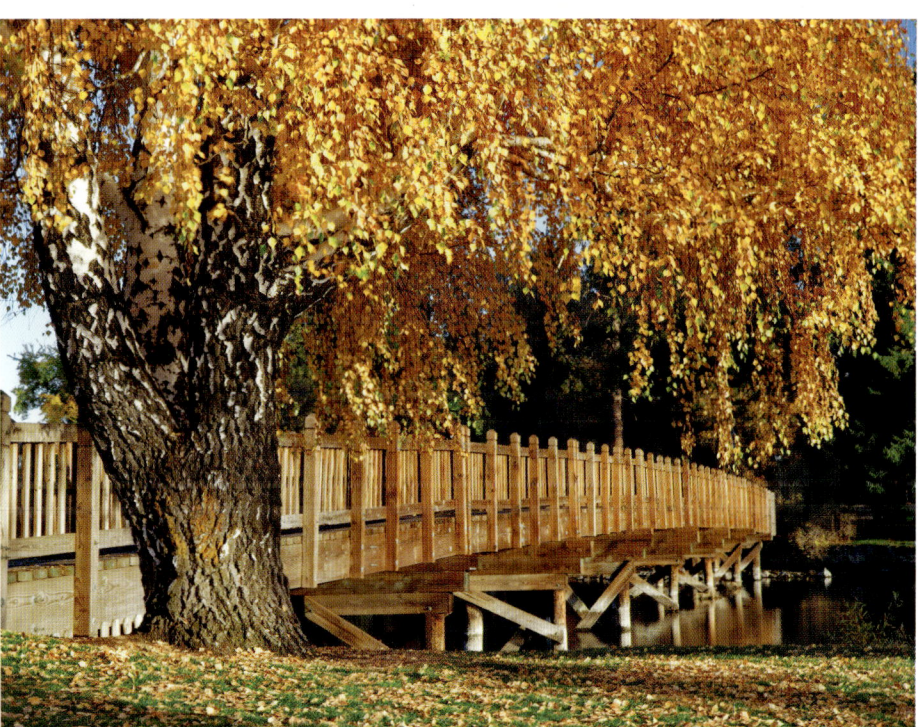

Above, top: Oregon is the third-largest wine growing region in the United States, producing 72 varietals from 17 diverse grape growing zones.

Above, bottom: The Deschutes River winds through downtown Bend's Drake Park, where cyclists and strollers share the tree-lined paths.

Left: After the apple and pear harvests, foliage is the focus in the Hood River Valley.

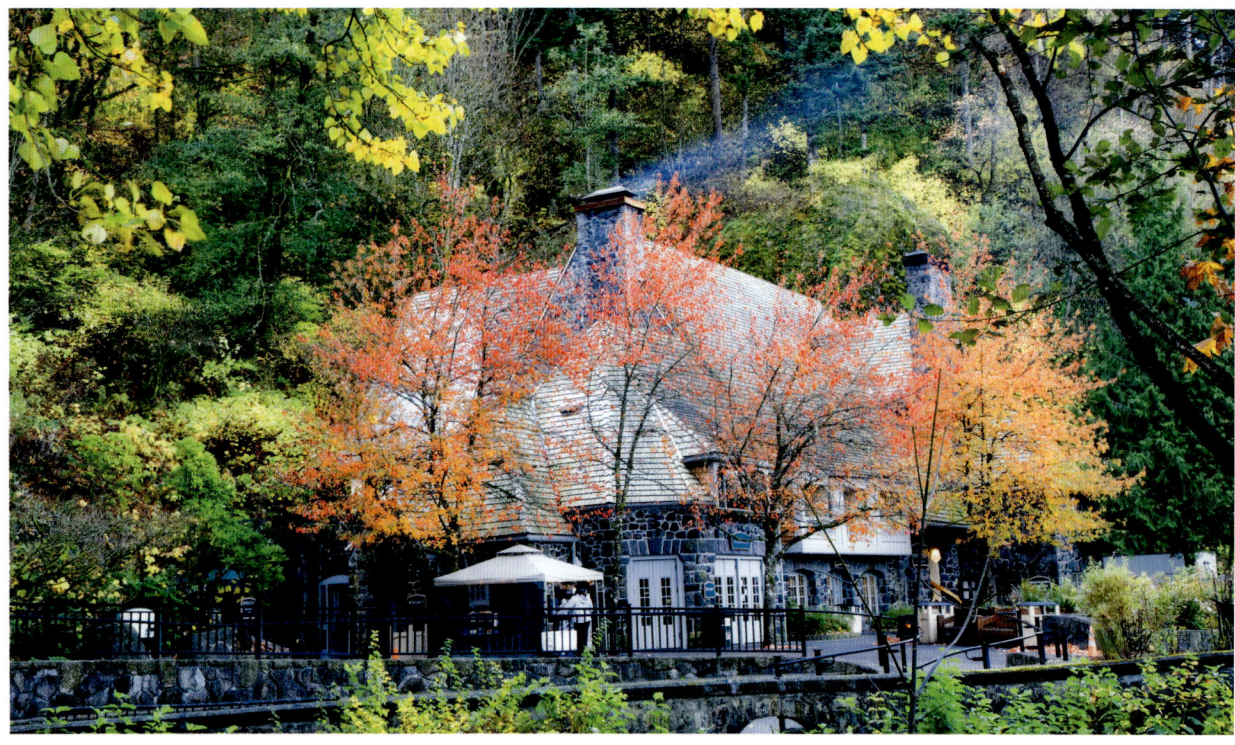

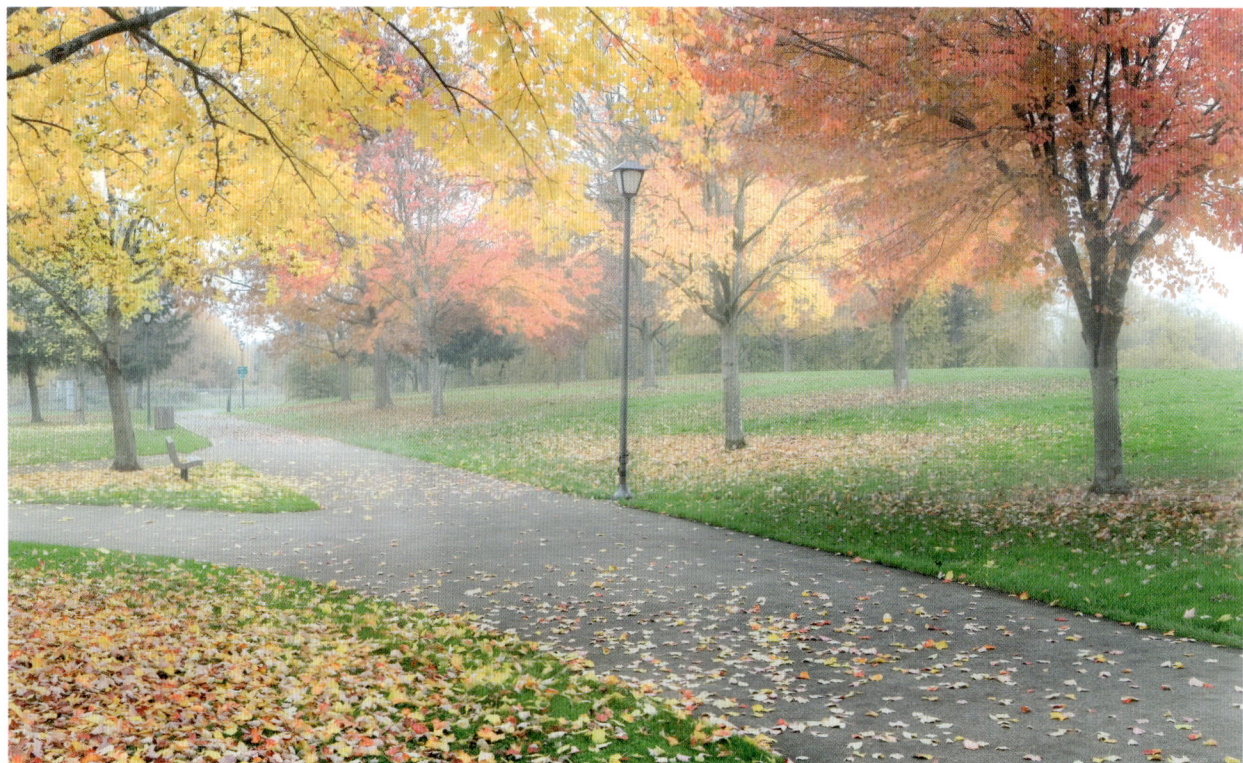

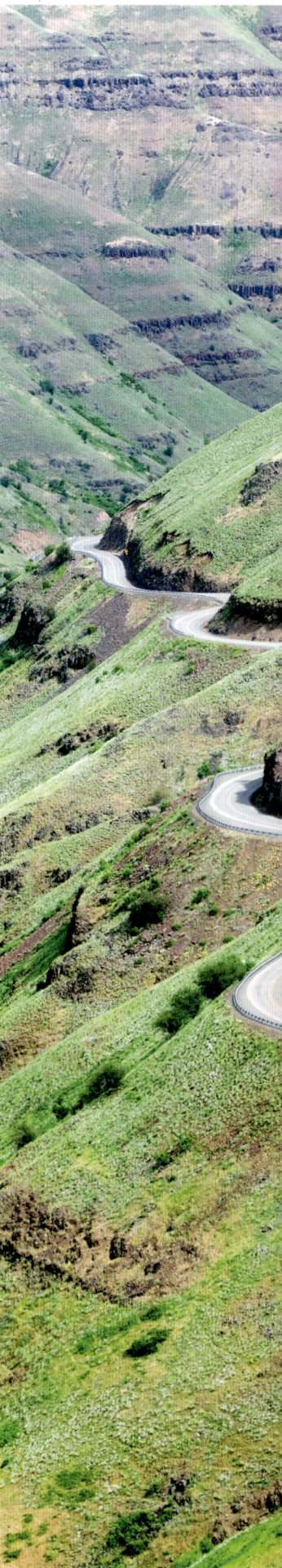

Above, top: Multnomah Falls Lodge was built in 1914 at the base of the famous waterfall in the Columbia River Gorge. The lodge is on the National Register of Historic Places and is a stopping point for 2.5 million travelers per year.

Above, bottom: At 100-acre Skinner Butte Park in Eugene, visitors can choose a view to match every mood, from tree-lined walkways to stellar cityscapes. The city and the park both trace their name to Eugene Franklin Skinner, who founded the city in 1853.

Right: With more twists and turns than a slithering snake, Highway 129 outside of Enterprise is a favorite among motorcyclists.

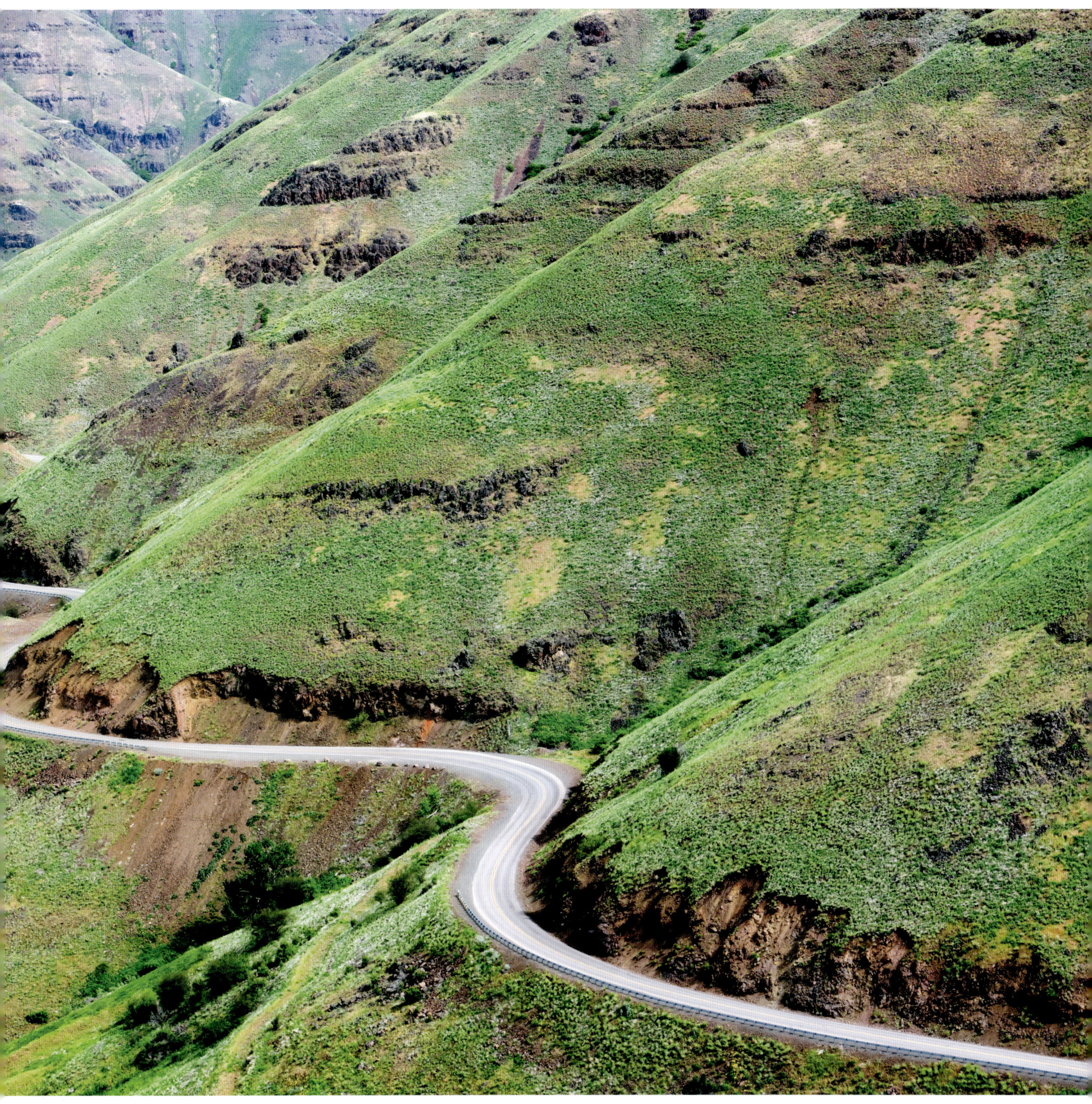

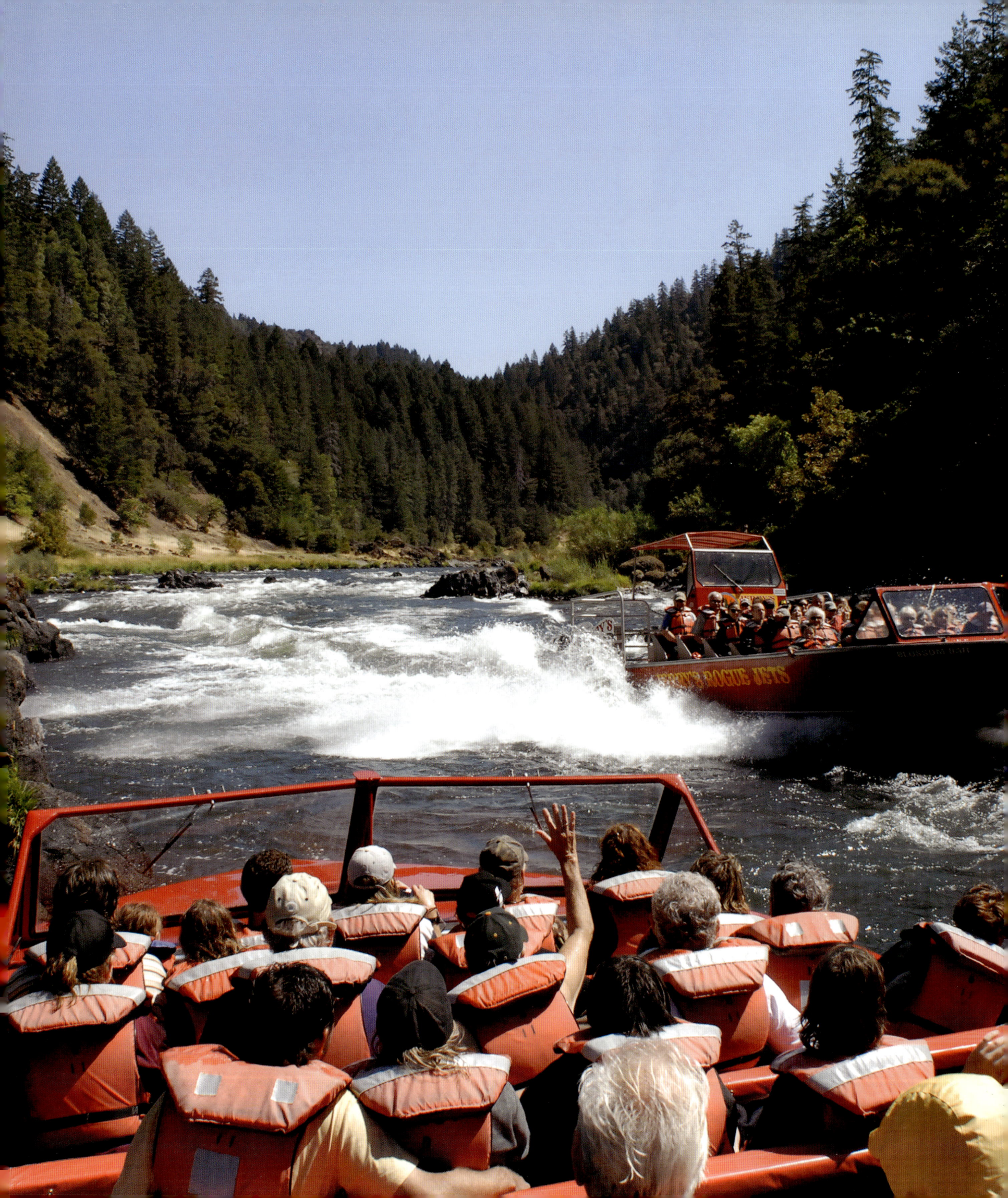

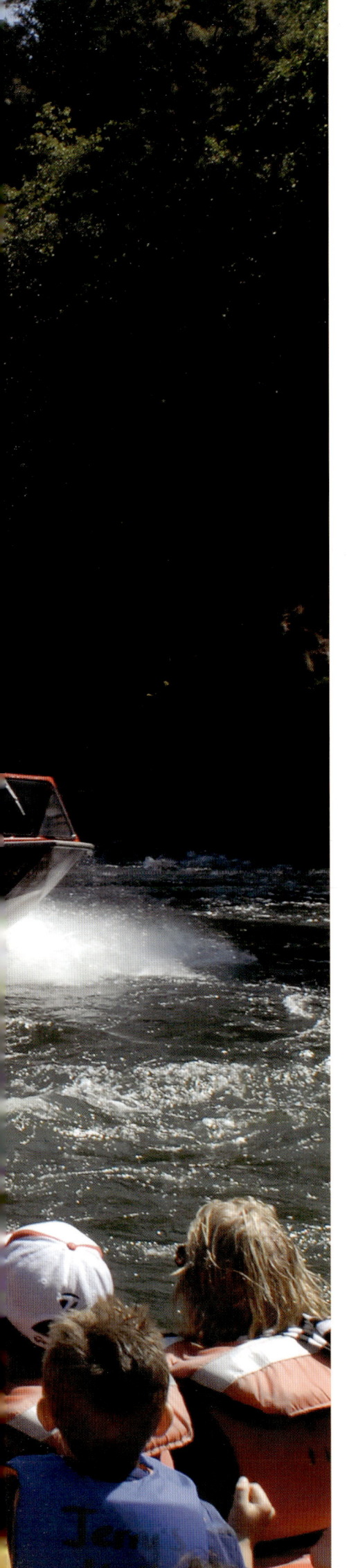
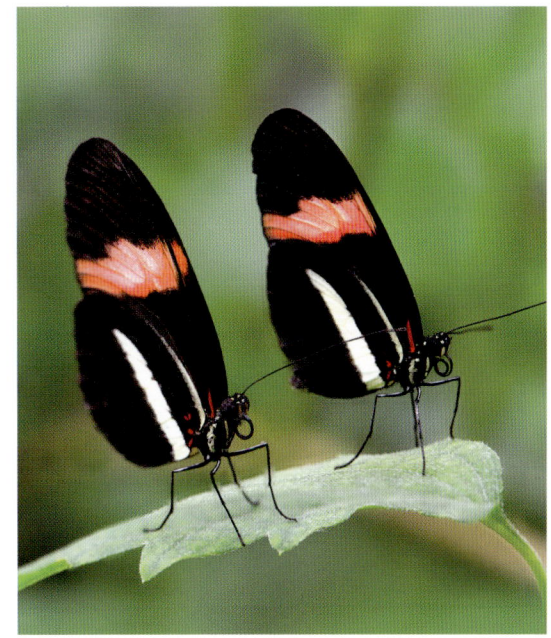
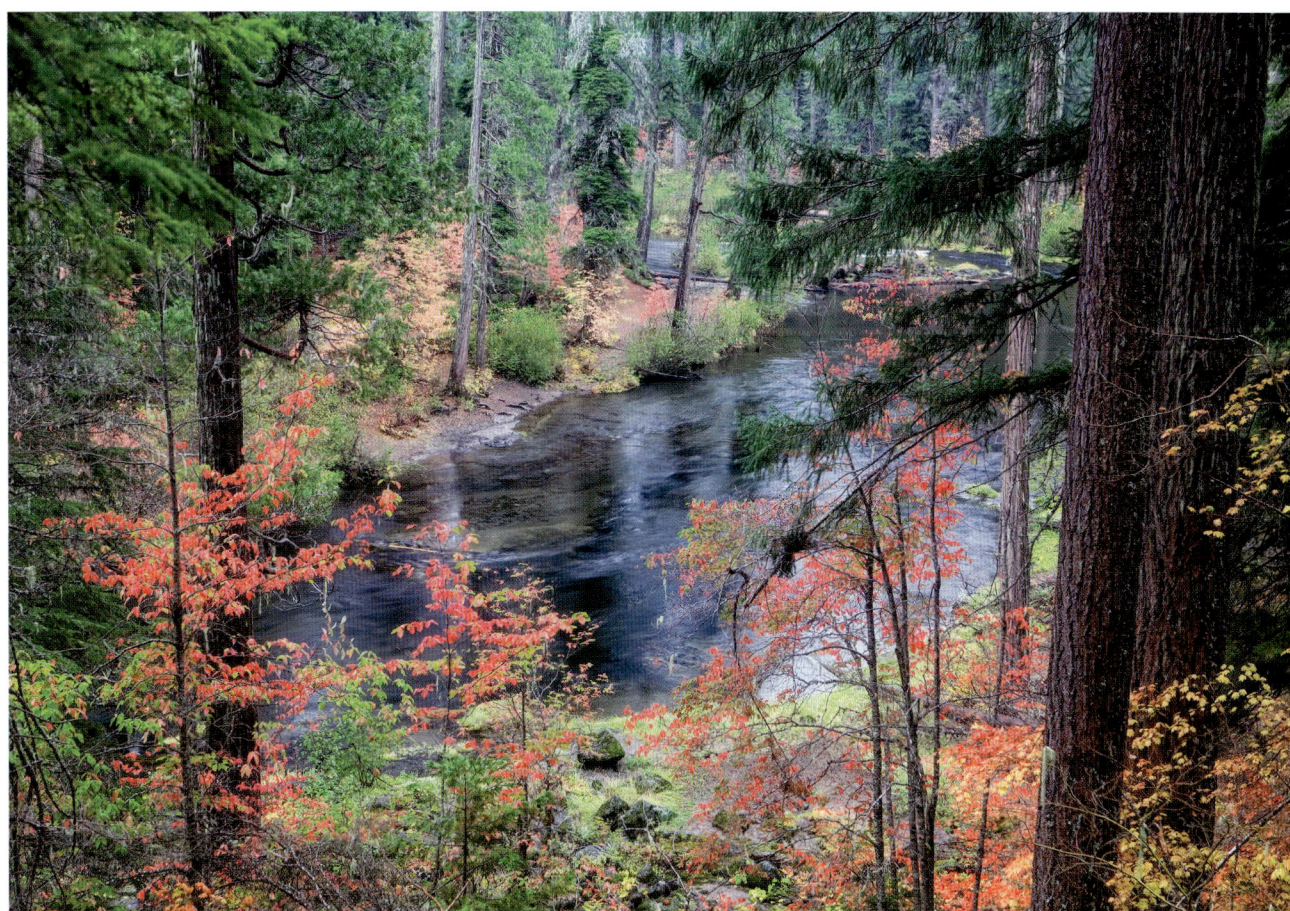

Above, top: The postman butterfly is one of many delicate beauties from Central and South America in the Oregon Zoo's Winged Wonders exhibit in Portland.

Above, bottom: The Rogue River cuts through the Cascade and coastal Klamath mountain ranges on its route to the Pacific Ocean.

Left: Jet boat tours are a favorite mode of transportation on the Wild and Scenic Rogue River. Sightseeing and whitewater trips leave from Gold Beach and Grants Pass. PHOTO COURTESY OF JERRY'S ROGUE JETS

Right: The clear waters of the Little North Santiam River in the Opal Creek Scenic Recreation Area east of Salem are a local hangout for swimming, hiking, and fishing.

Far right: Spruce trees draped in velvet-green moss line the Trail of Ten Falls in Silver Falls State Park east of Salem. The designated National Recreation Trail passes above a 100-foot waterfall before descending to a creek at the base of the canyon. The forested landscape is a sought-after destination for photographers, hikers, and waterfall enthusiasts.

Below: With Eugene's progressive outlook, there's nothing wrong with 50 inches of annual precipitation, as long as you have colorful boots, a friend, and a puddle.
PHOTO COURTESY OF HALEY GRAHAM

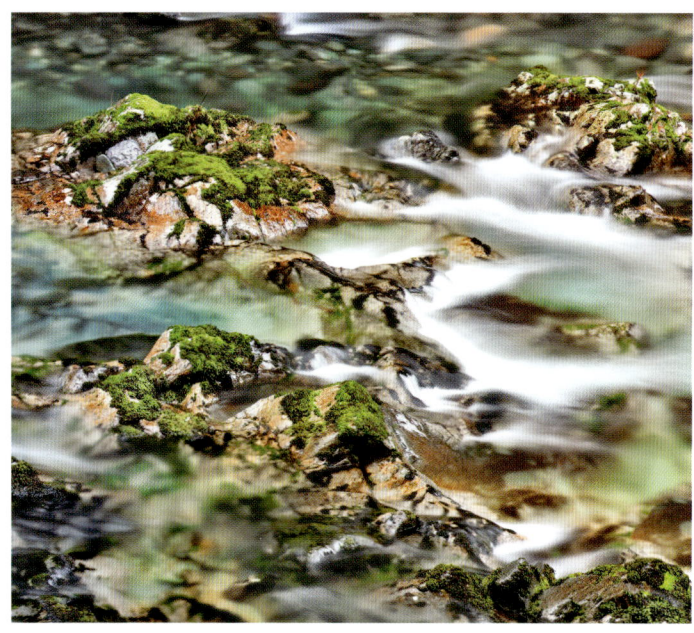
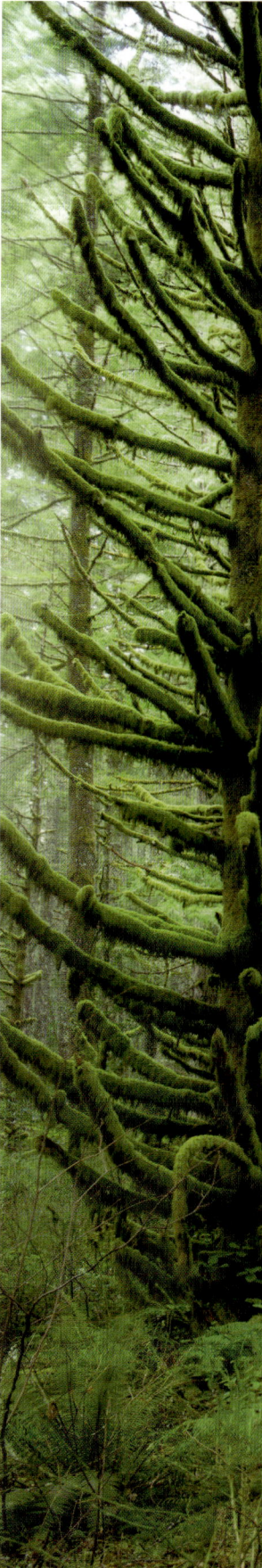
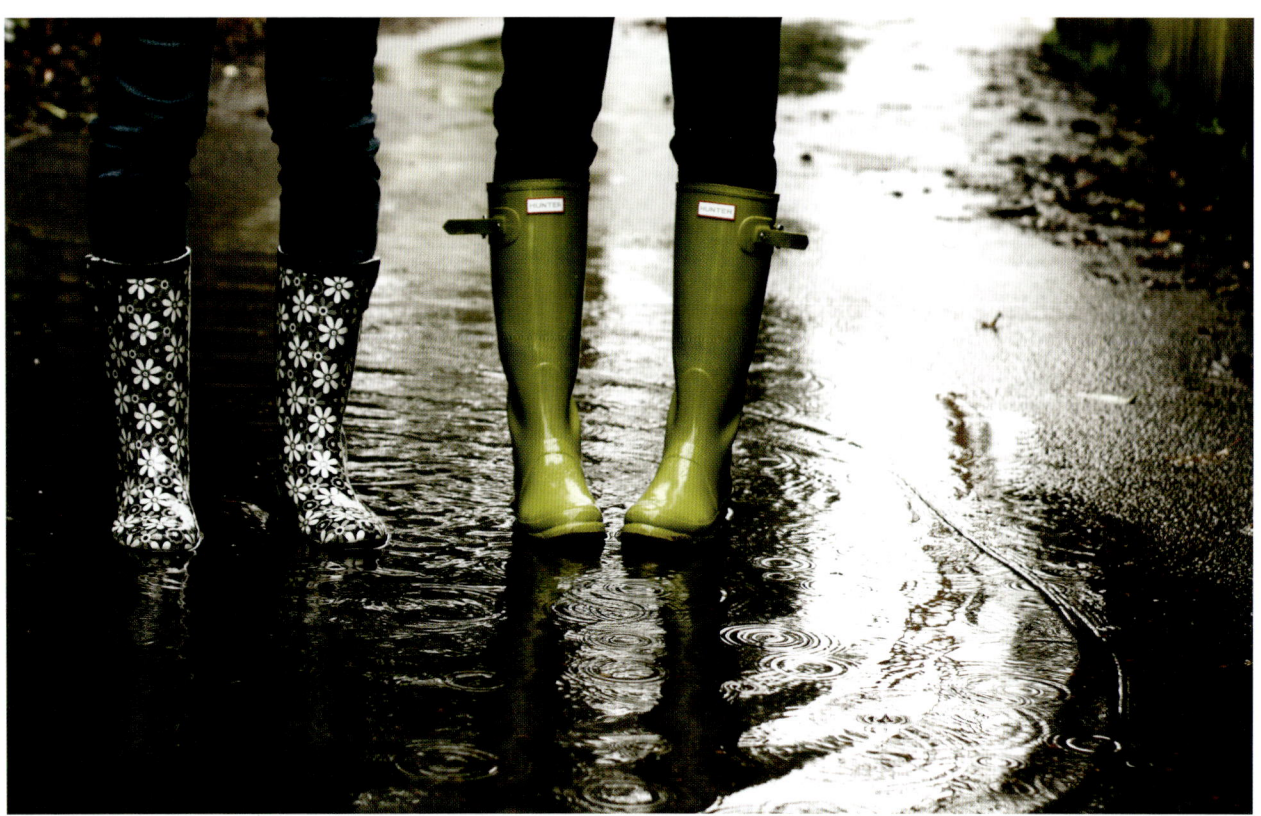

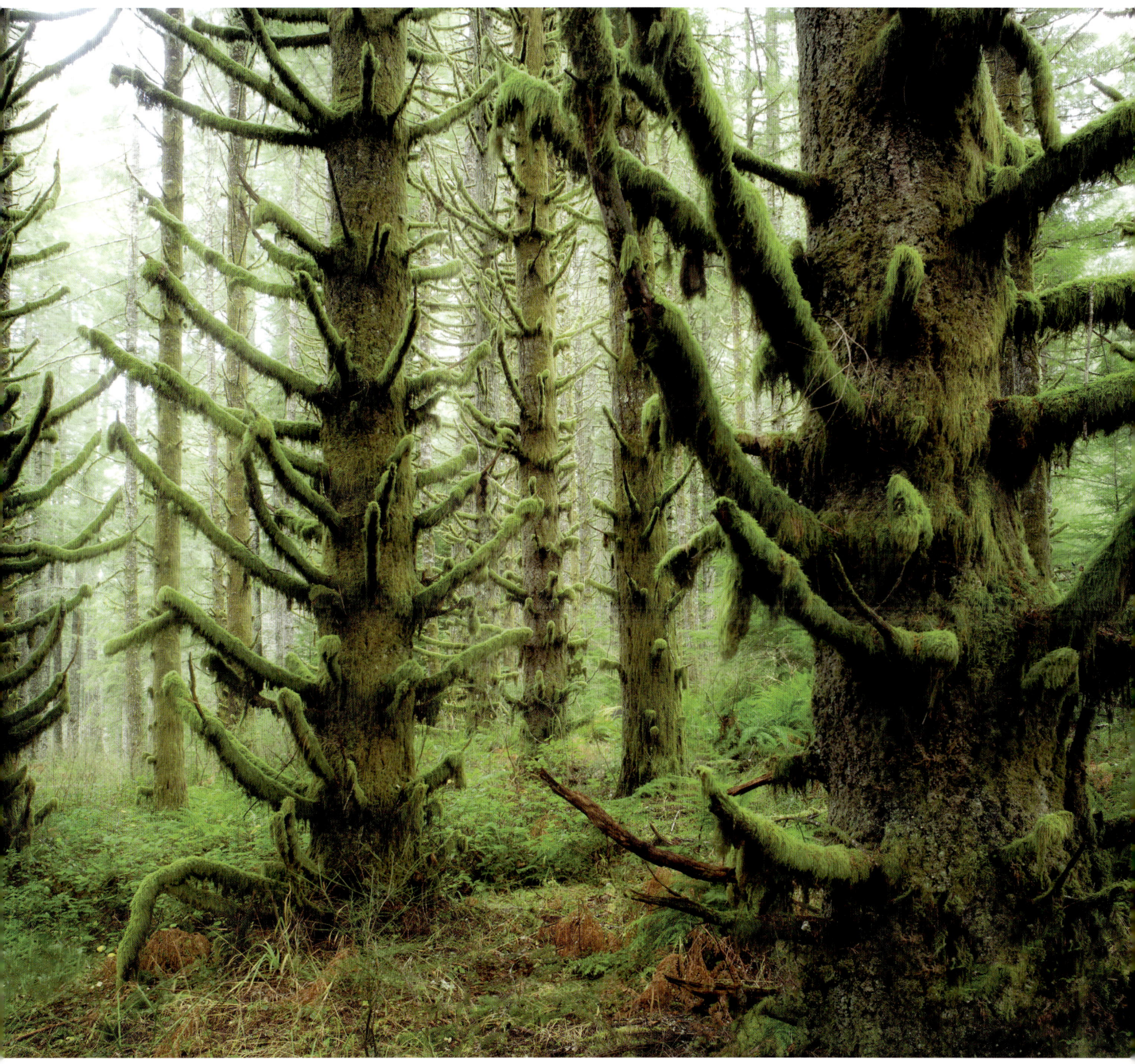

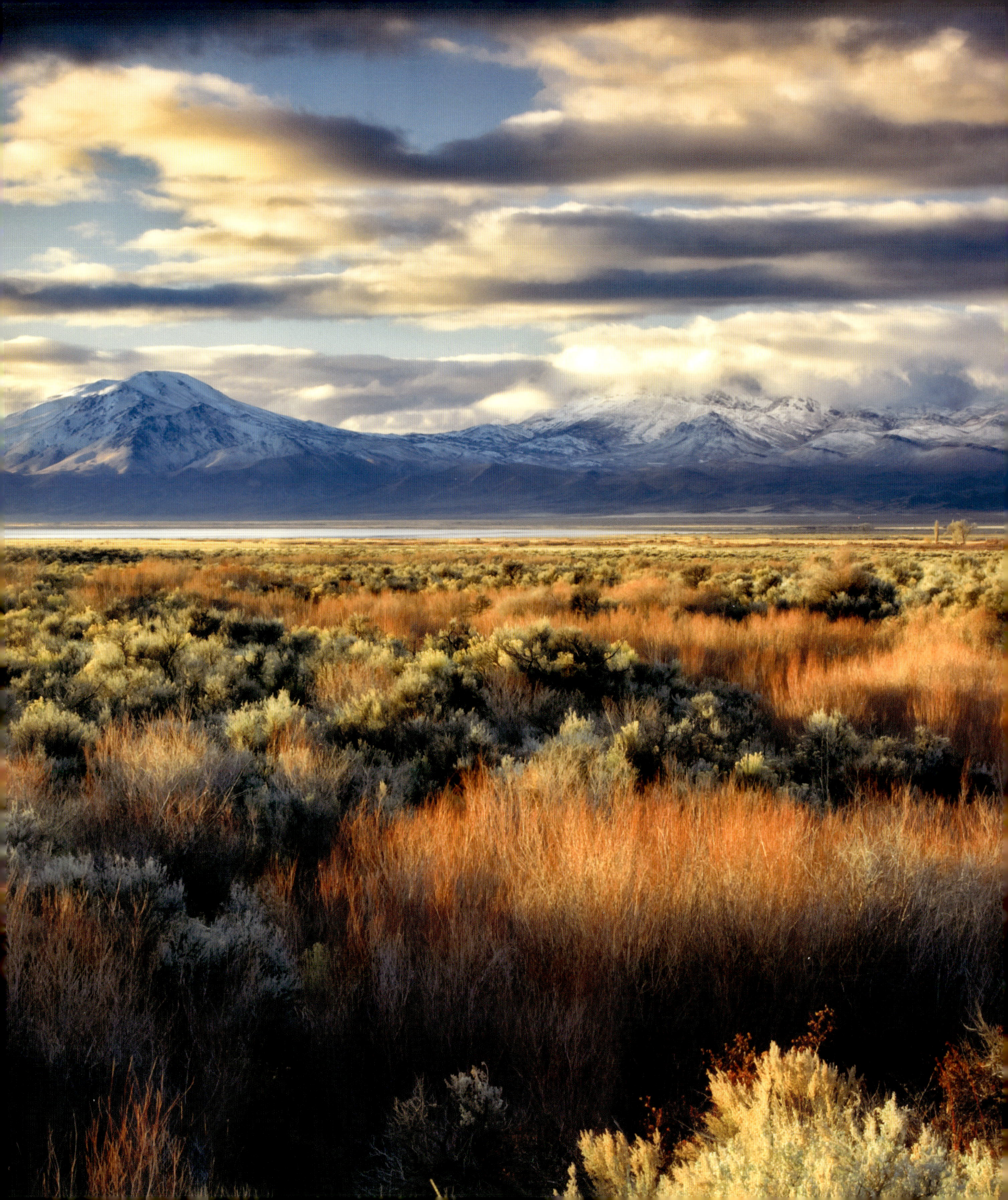

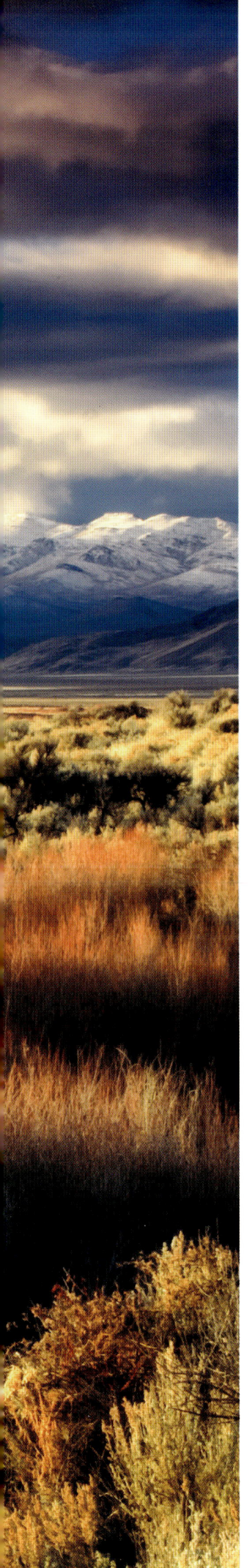

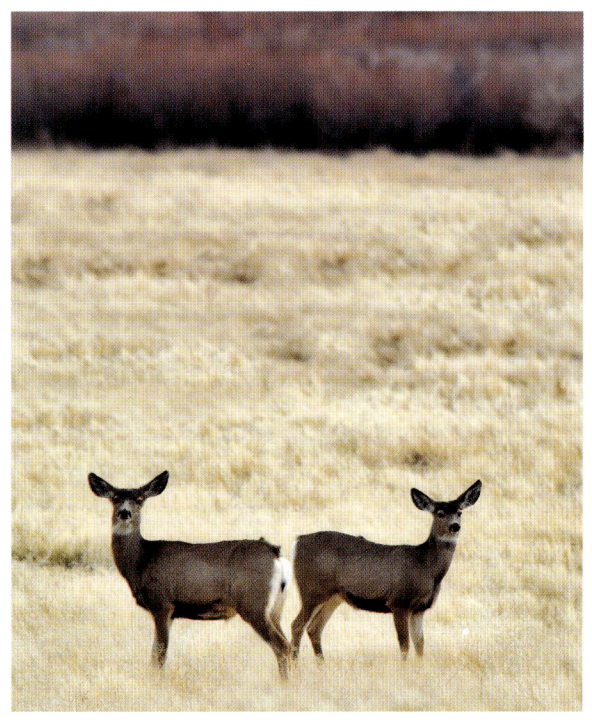

Left: Deer, pronghorn, wild horses, and elk are just a few of the animals that make their home in the southeastern corner of Oregon near Steens Mountain. A 52-mile Backcountry Byway travels through glacier-carved gorges and stunning wilderness where wildlife often share the roadway.

Far left: Sunrise reveals the stark beauty of the Pueblo Mountains, which straddle the border between Nevada and Oregon. Though desolate, the meadows, aspen groves, and talus slopes at the northern end of the Black Rock Desert piece together a mosaic of habitats rich with wildlife.

Below: Winter is a quiet time on the wild and scenic Owyhee River in the southeastern corner of the state. Dubbed the "Grand Canyon of Oregon," the river cuts through a steep-walled gorge riddled with hoodoos—tall, narrow spires of rock rising from the basin floor. In the summer, whitewater rafters maneuver through the currents past ancient rock carvings made by the native peoples who once inhabited the region.

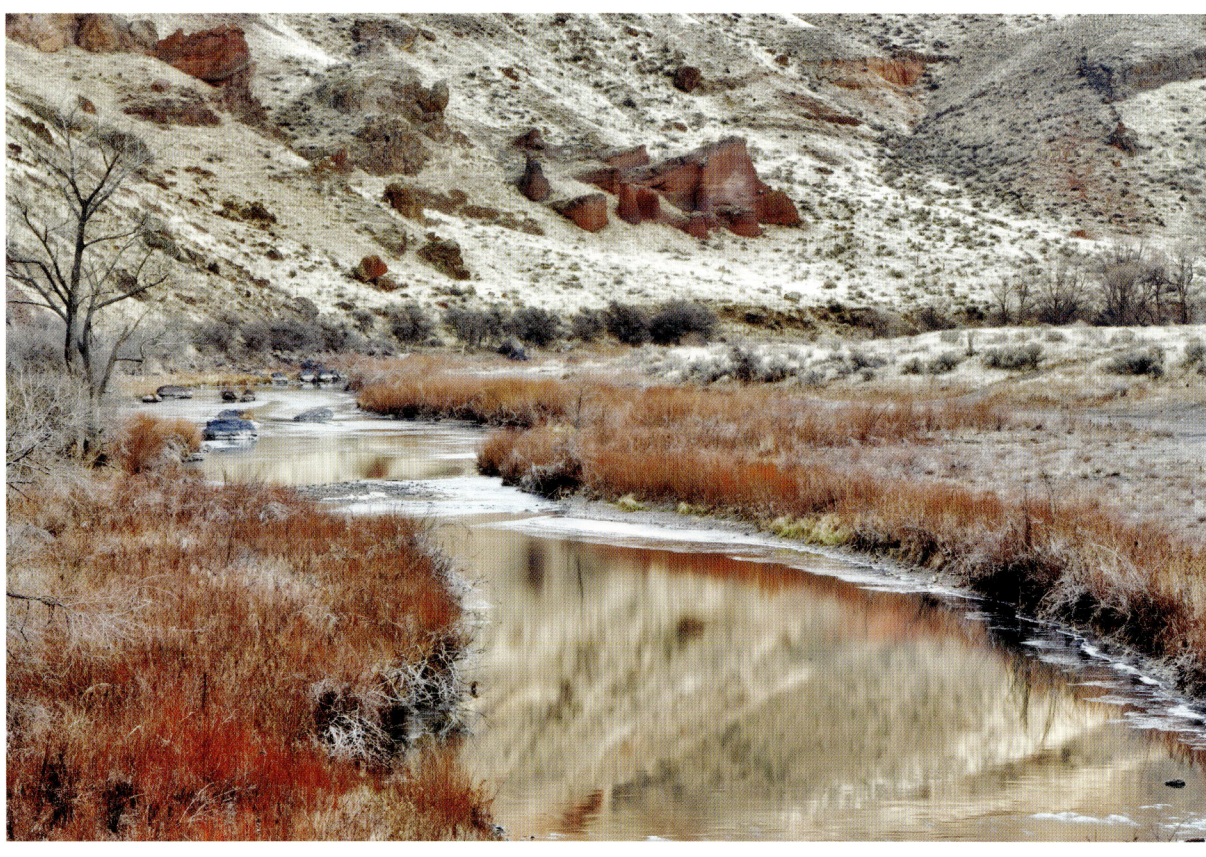

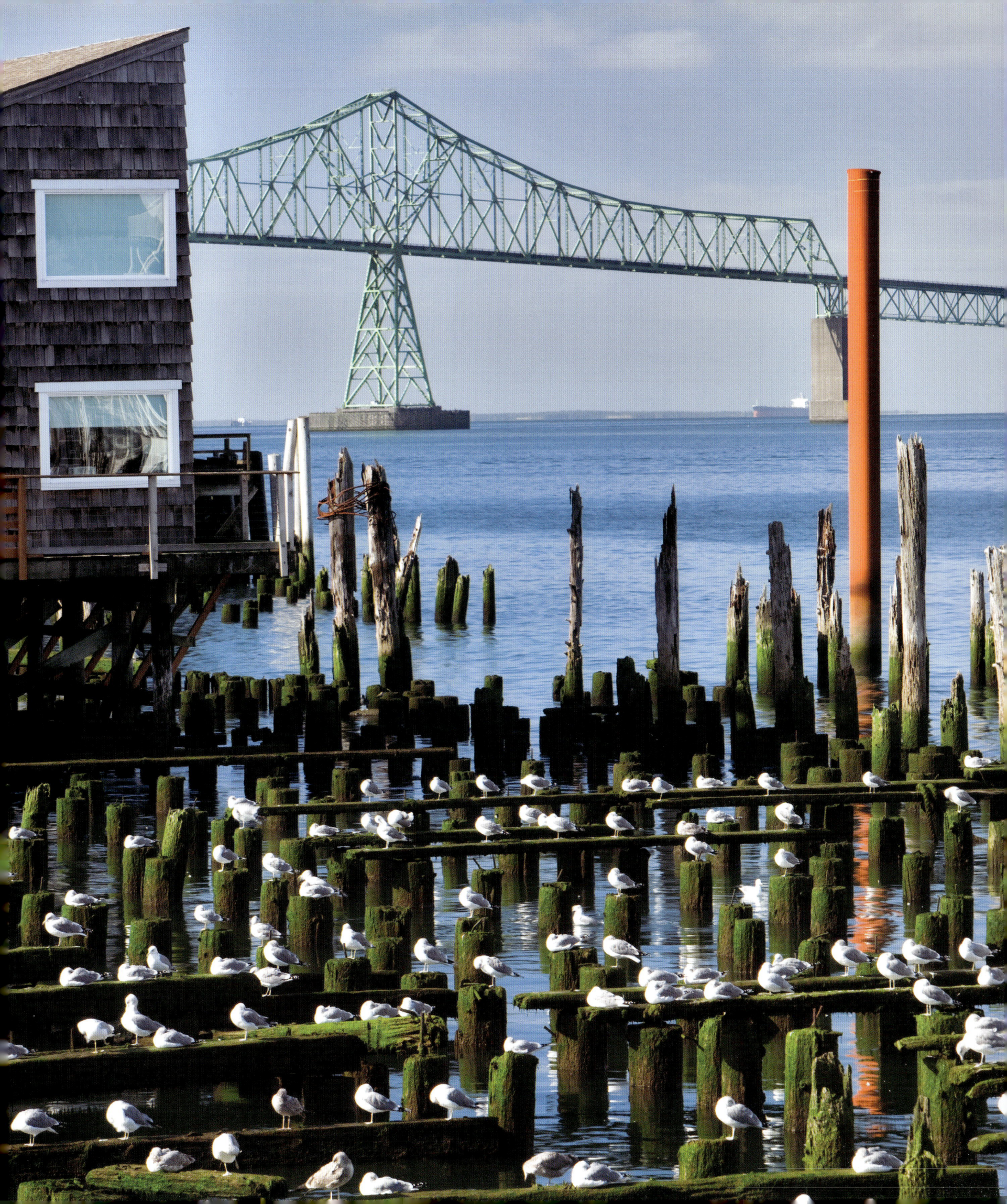

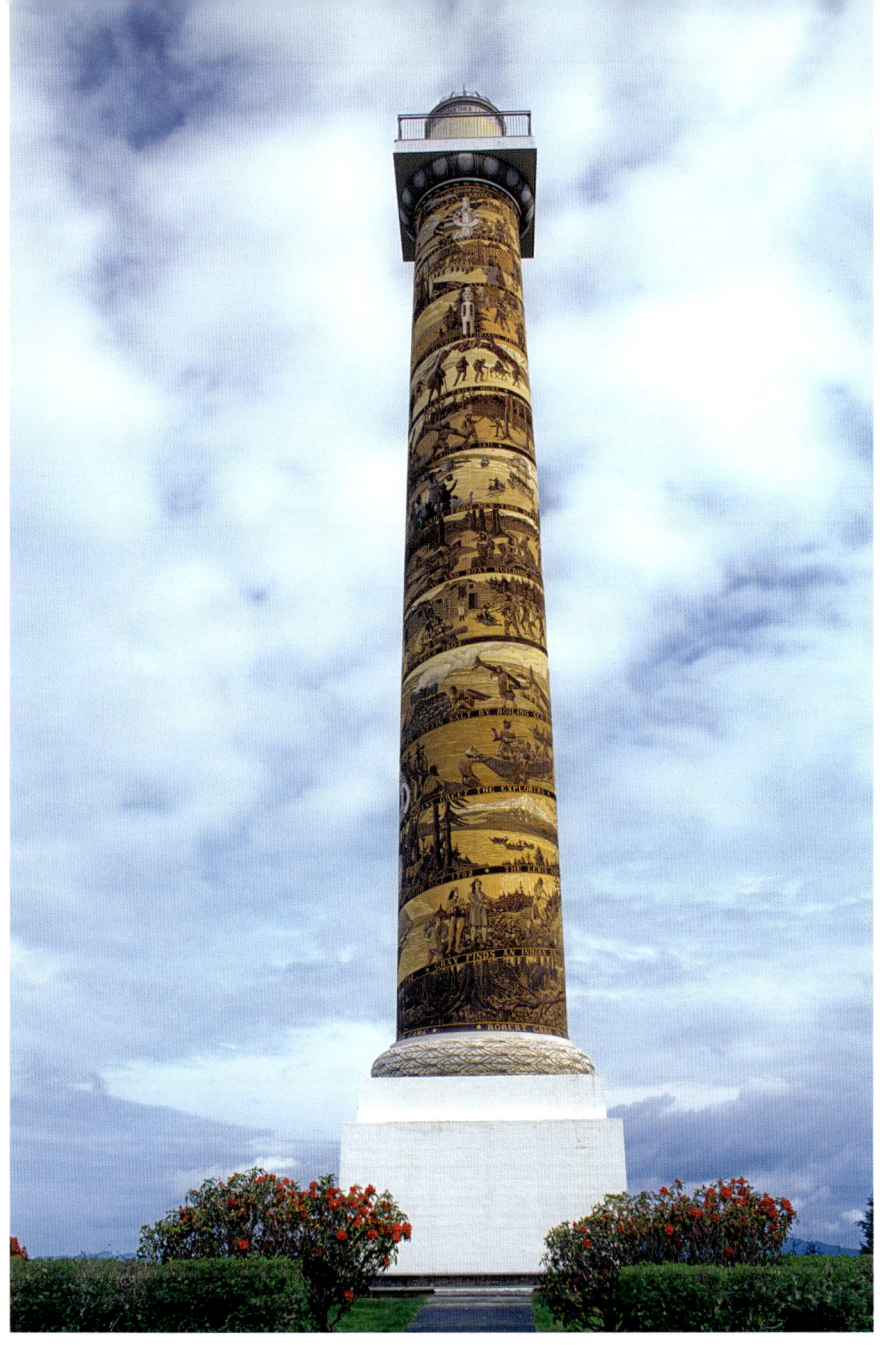

Left: The Astoria Column rises 125 feet from the top of Astoria's Coxcomb Hill. Completed in 1925, the concrete structure offers stunning views of the Pacific Ocean, Columbia River, Cascade Mountains, and Astoria itself.

Facing pages: The 4.1-mile Astoria-Megler Bridge carries U.S. Highway 101 across the mouth of the Columbia River from Astoria to Point Ellice, Washington. At 1,232 feet, its main span is the longest continuous truss in the nation.

Below: Portland's historic Old Town, the city's first neighborhood, is home to Lan Su Chinese Garden, Japantown, and the Portland Saturday Market.

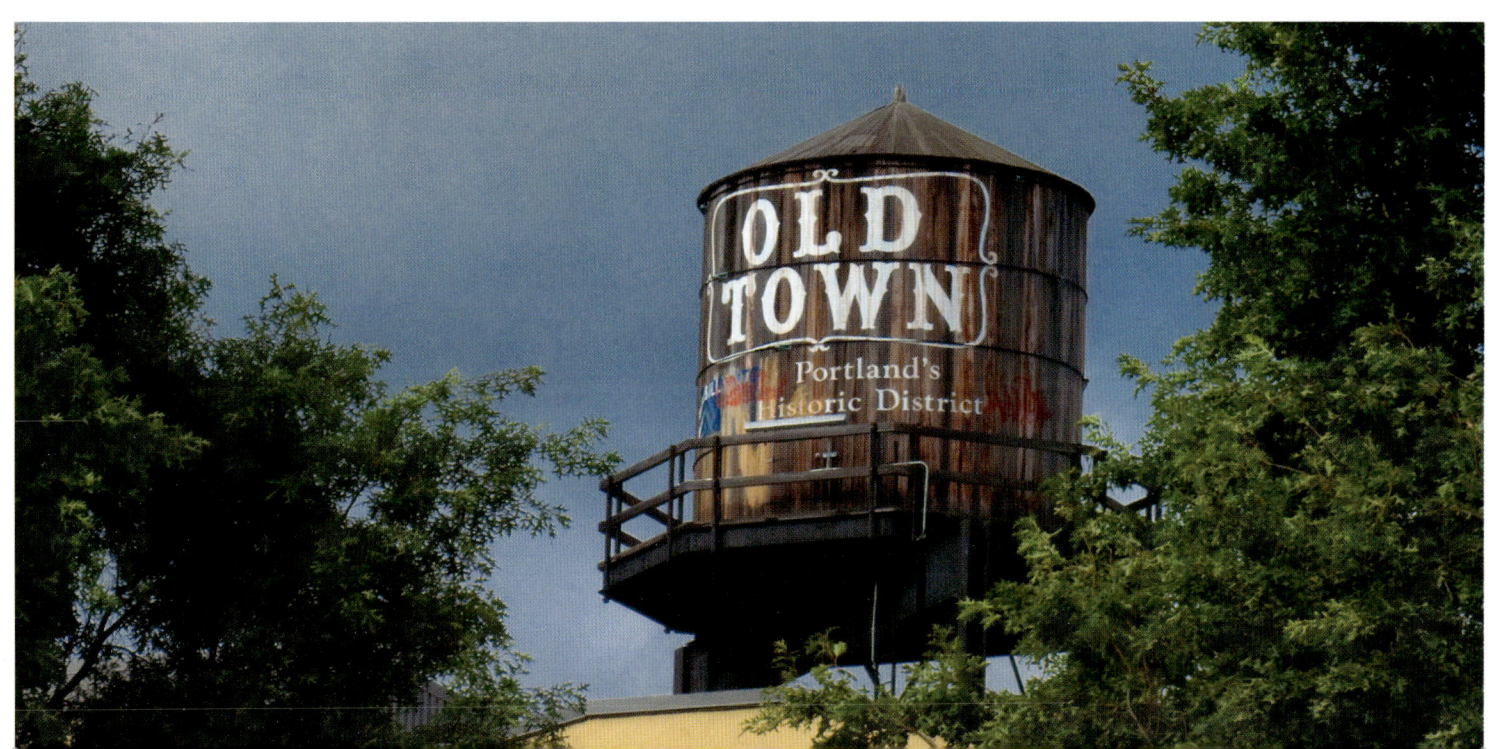

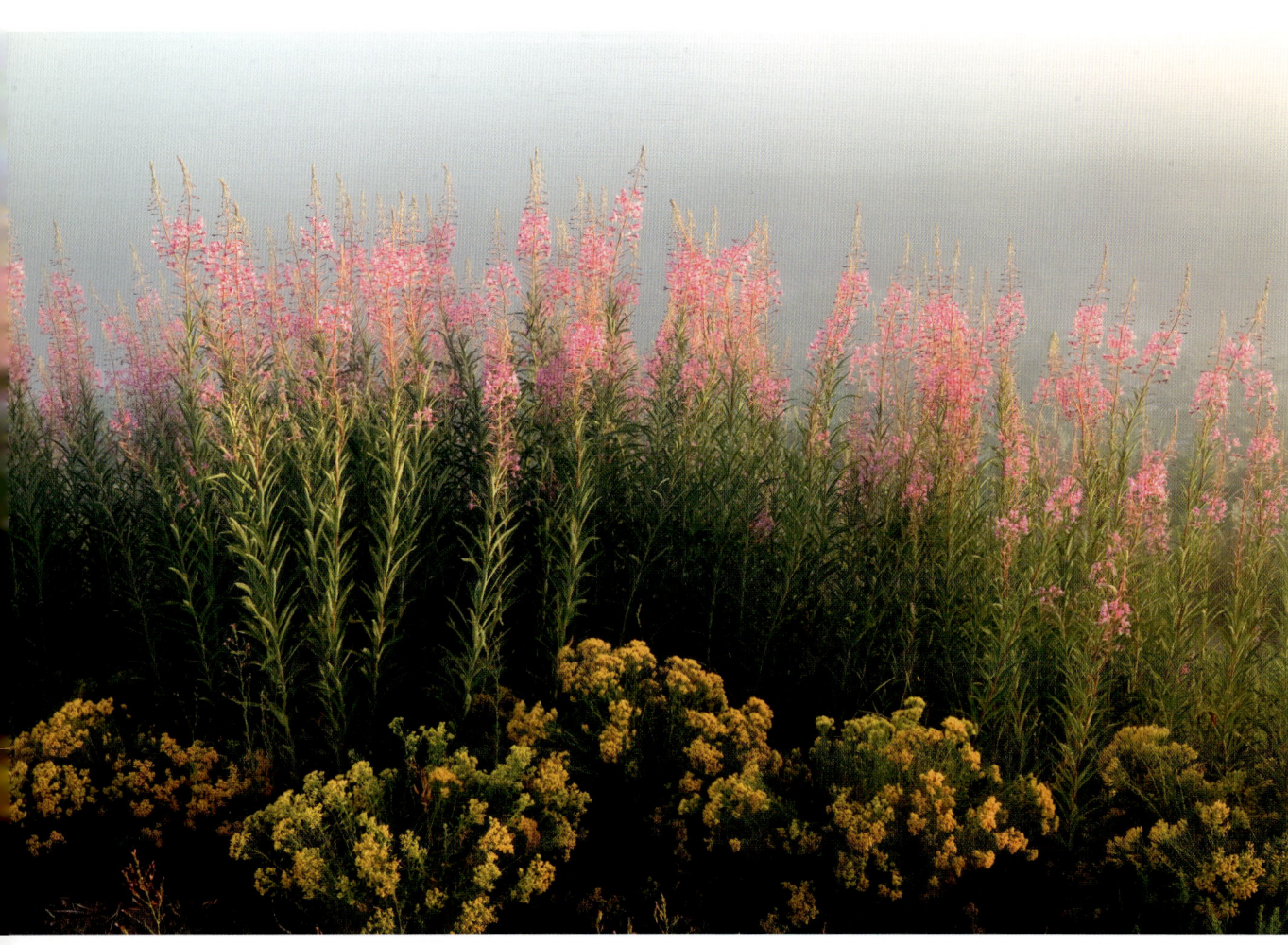
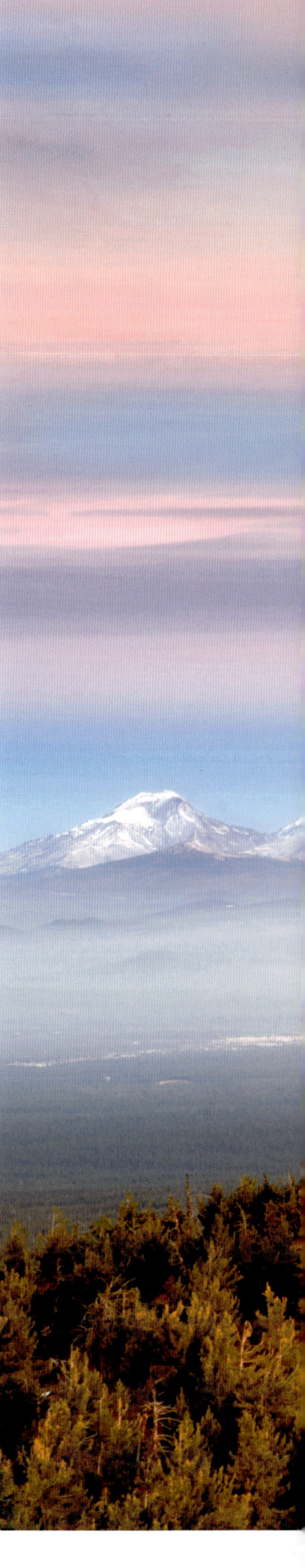

Above: Fireweed and rabbitbrush are part of the diverse habitat at the Klamath Marsh National Wildlife Refuge. With its natural marshes and wooded uplands, the refuge is a feeding and nesting ground for several species of waterfowl, including American white pelicans. Bald eagles, sandhill cranes, and great gray owls can also be found there.

Right: An early morning hike up Paulina Peak in Newberry National Volcanic Monument reveals views of the Cascade Mountains, including the triple peaks of the Three Sisters. At 7,985 feet, Paulina is the highest point on a 21-mile rim of a crater—the remains of one of the largest shield volcanoes in North America. Visitors pass cinder cones, obsidian flows, and jagged cliffs on the way to the summit.

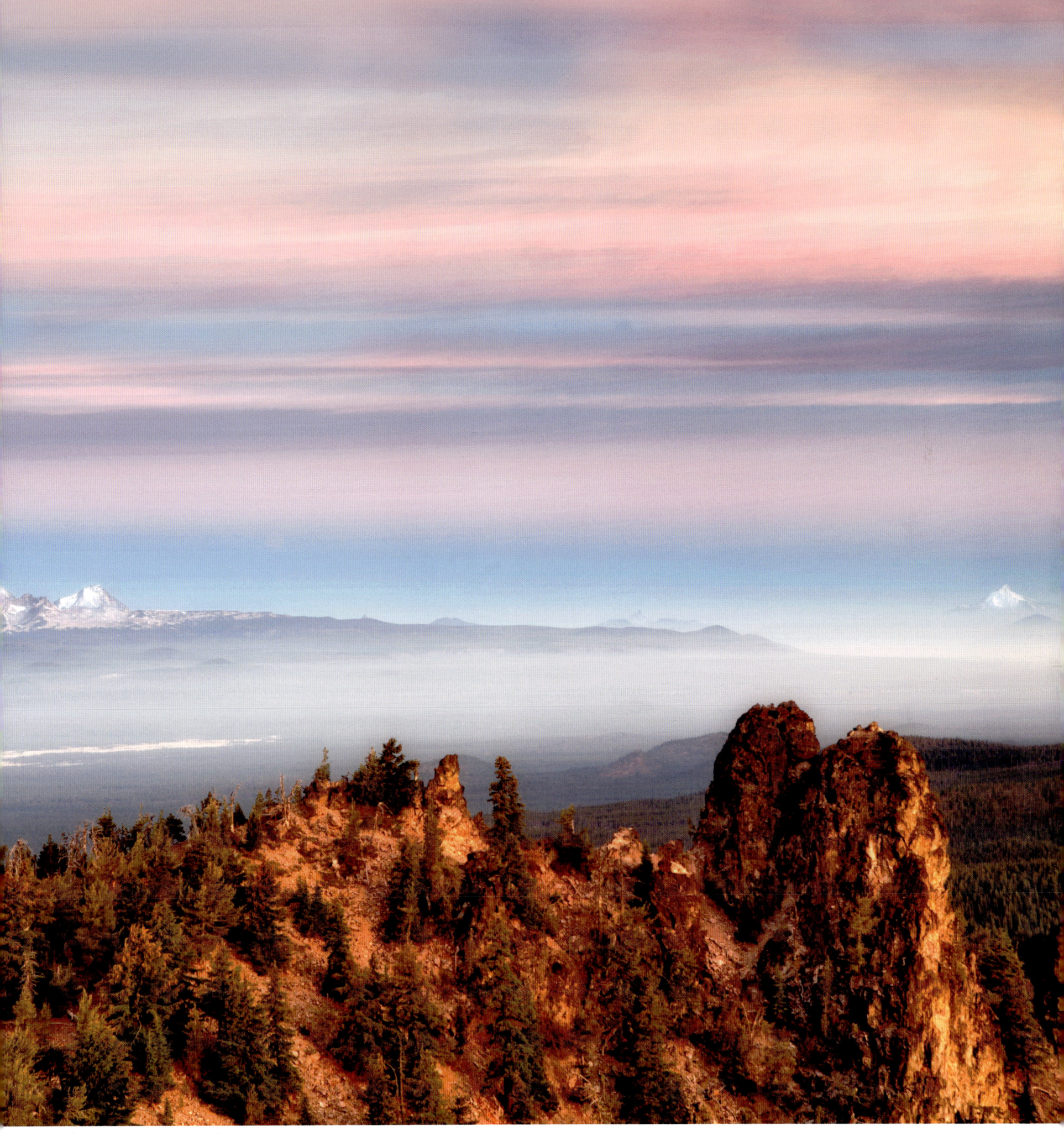

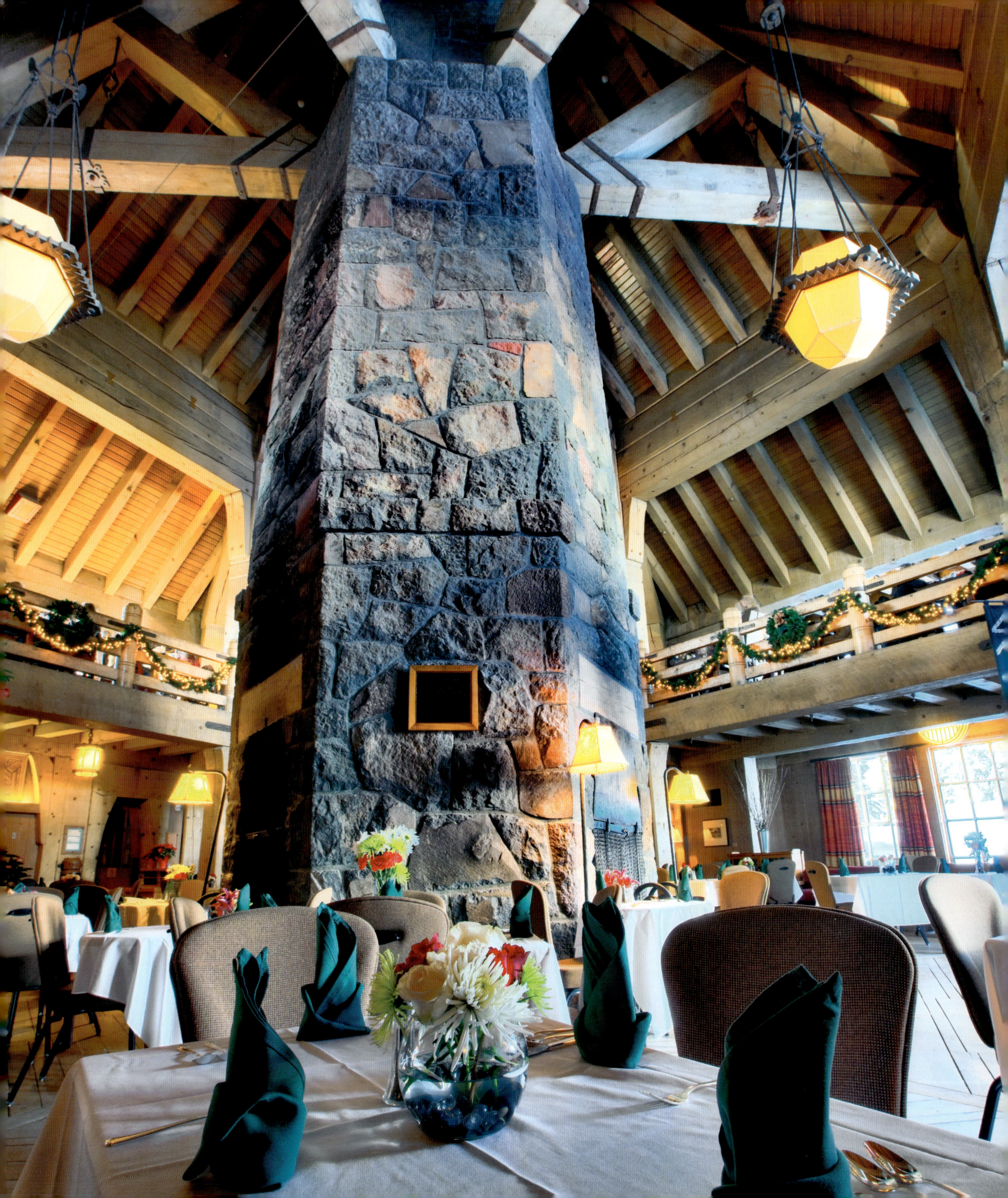

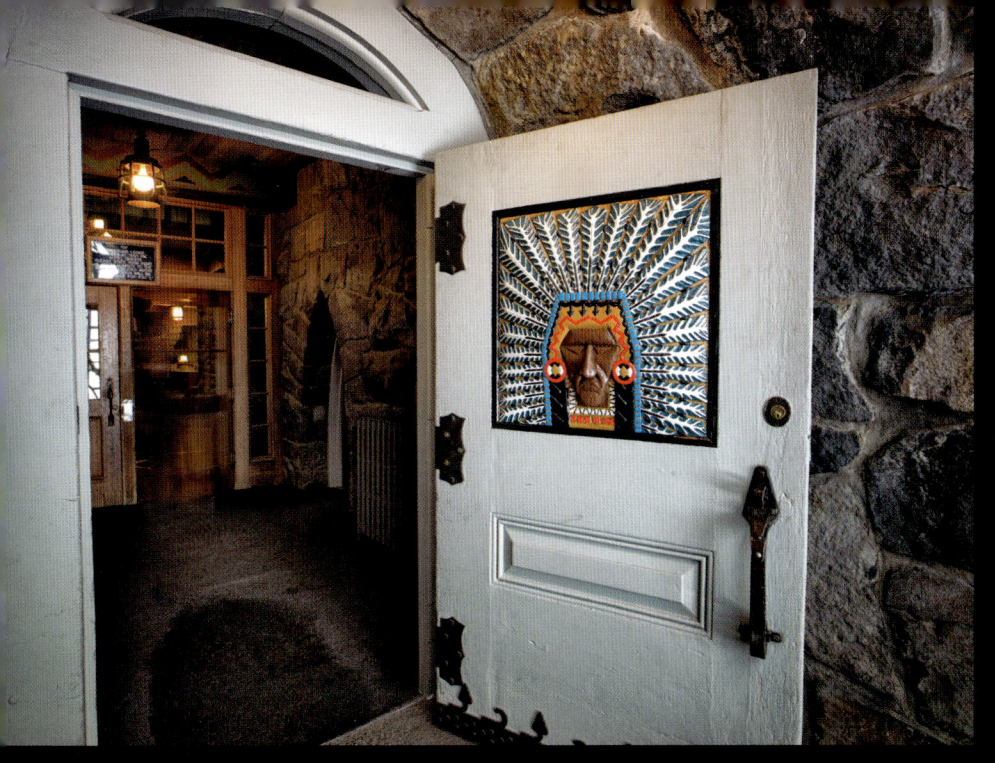

Left: Since the lodge's completion in 1937, countless skiers have entered Timberline Lodge via the Indian Head Door. Named for its carving, the door, complete with an arrow-shaped handle, is one of thousands of original creations handcrafted by Works Progress Administration (WPA) workers who built the lodge during the Great Depression.

Far left: Whether the snow is falling or the sun is shining on Mt. Hood, there is always a comfortable spot for relaxing at Timberline Lodge. The iconic ski lodge and historic landmark is a cozy location for dinners, weddings, and mountain getaways year-round.

Below: Winter on the Metolius River is a time to stoke the fire, listen to the rush of the river, and dream of fly fishing, hiking, and mountain biking when spring returns to Central Oregon.

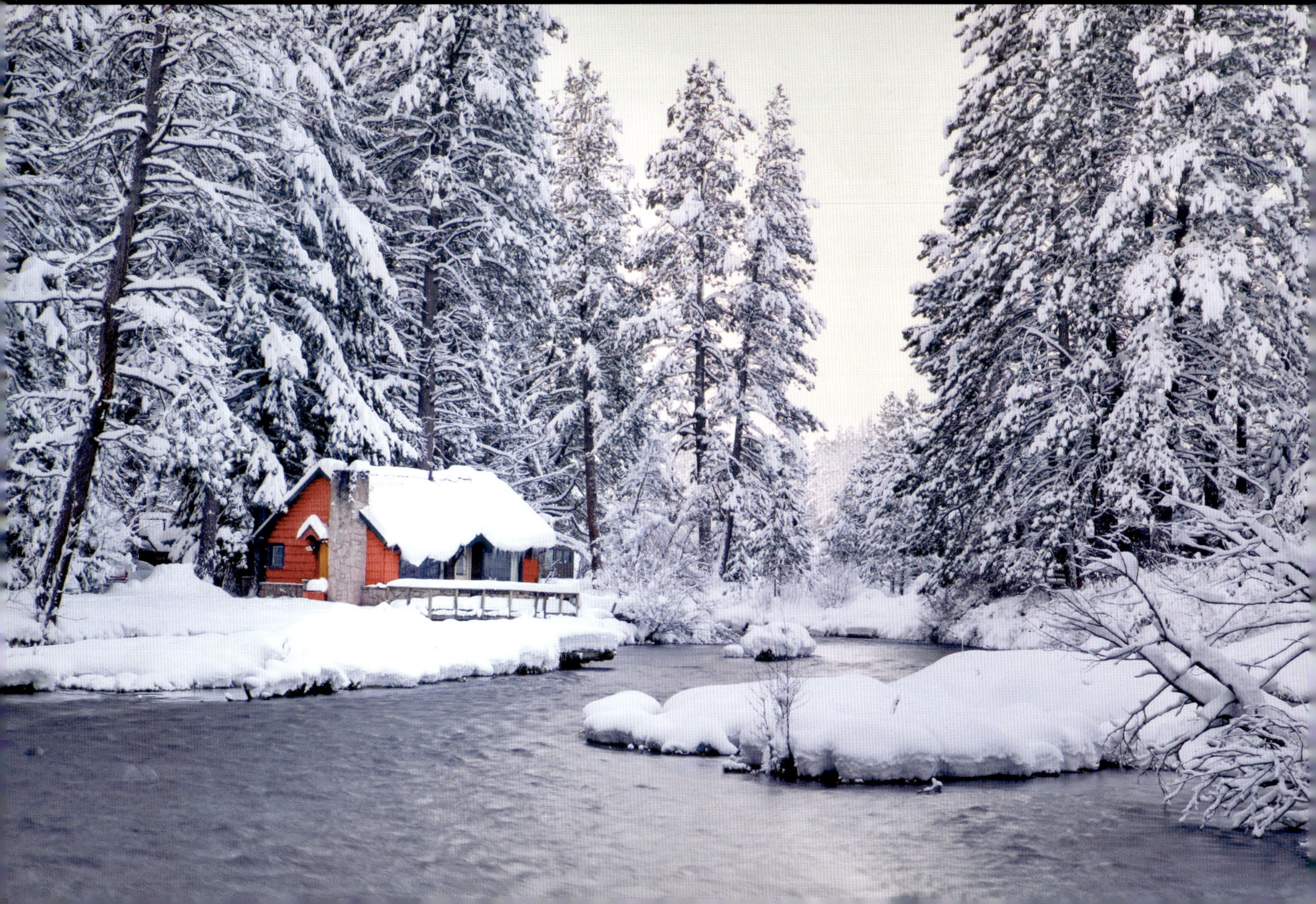

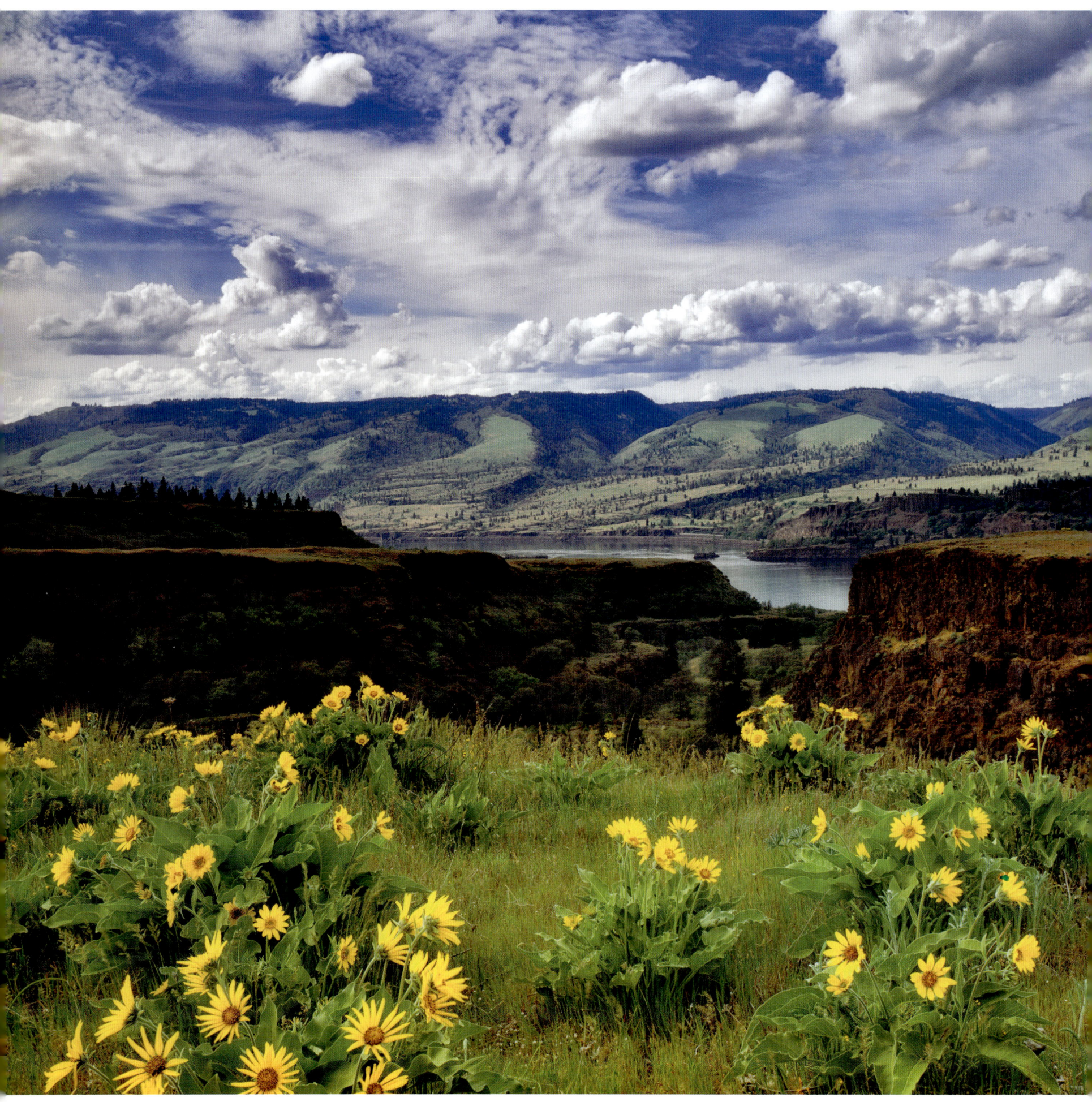

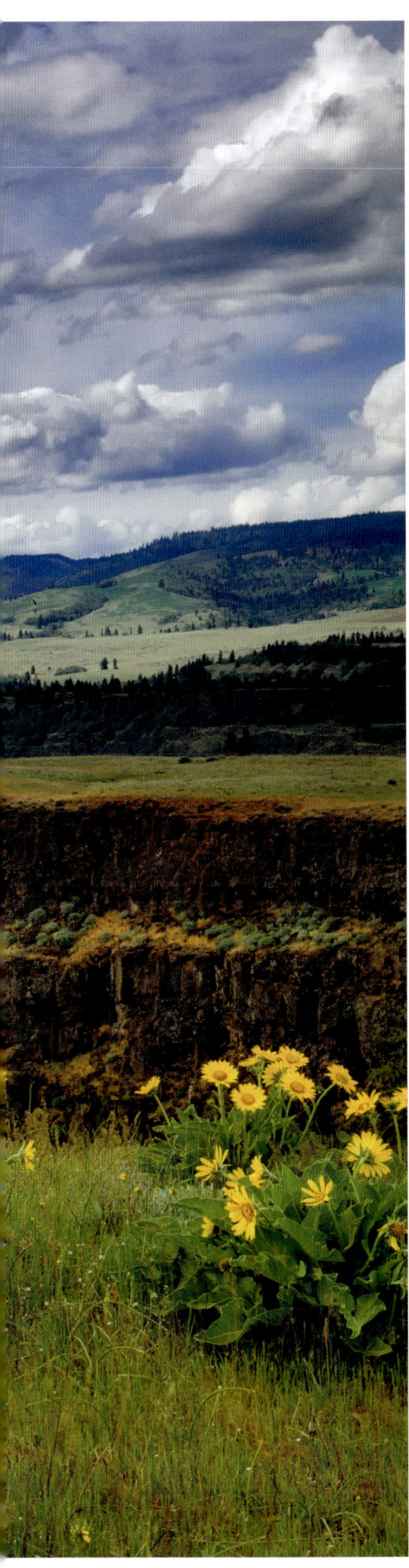

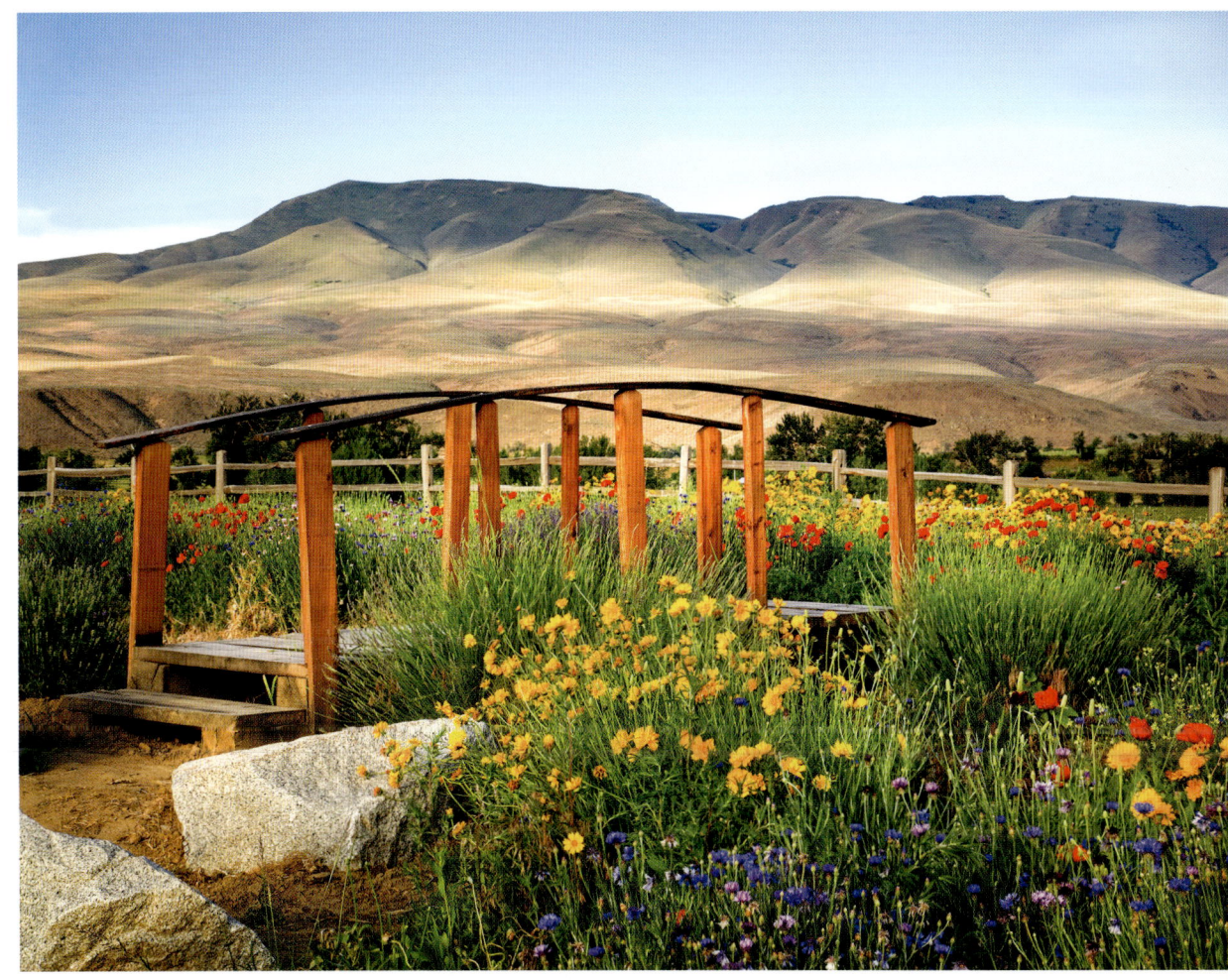

Above: Once merely a weed patch, this site along the Hells Canyon National Scenic Byway now blooms with native wildflowers thanks to the efforts of the Richland Wildflower Project.

Left: Sunny arrowleaf balsamroot is one of several native wildflower species that heralds spring at the Tom McCall Preserve in the Columbia River Gorge.

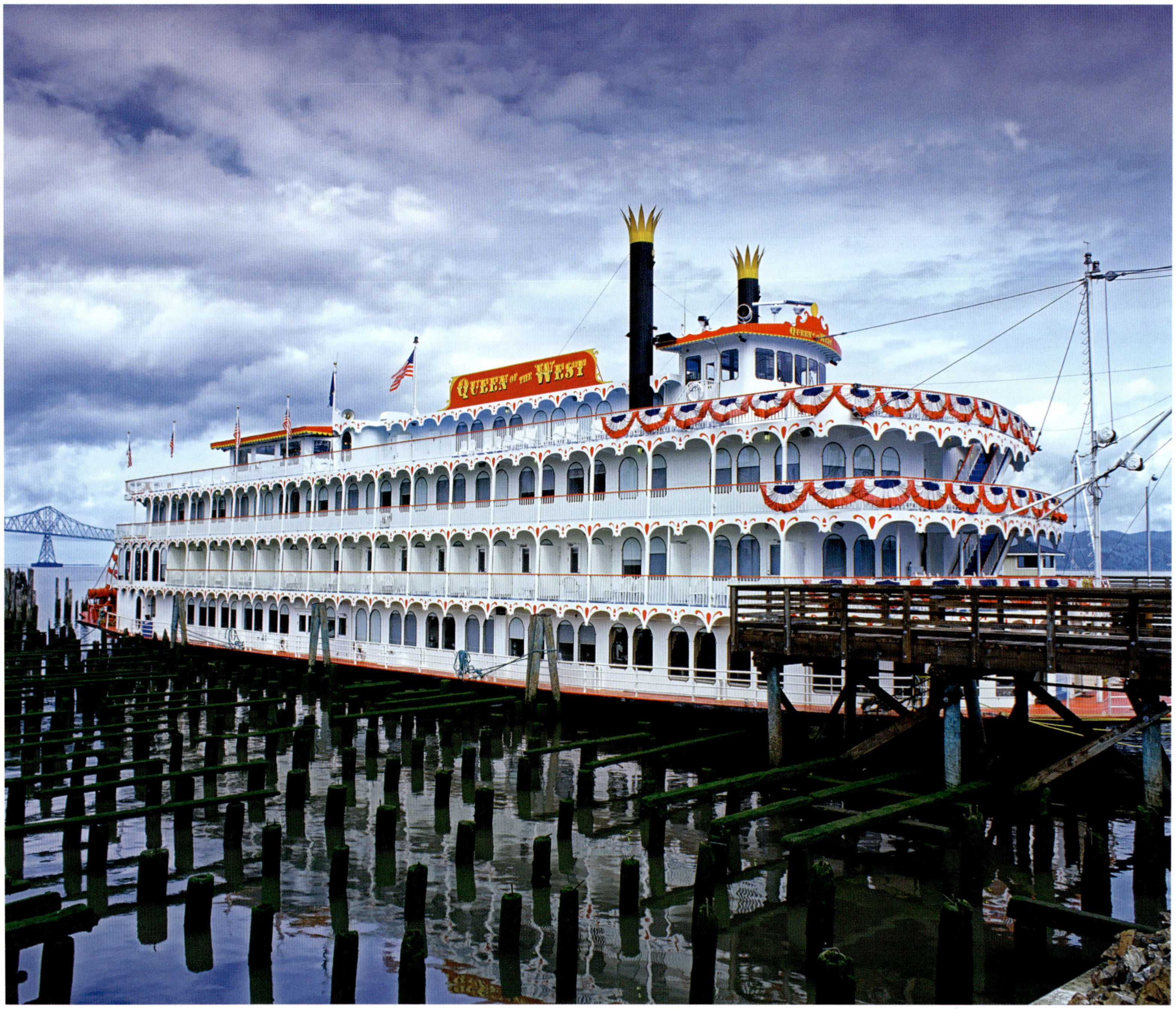

Above: The Queen of the West offers weeklong cruises along the waterway that led Lewis and Clark to the Pacific Ocean. Propelled by a three-story paddlewheel, the ship makes its way to Astoria and then heads east along the Columbia River to the twin cities of Clarkston, Washington, and Lewiston, Idaho.

Right: The colorful floats of crab pots are a common sight in many coastal towns. In Yaquina, Alsea, Tillamook, and Coos Bay, commercial crabbers and recreational enthusiasts hunt for the delicious Dungeness crabs native to local waters.

Facing page: Commercial fishing vessels deliver 200-300 million pounds of fish and shellfish to Oregon ports each year. The state's salmon, Dungeness crab, pink shrimp, and albacore tuna are among the most sustainably harvested catches in the United States.

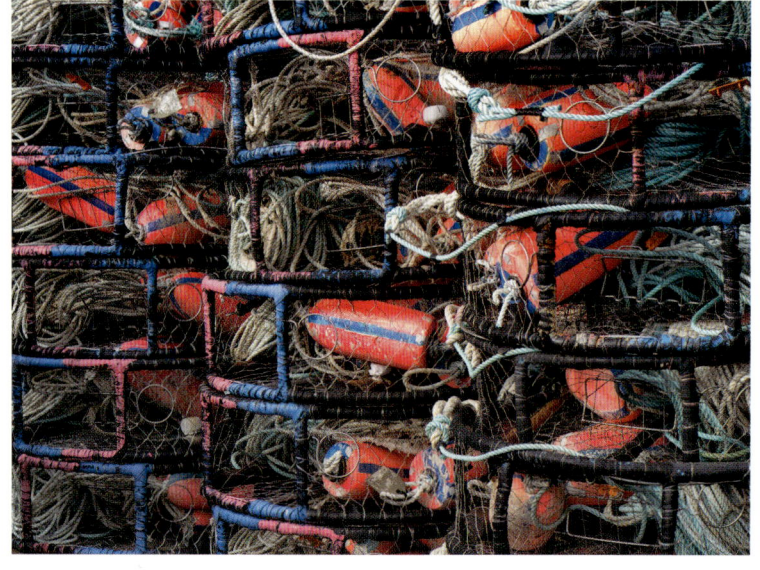

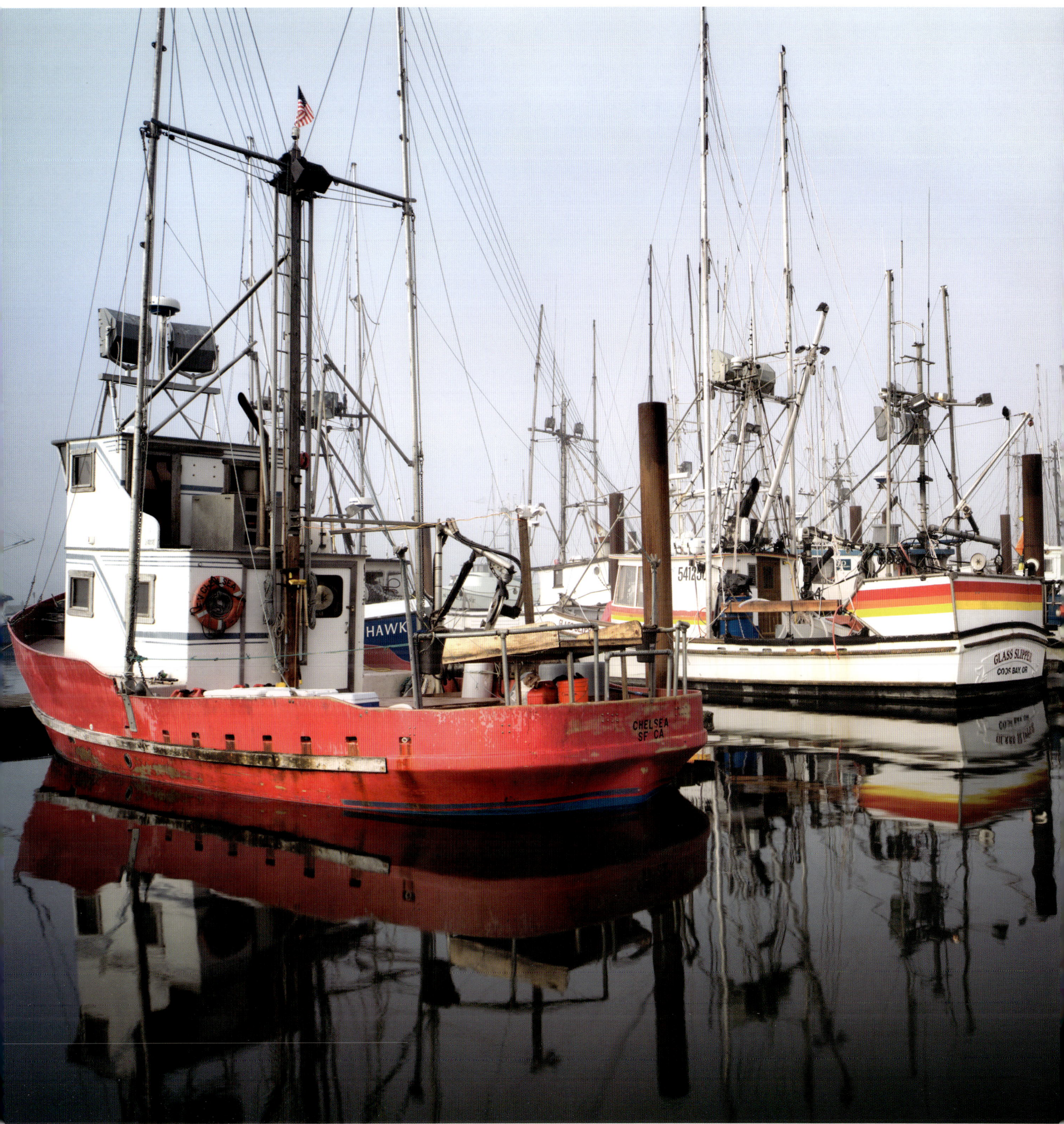

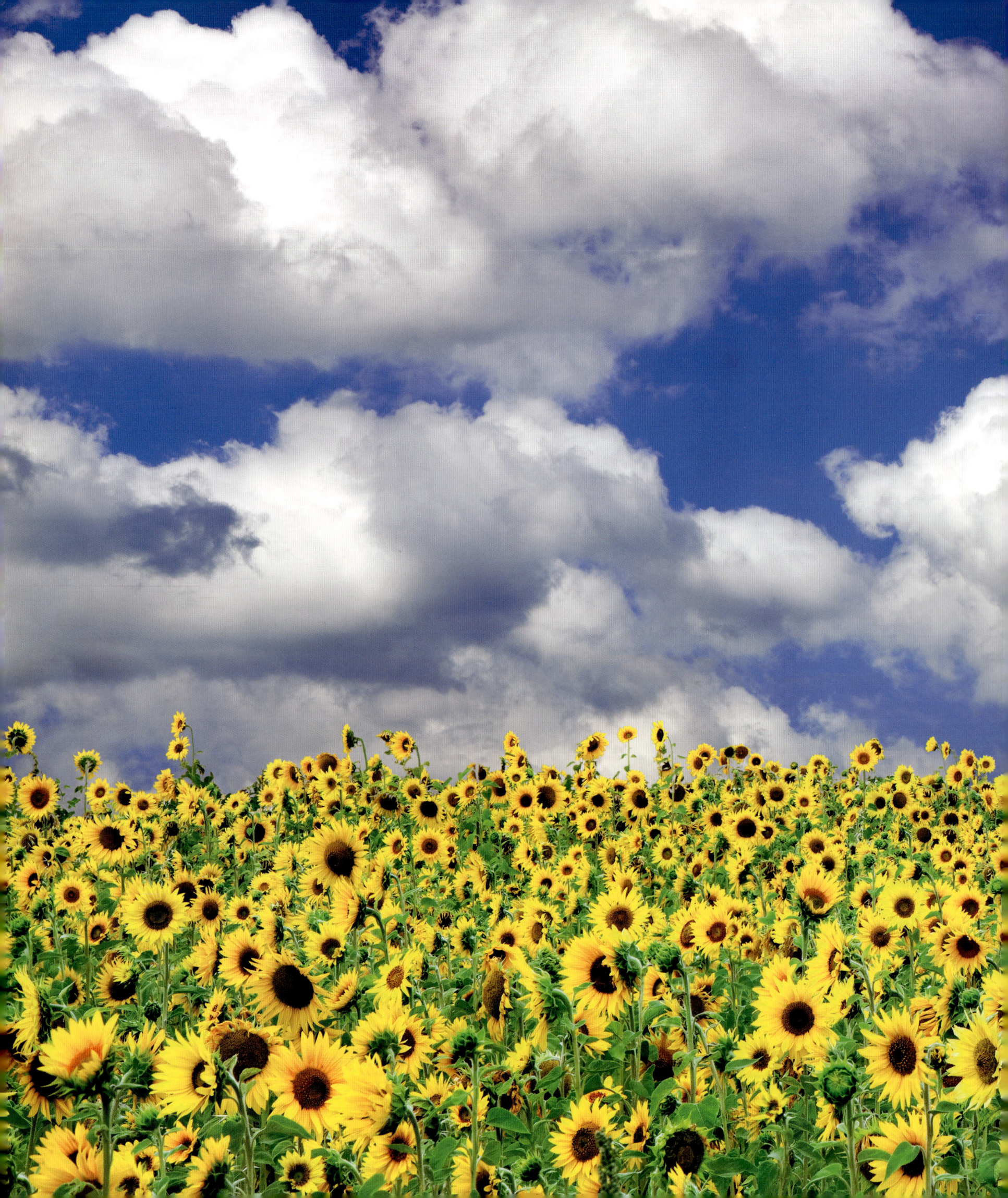

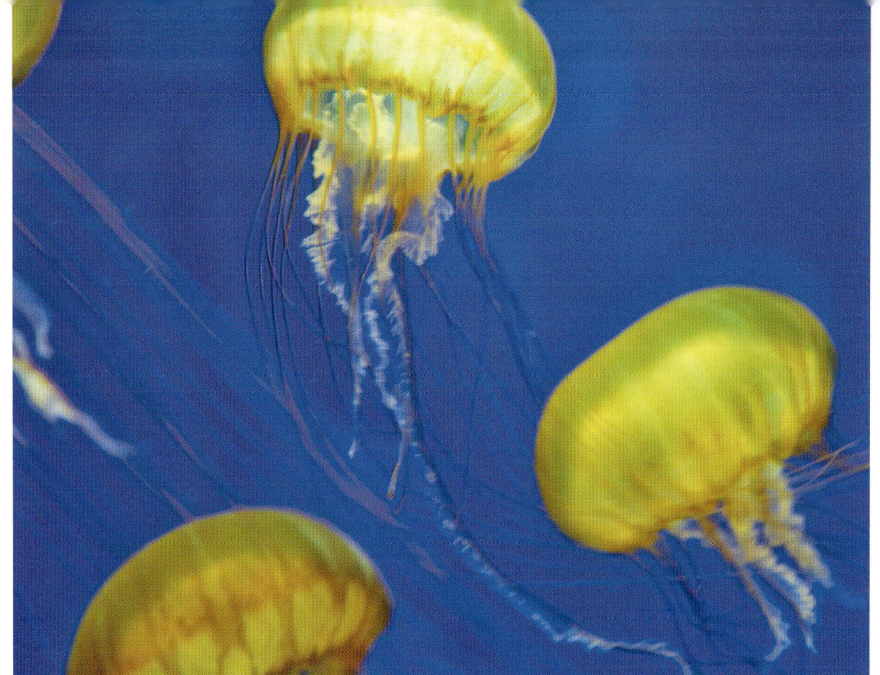
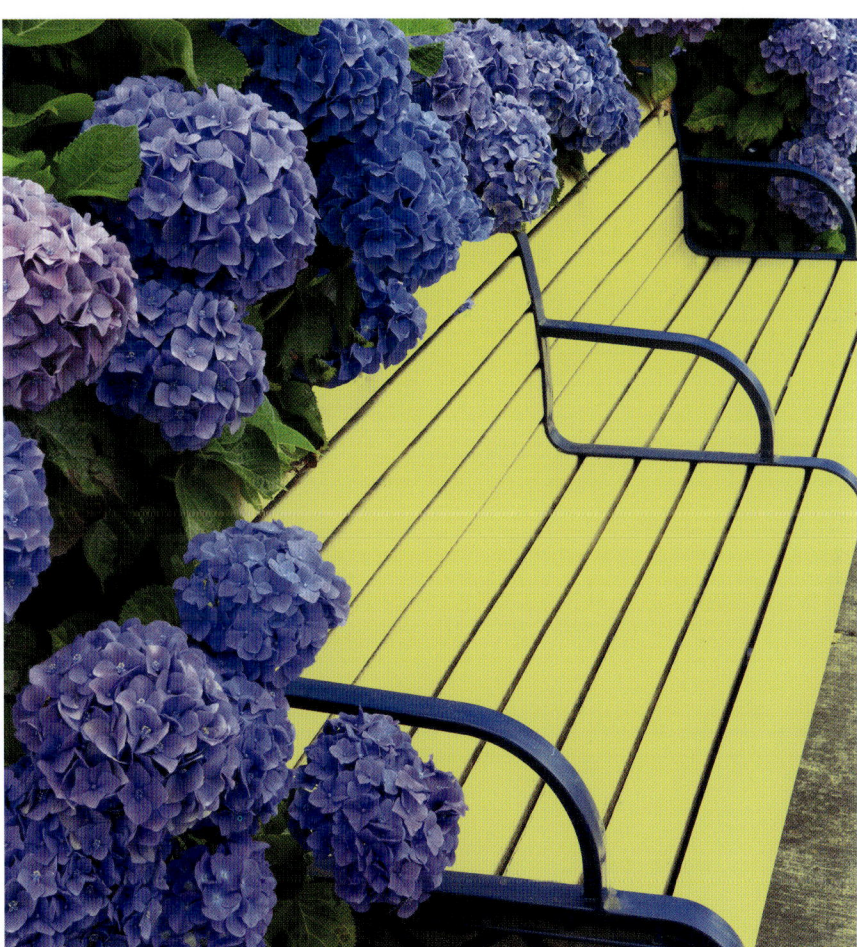

Above, top: The rhythmic undulations and lacy tentacles of the Pacific sea nettle make the jellyfish a crowd favorite at the Oregon Coast Aquarium in Newport. These beauties drift on ocean currents, spreading their tentacles to catch and sting unsuspecting prey.

Above, bottom: Hydrangeas, with their massive, periwinkle-blue heads, thrive in the temperate climates west of the Cascade Mountains. The plants can stretch to six feet tall and eight feet wide.

Left: Perky sunflowers raise their heads to the summer sky near Sherwood. Known for their stunning array of colors, ranging from pale yellow to orange and rust, these sturdy blooms are a popular item at farmers markets and pick-your-own farms in the western valleys.

Right: A yellow and rose-orange bloom of the "September Morn" variety grows in the rich Willamette Valley soil at Swan Island Dahlias in Canby. Oregon is among the nation's top producers of fresh flowers.

Far right: Heceta Head is both a bed and breakfast and a working lighthouse, serving up breakfast with views of nesting cormorants and migrating whales, while ensuring maritime safety to passing ships.

Below: The sky just seems larger in Wallowa County. Farmers and artists alike thrive in the fresh mountain air in the far northeast corner of Oregon, home to Wallowa Lake, the Eagle Cap Wilderness, and Hells Canyon National Recreation Area.

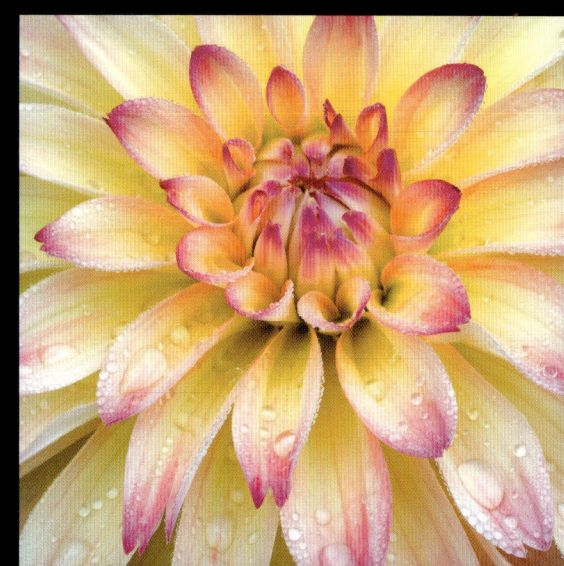

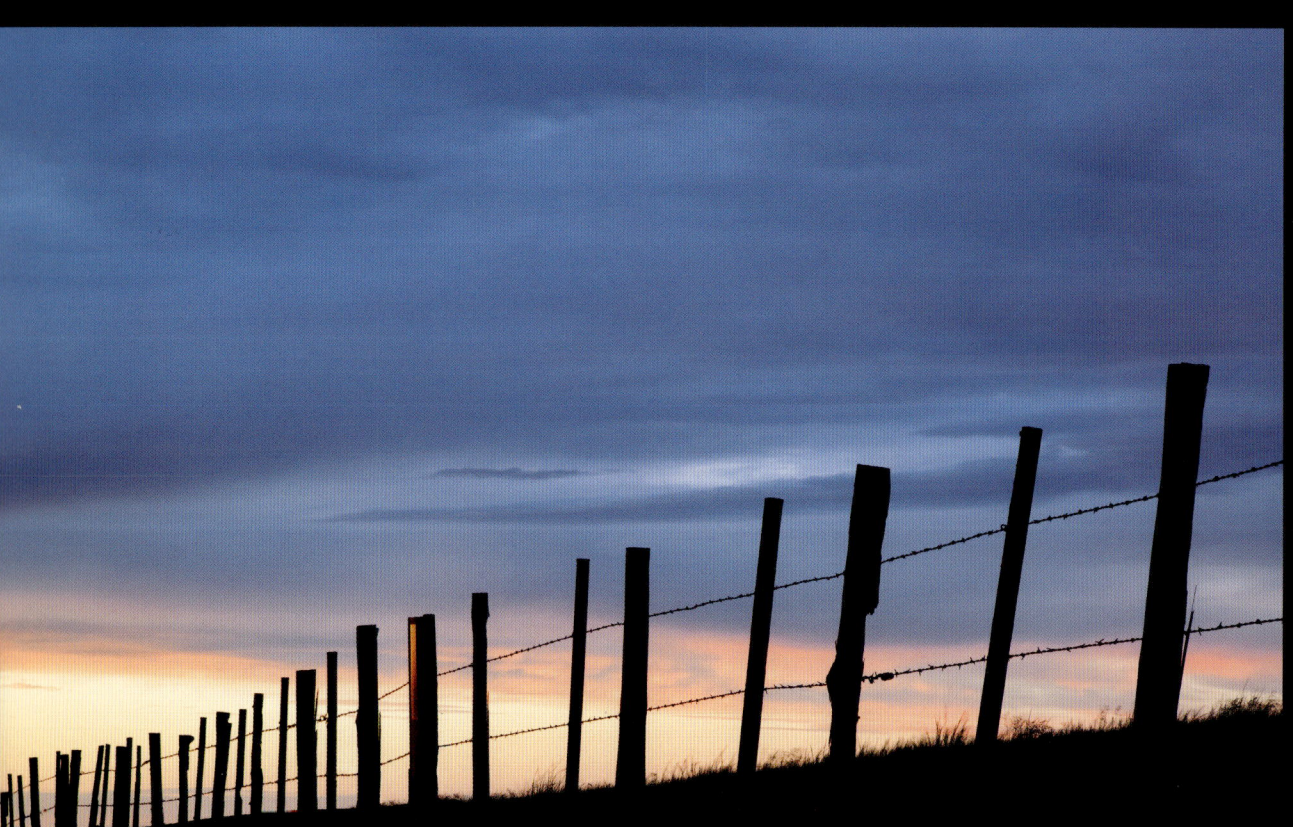

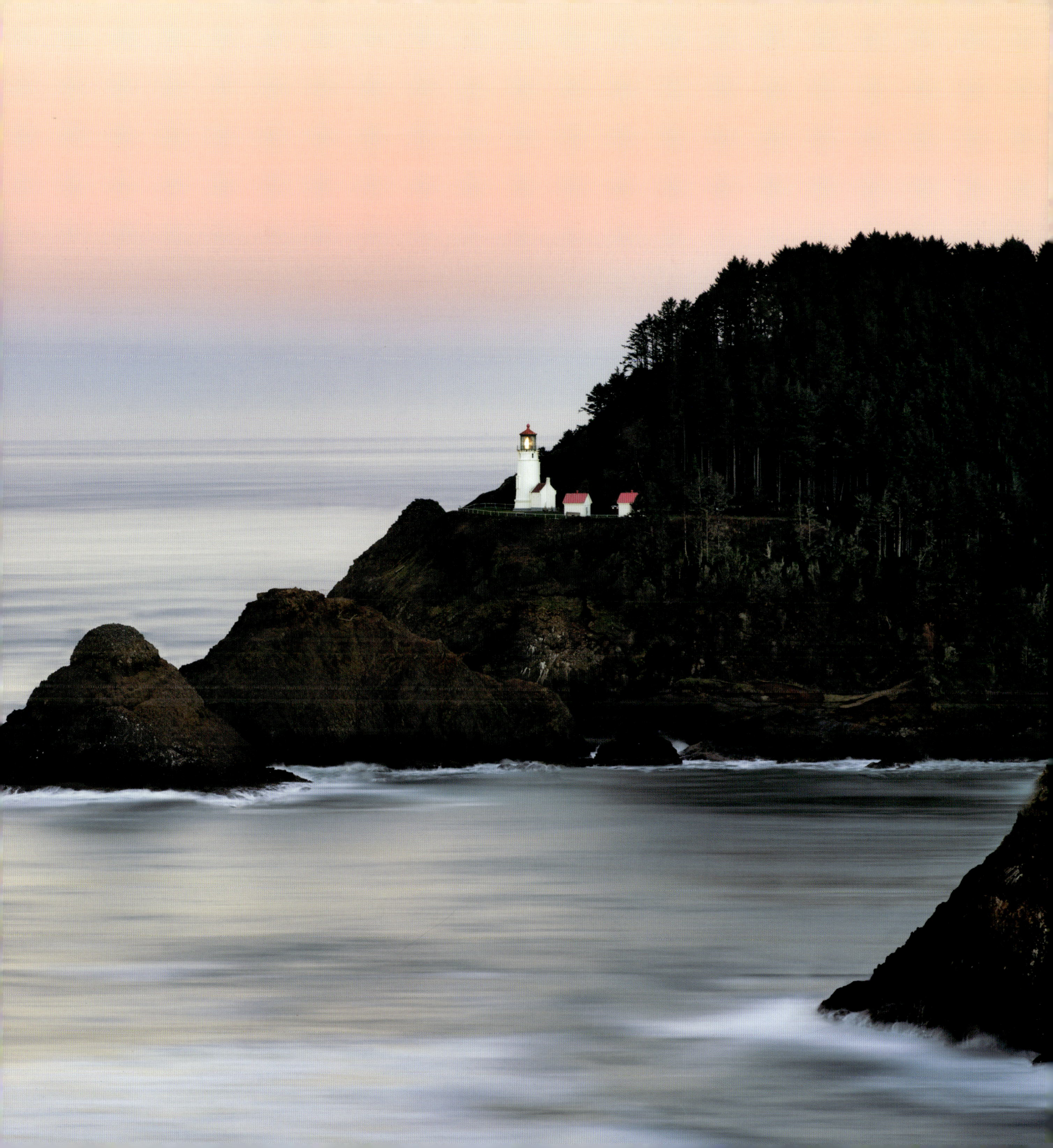

Right: When temperatures rise, Asian elephant Rose-Tu and her calf Lily take a dip in the pool at the 64-acre Oregon Zoo. The youngster's name was chosen by public vote shortly after her birth. Visitors to the zoo may also view 260 species of creatures and over 1,000 species of exotic plants. PHOTO COURTESY OF THE OREGON ZOO

Below, top: Love them or hate them, raccoons are part of the Oregon landscape. Raccoons are supremely adaptable, and are known to lift hatches and open gates to gain entry to houses and barns. However, the black-masked bandits often charm their human neighbors despite the trouble they cause.

Below, bottom: The spring-fed lake at Crystal Springs Rhododendron Garden in Portland attracts many species of birds and waterfowl, including Canada geese. These birds create strong family bonds and tend to return to their place of birth to nest.

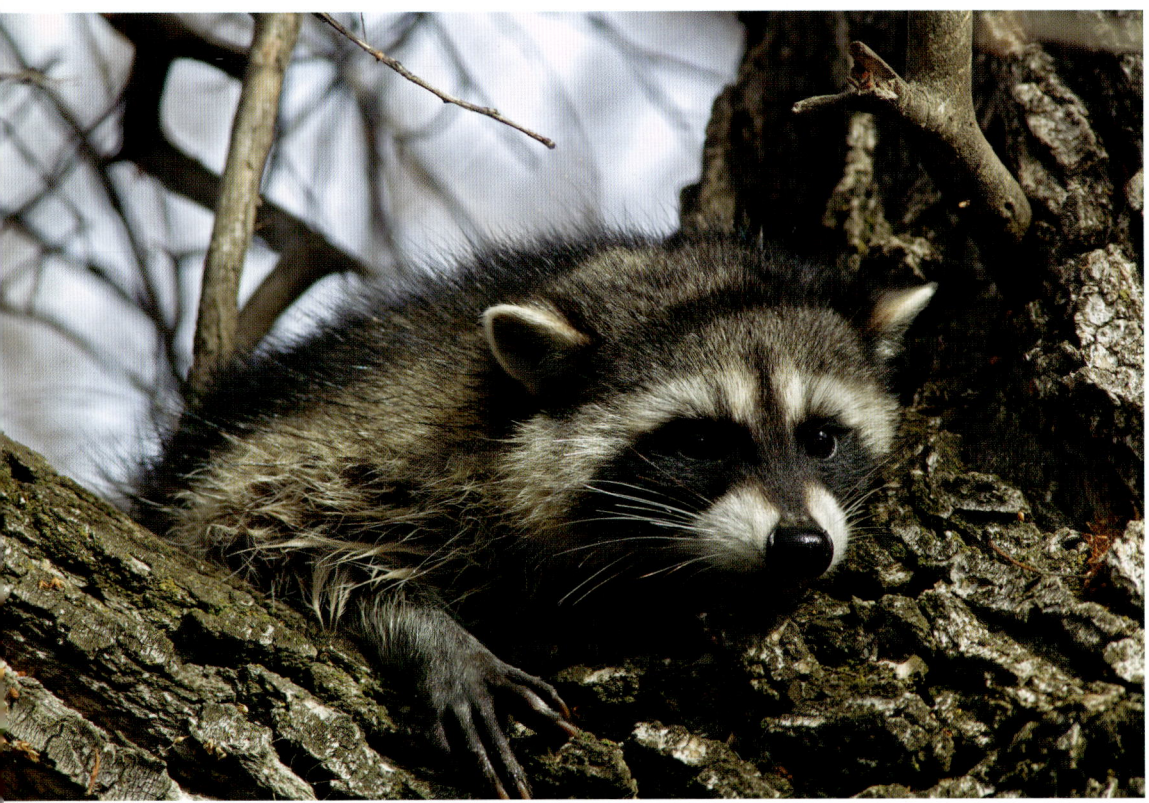

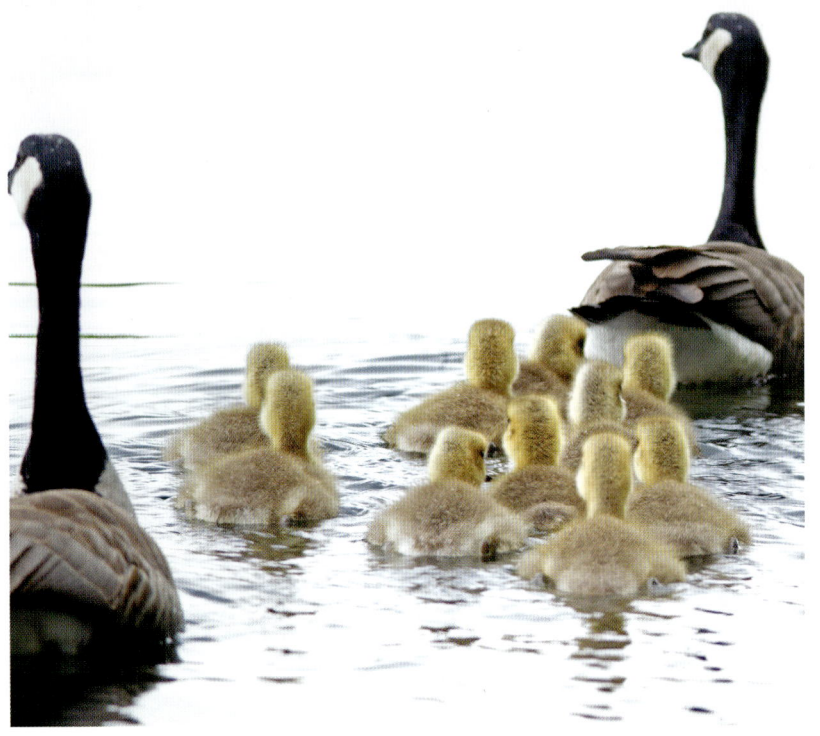

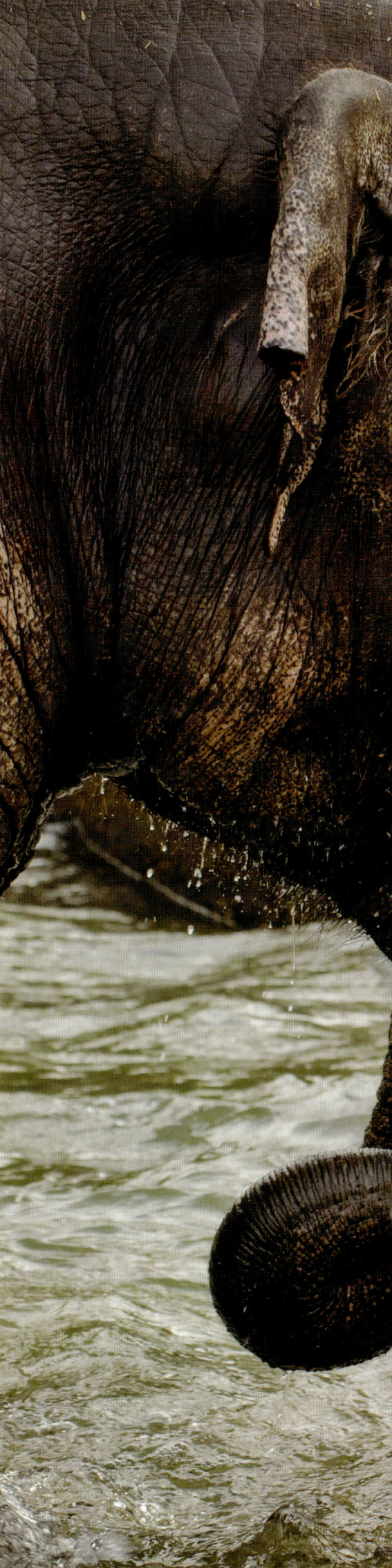

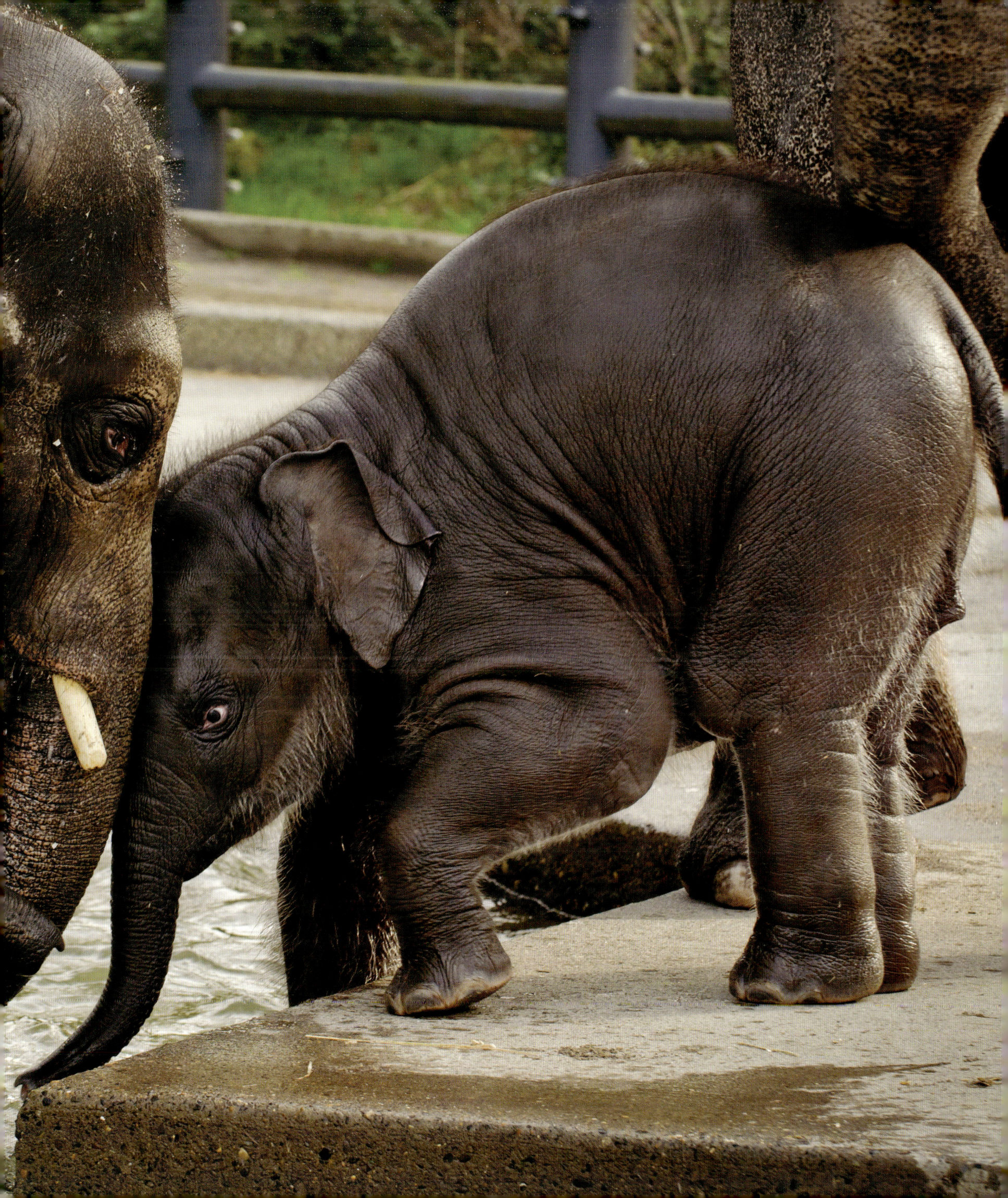

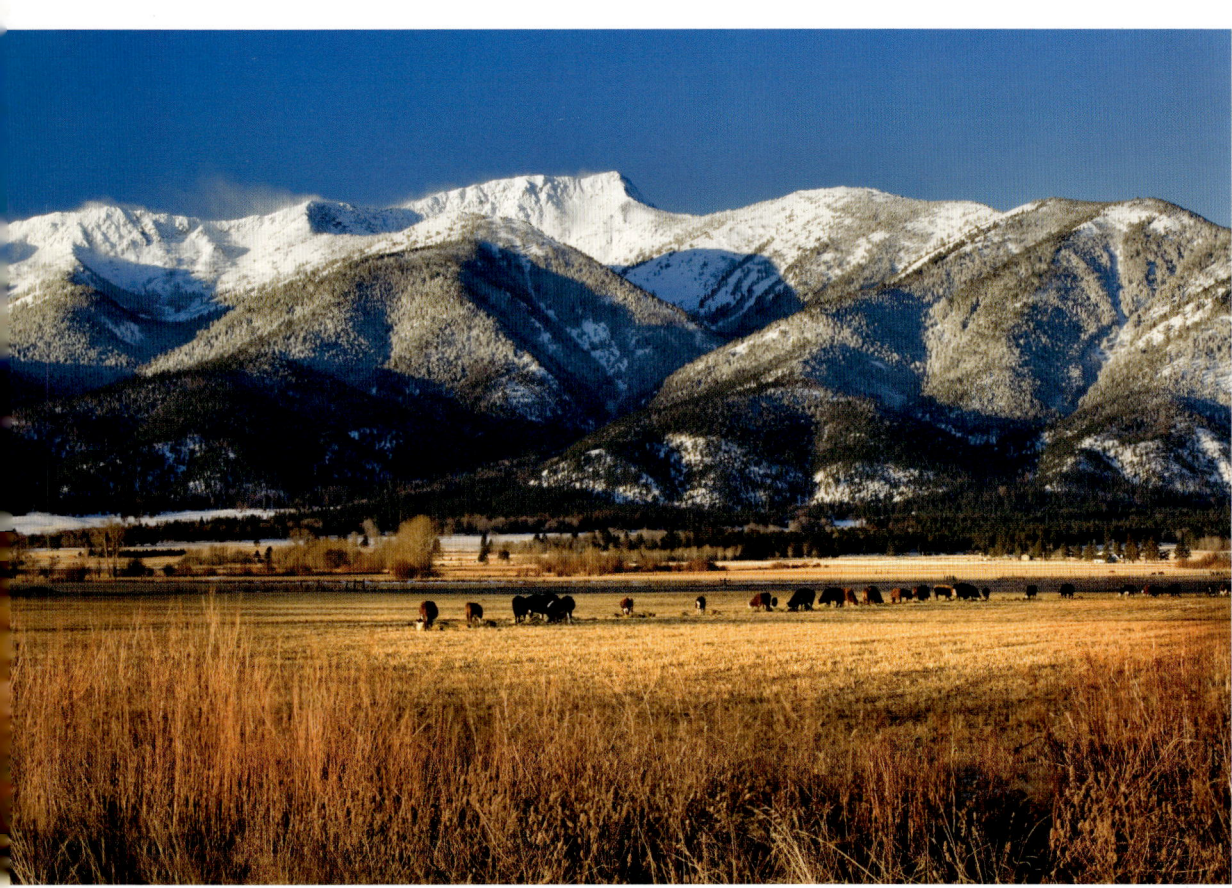

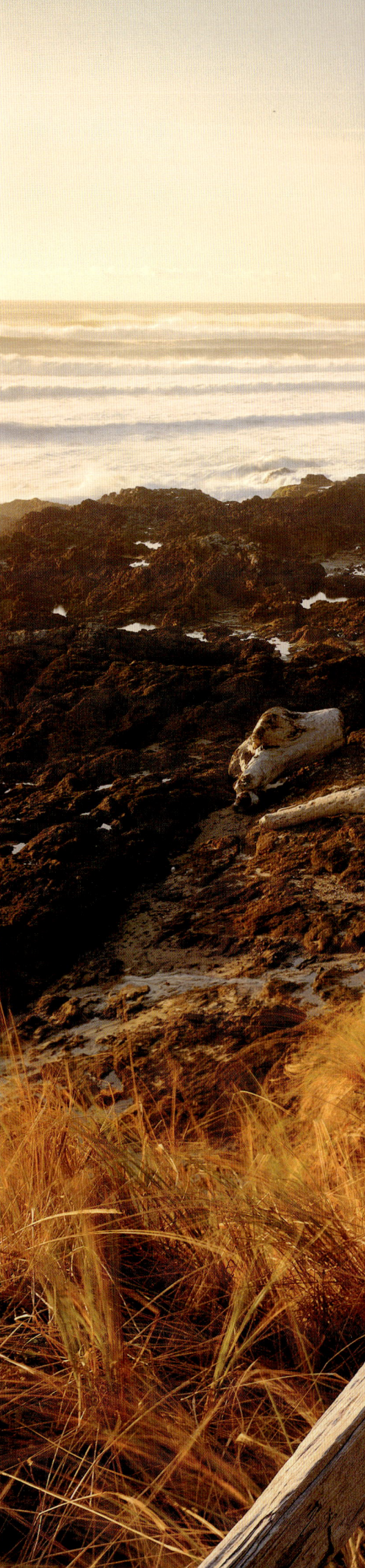

Above: Many who traveled the Oregon Trail sought to make their fortune mining for gold in the jagged Elkhorn range of the Blue Mountains. The Elkhorn Scenic Byway begins in Baker City and meanders past the former mining towns of Sumpter and Granite.

Right: Oregon law guarantees the public free and uninterrupted use of the beaches along the state's 363 miles of coastline. This path leads beachgoers to high tide near Yachats, the name of which was taken from a Chinook word meaning "dark waters at the foot of the mountain."

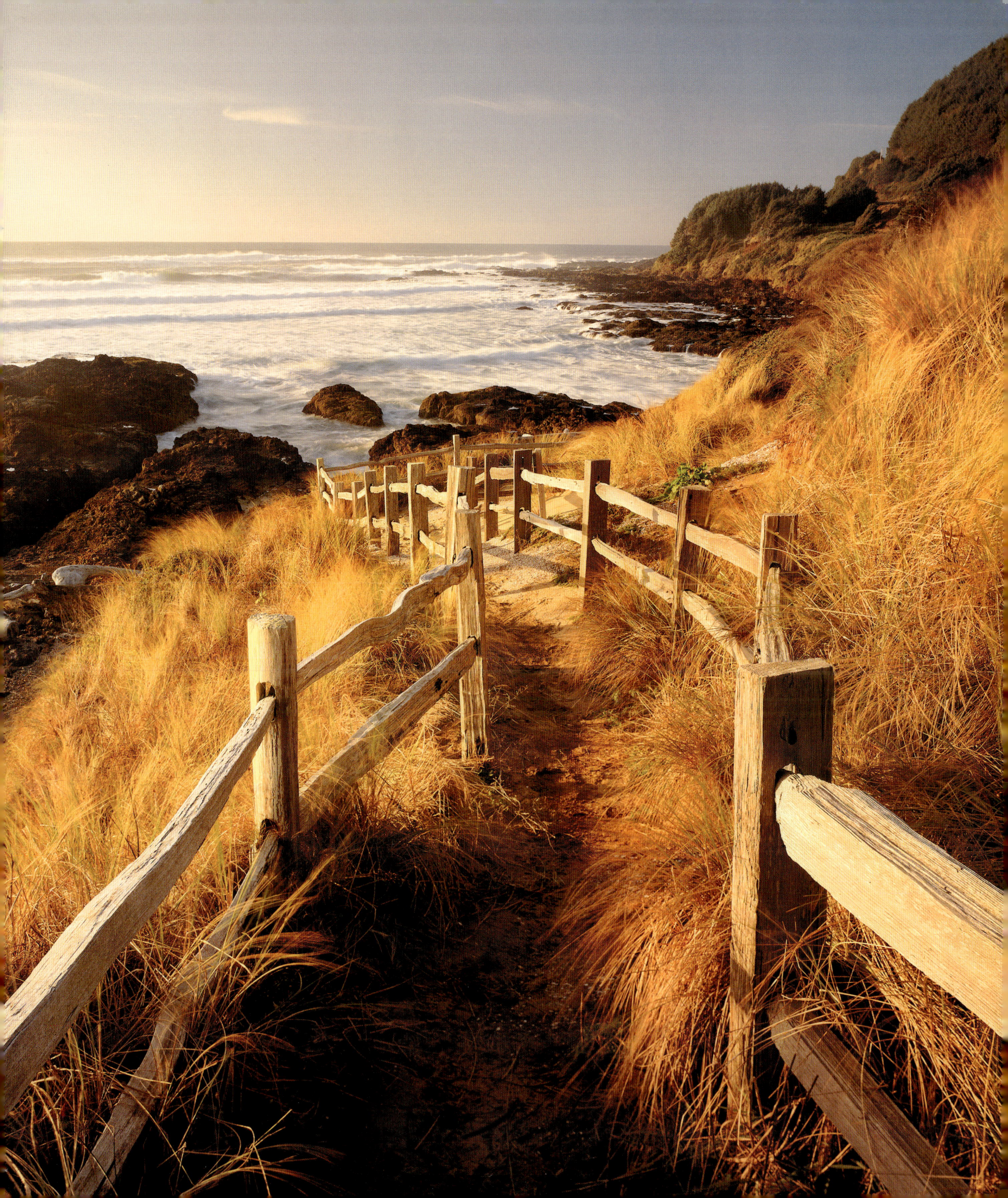

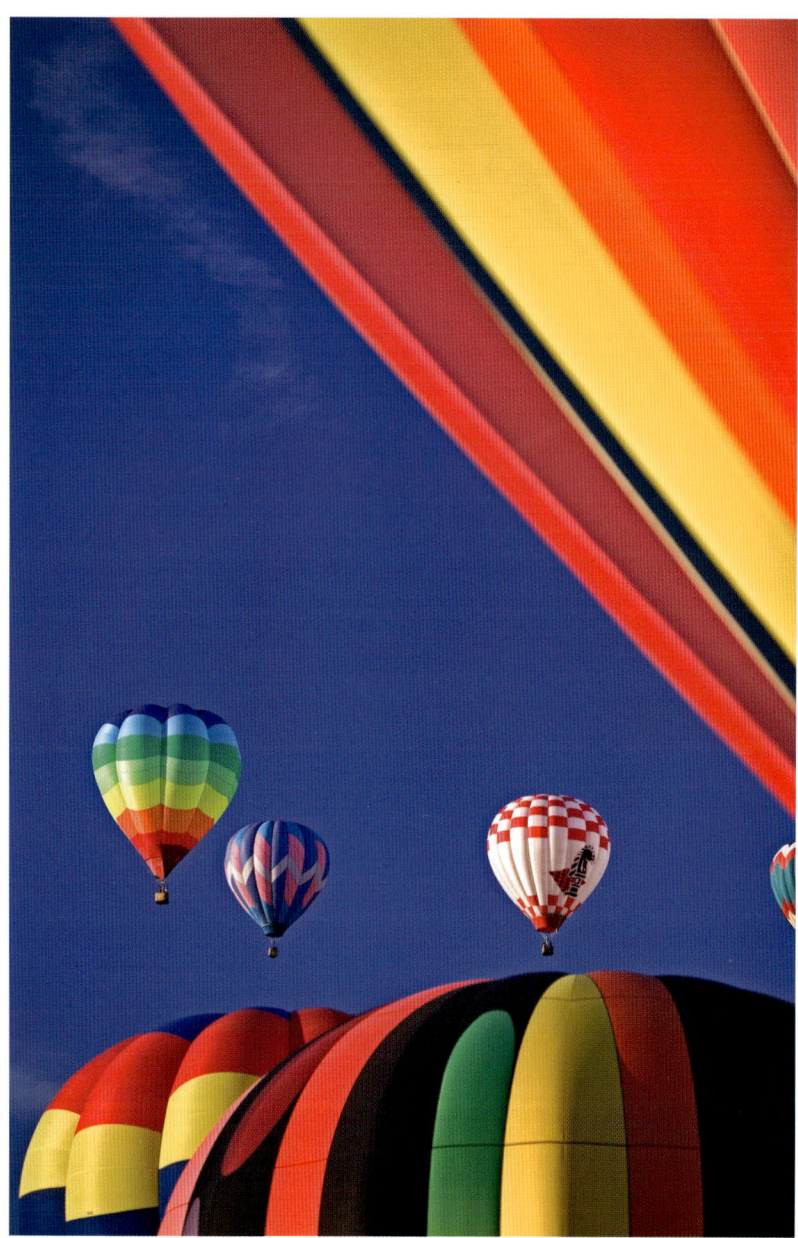

Above: It is the early bird that catches sight of the hot air balloons at the Northwest Art and Air Festival in Albany. Dozens of balloons lift off every morning during the three-day event the last weekend of August.

Right: Spring wildflowers blanket the meadows below 5,601-foot Echo Mountain near Santiam Junction in the Willamette National Forest of Oregon's central Cascades.

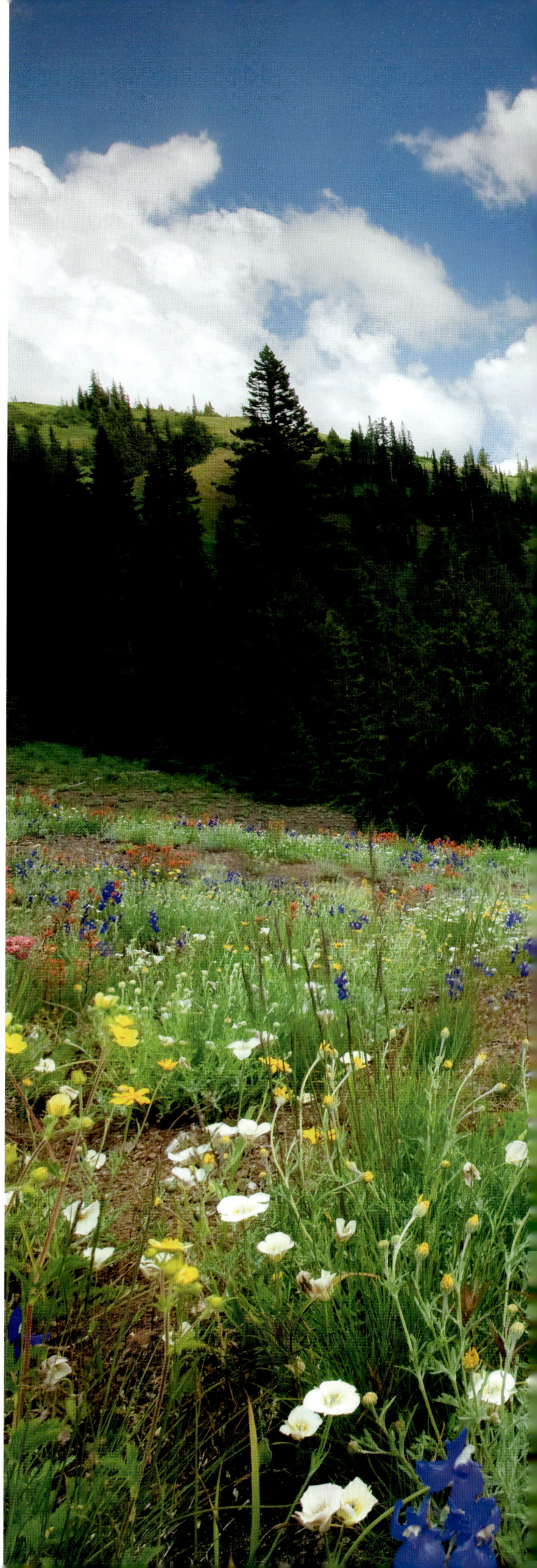

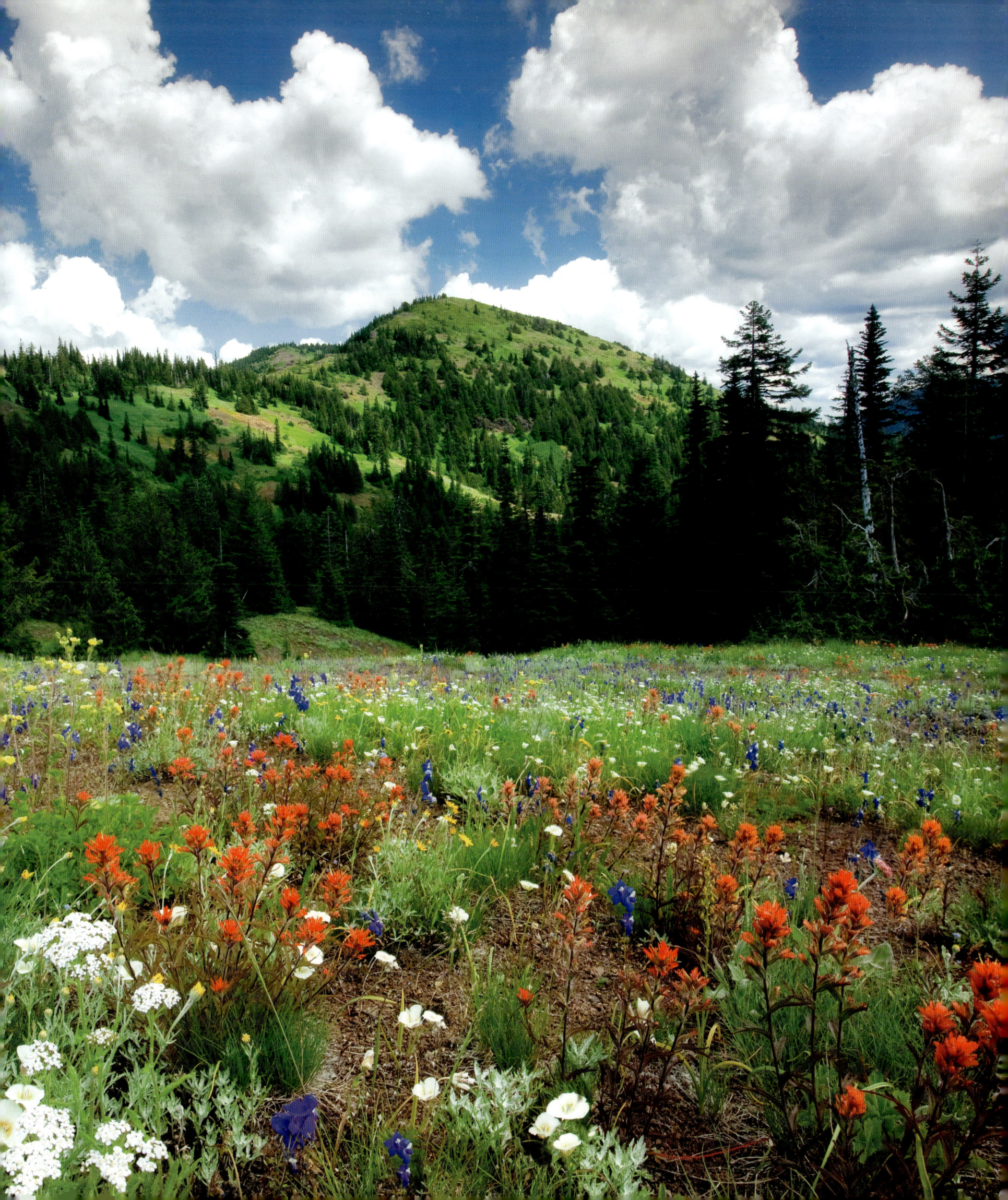

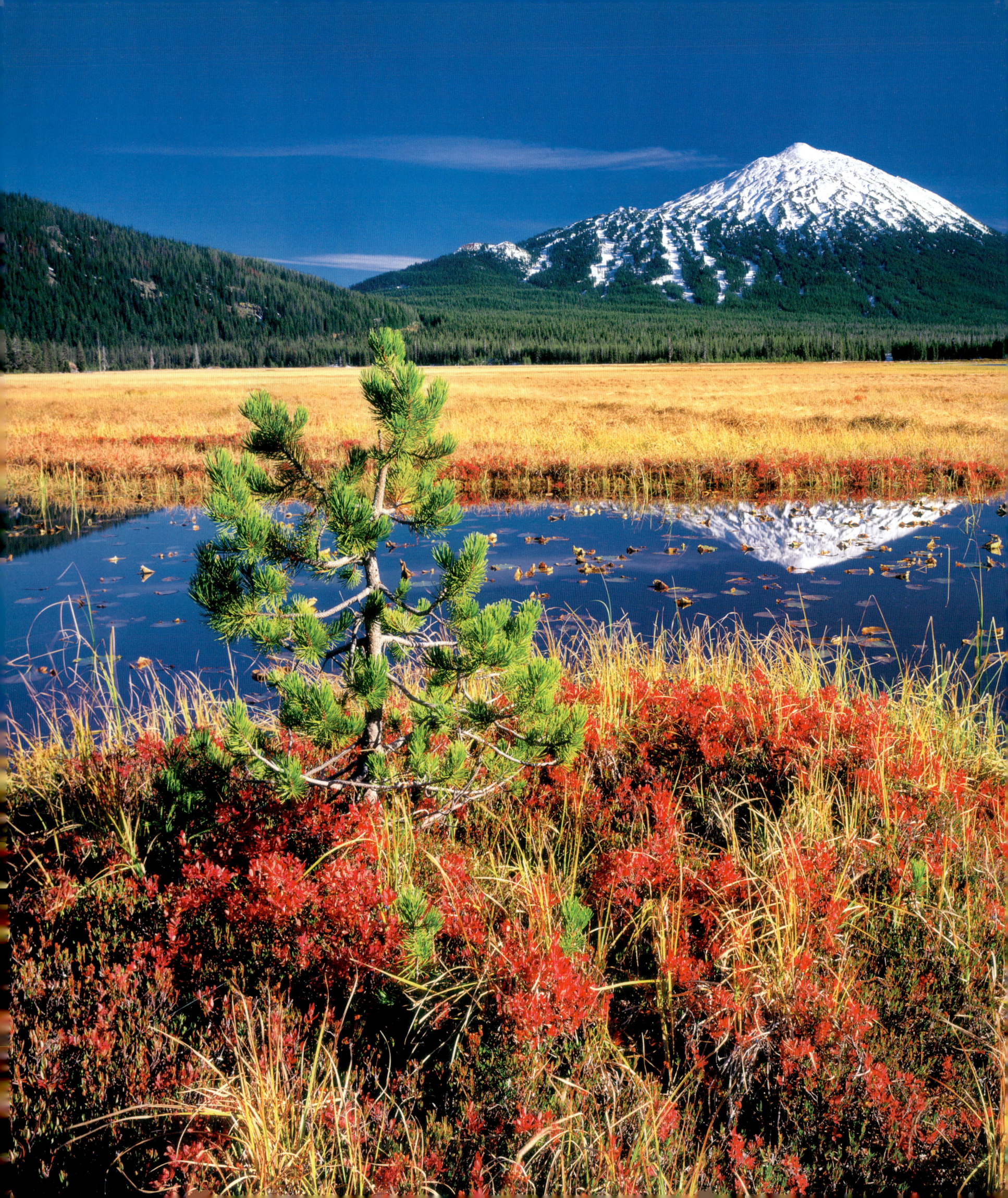

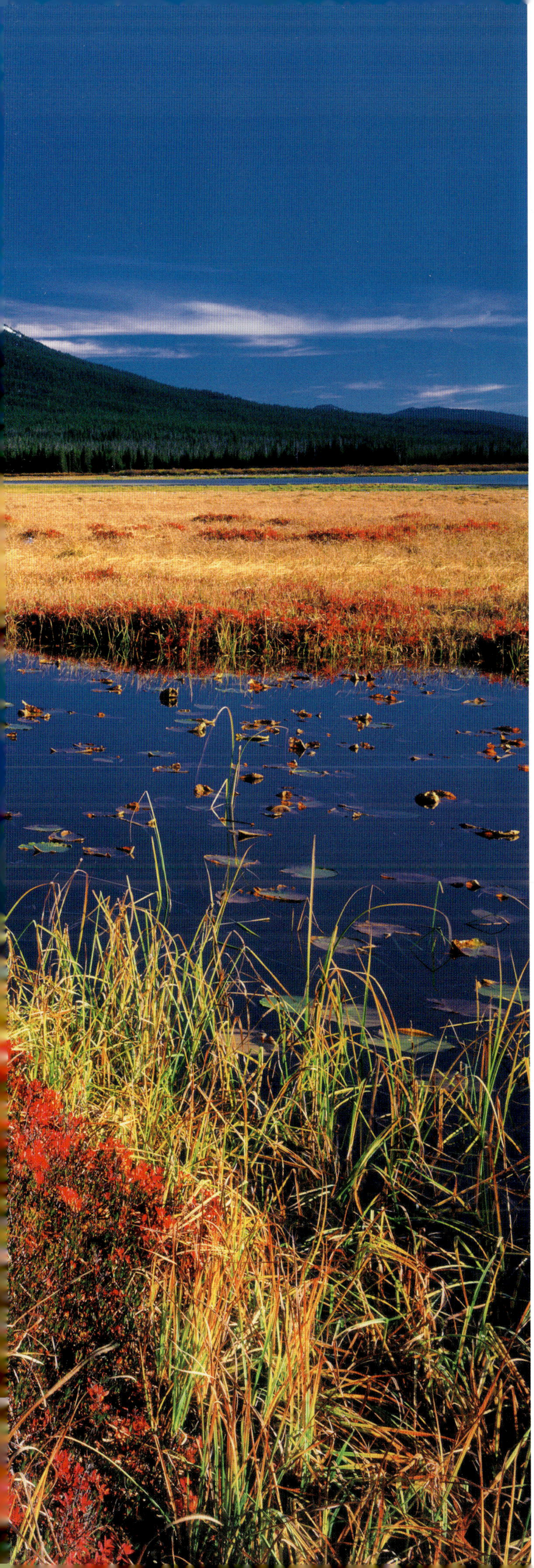

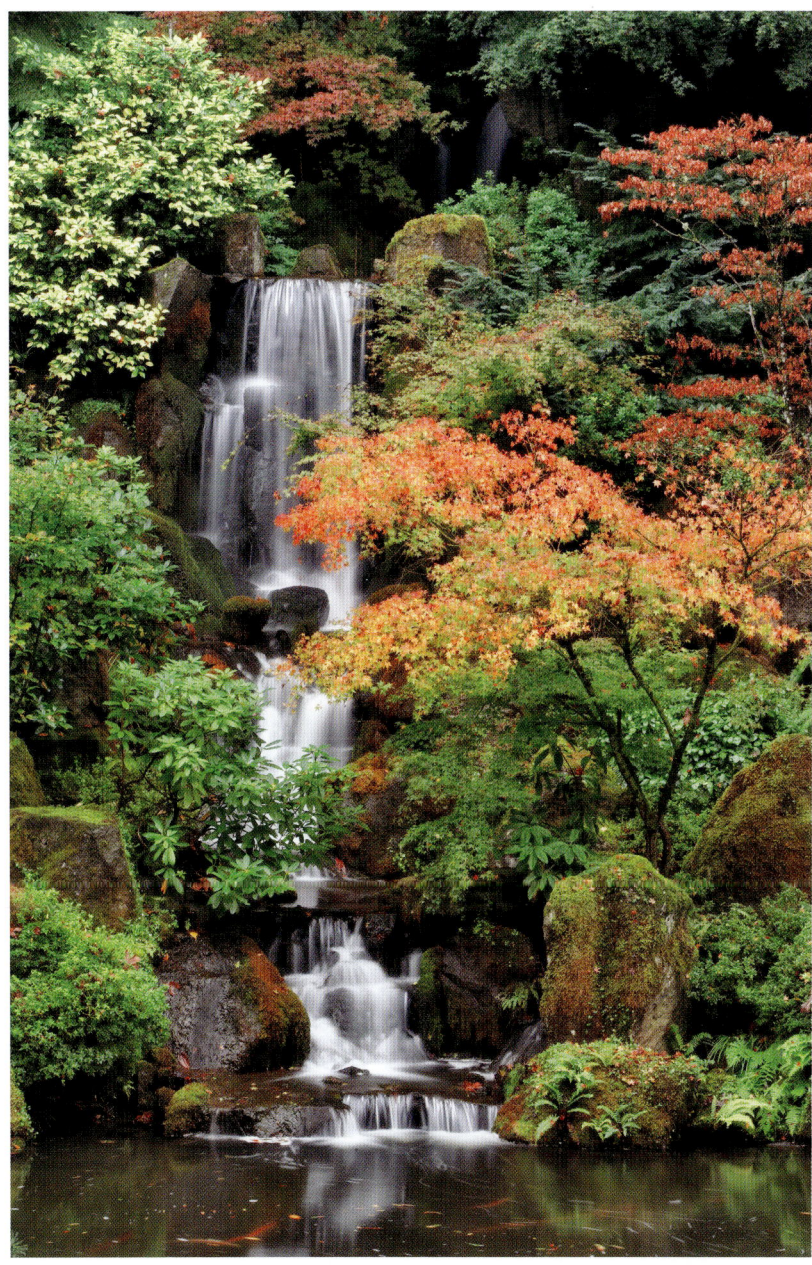

Above: Hailed as "the most authentic Japanese garden outside of Japan," the Portland Japanese Garden is a masterpiece. The garden uses three essential design elements—stone, water, and plants—to create a tranquil corner amid Portland's bustling streets.

Left: The yellow-green needles of lodgepole pine and crimson leaves of wild huckleberry frame the reflection of Mt. Bachelor's 9,068-foot peak in central Oregon. A cousin to the blueberry, huckleberries grow well on sunny slopes at high elevations in the Cascade and Coast mountain ranges. Picking expeditions in late August and early September are a tradition for many Oregonians, who favor the slightly tart blue-black fruit.

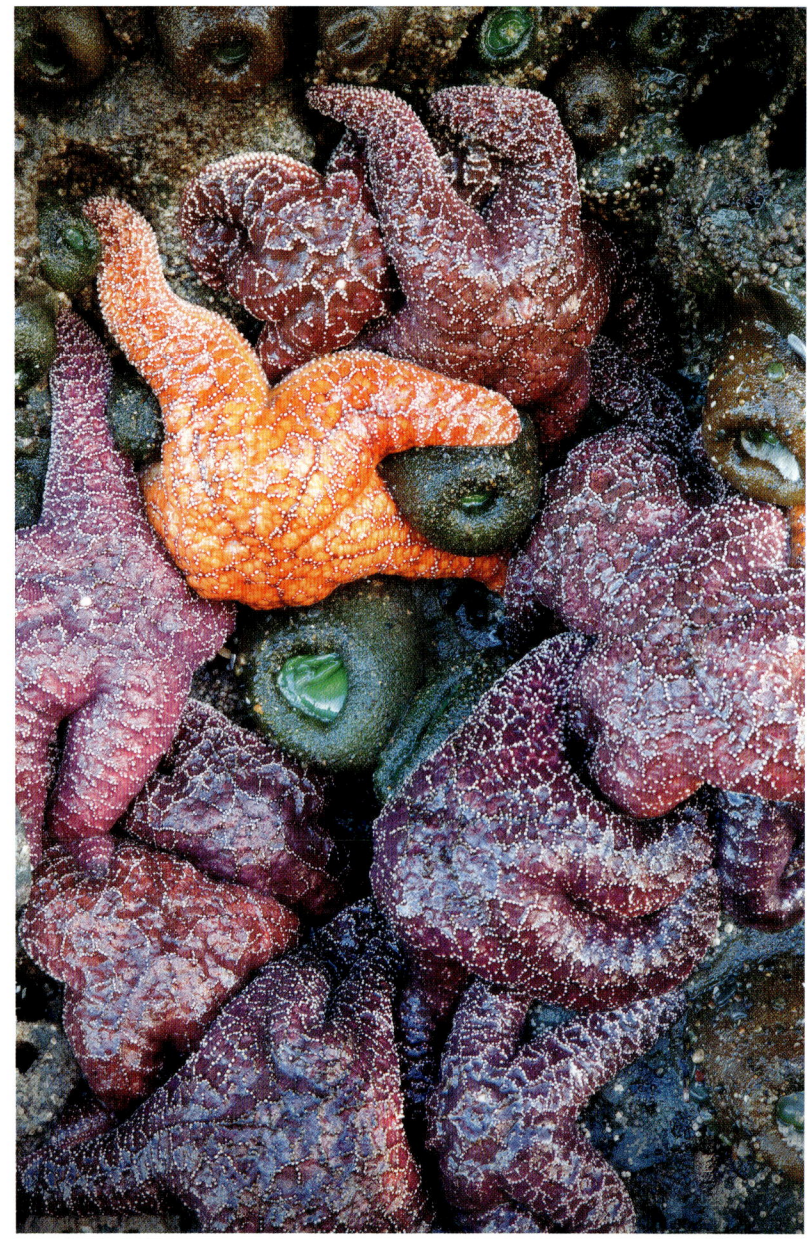

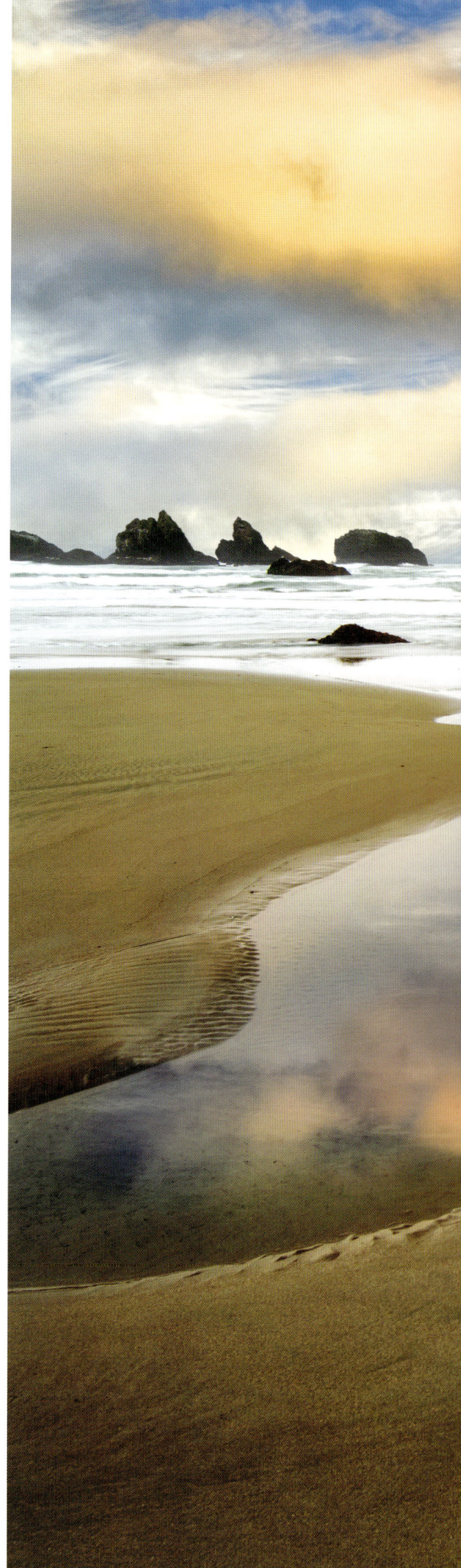

Above: Low tide is the best time to view starfish, sea anemones, and other intertidal marine creatures that live on the rocks and in the shallow pools along the coast.

Right: Some tide pools are easier to explore than others. Interpretive programs at several locations along the Oregon coast teach visitors about the watery habitats and the species found there.

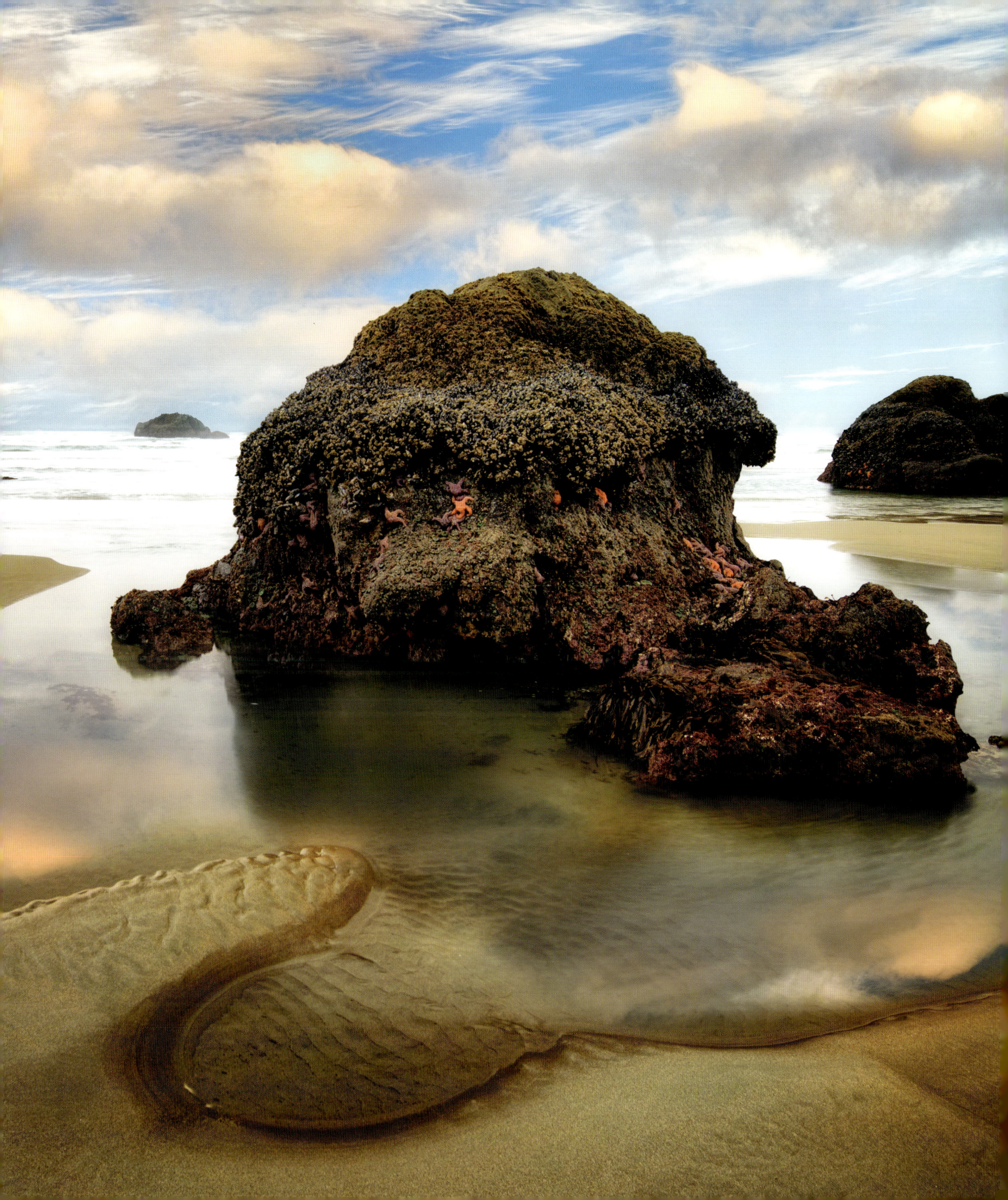

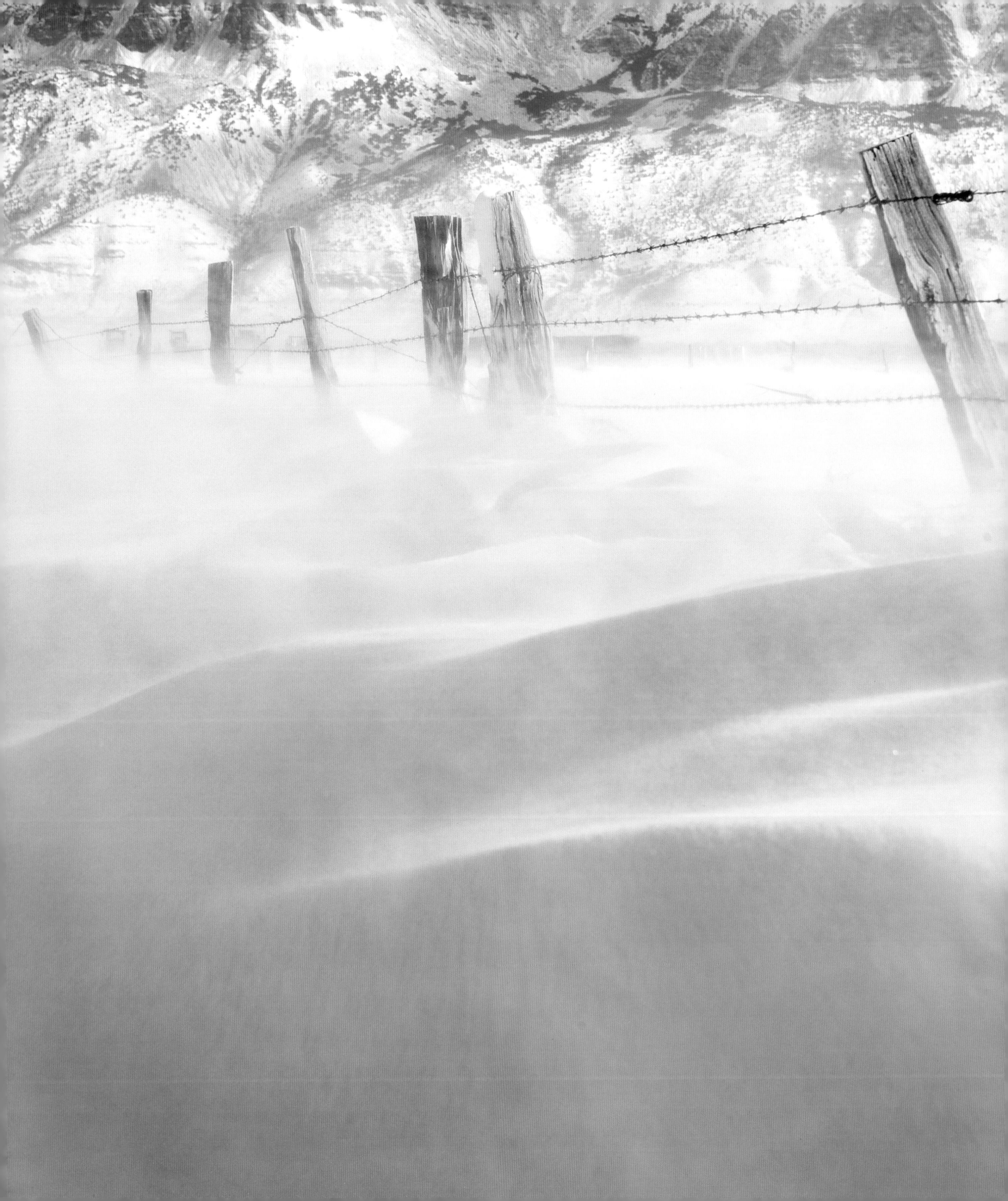

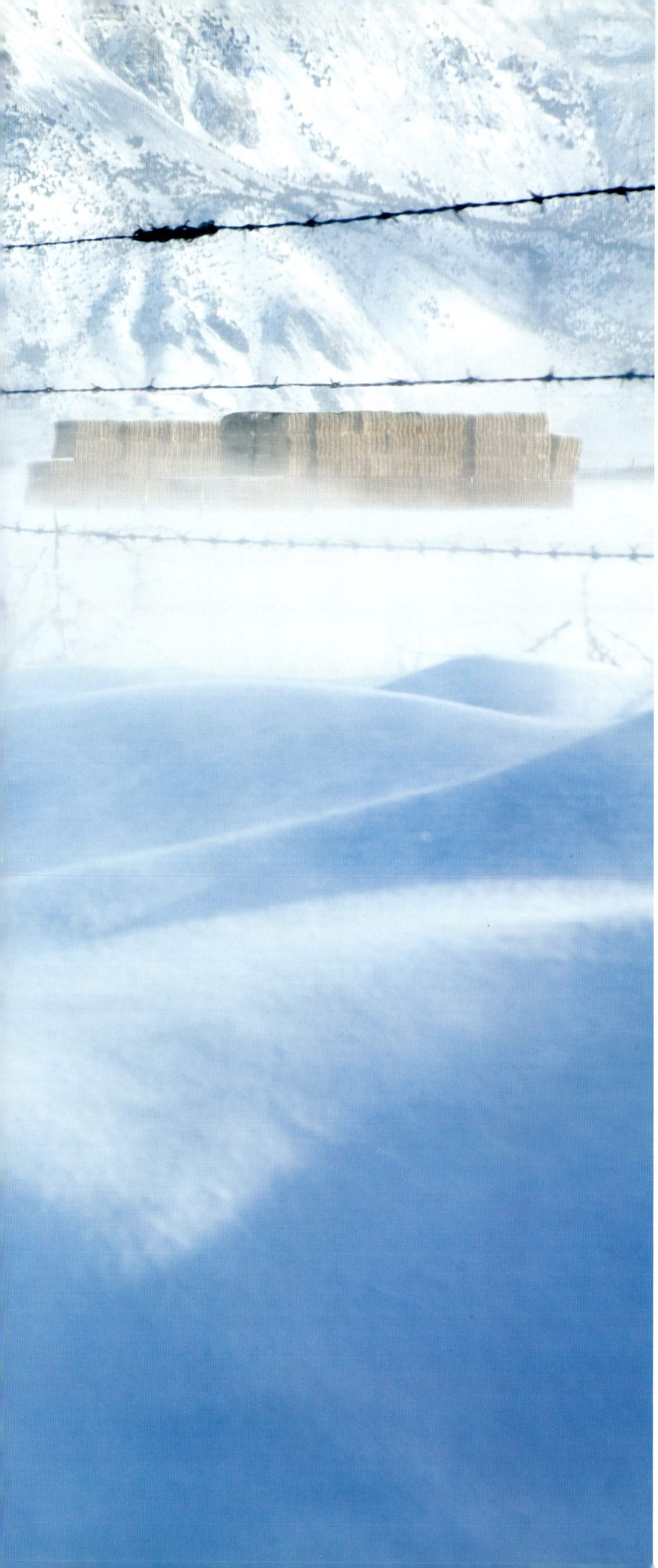

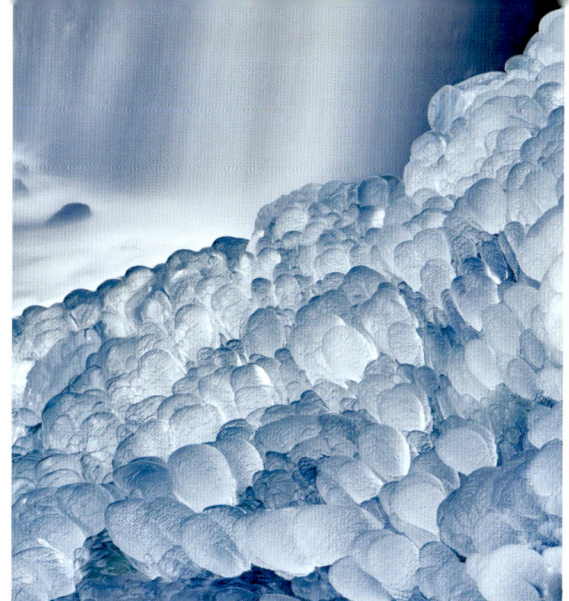

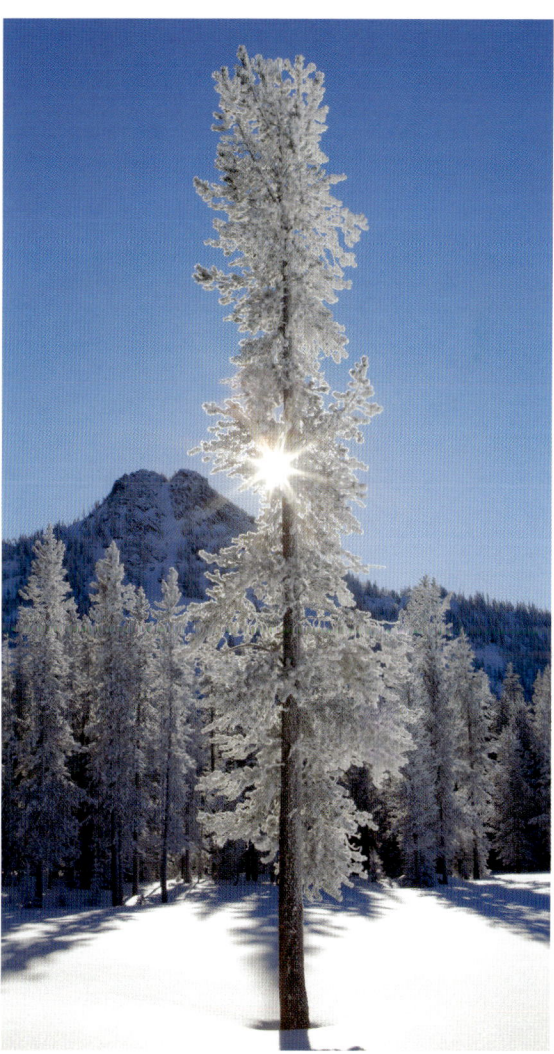

Above, top: Spray from Wahkeena Falls becomes a work of art each winter when freezing temperatures in the Columbia Gorge National Scenic Area turn water droplets to ice.

Above, bottom: With an average of 80 inches of the powdery white stuff a year and the highest base elevation in the state, Anthony Lakes is a gem of a ski resort hidden in the remote Elkhorn Mountains.

Left: A rare thick blanket of snow envelopes a ranch in Warner Valley. Western Oregon enjoys a mild, humid climate regulated by the Pacific Ocean, while the the region east of the Cascades is drier, with wider temperature extremes.

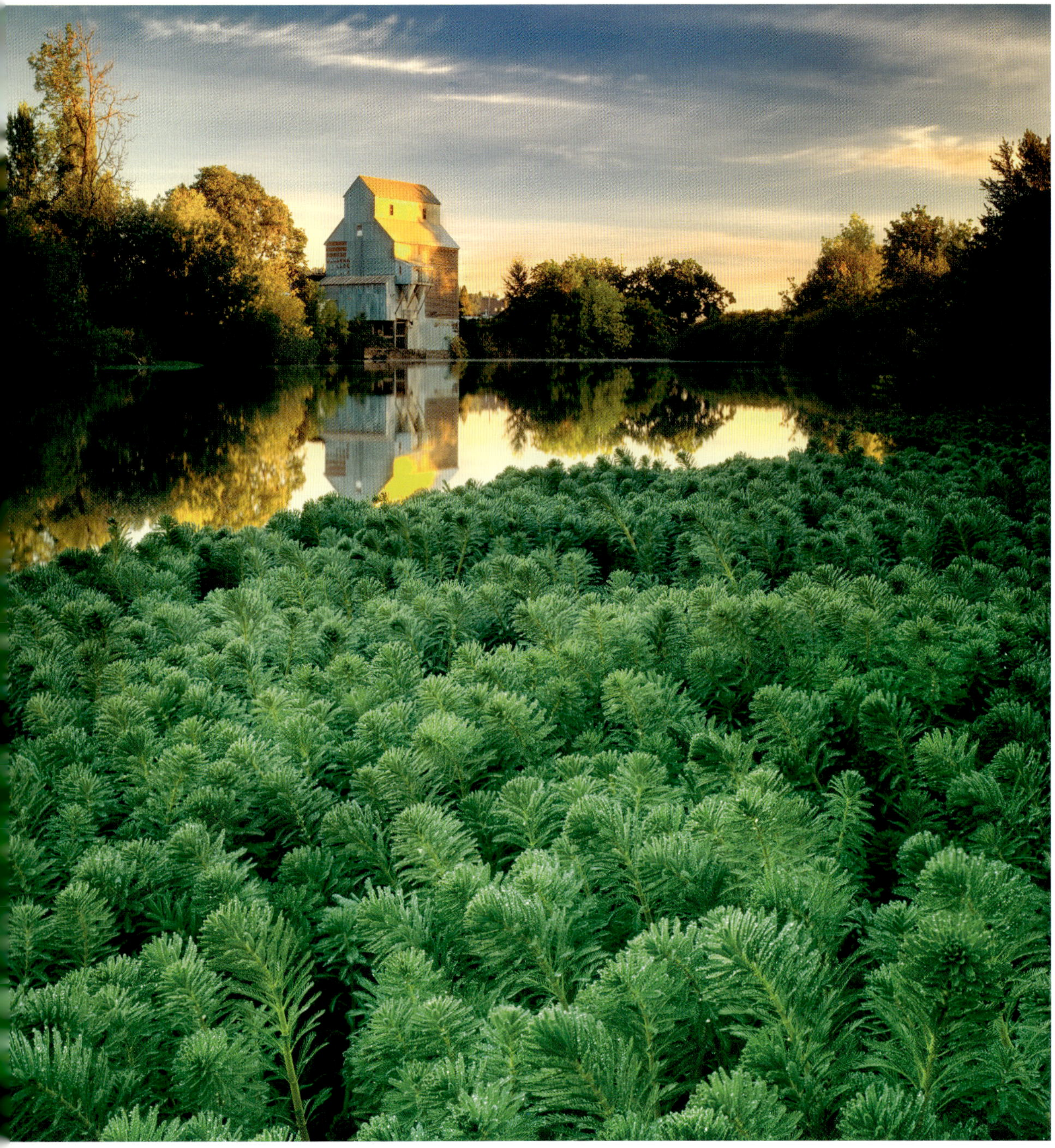

Above: The Kompf Grain Mill on the Long Tom River in Monroe stands as a reminder of bygone days when water-powered wheels ground the grain to feed local families in rural towns across the country.

Right: Time passes differently in pastoral Malheur County, one of the few counties in the United States split into two time zones.

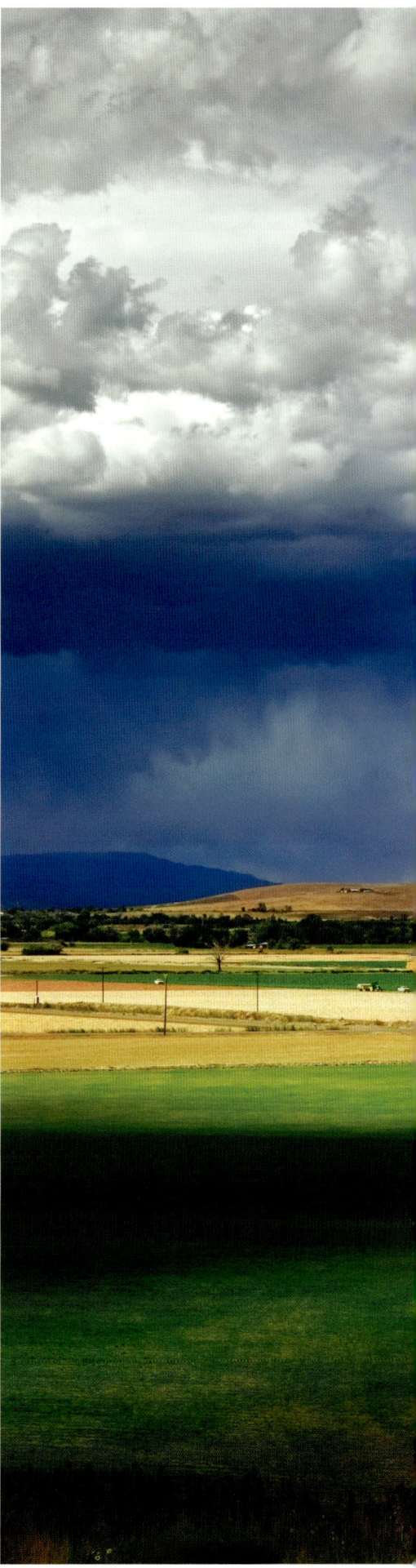

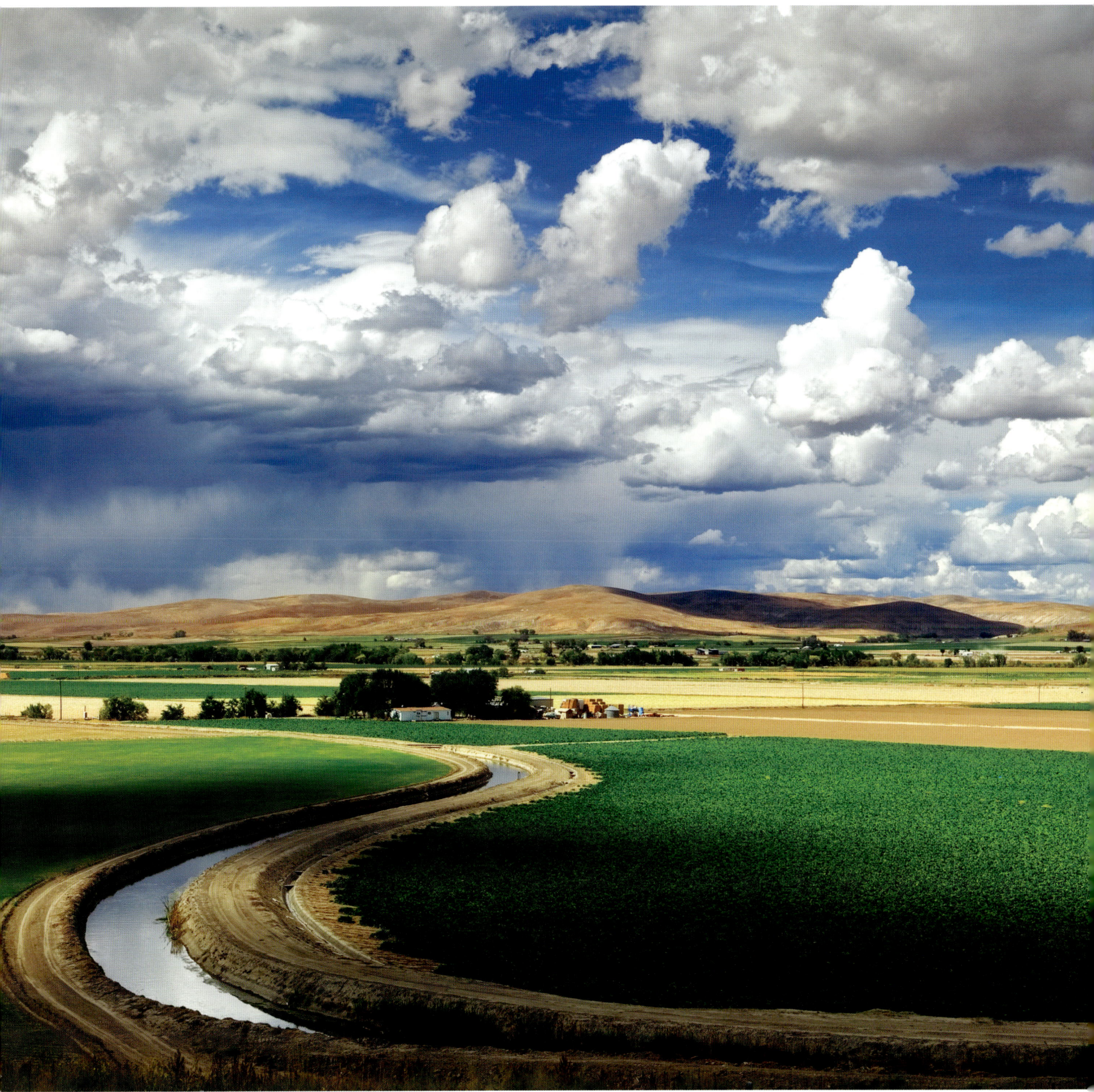

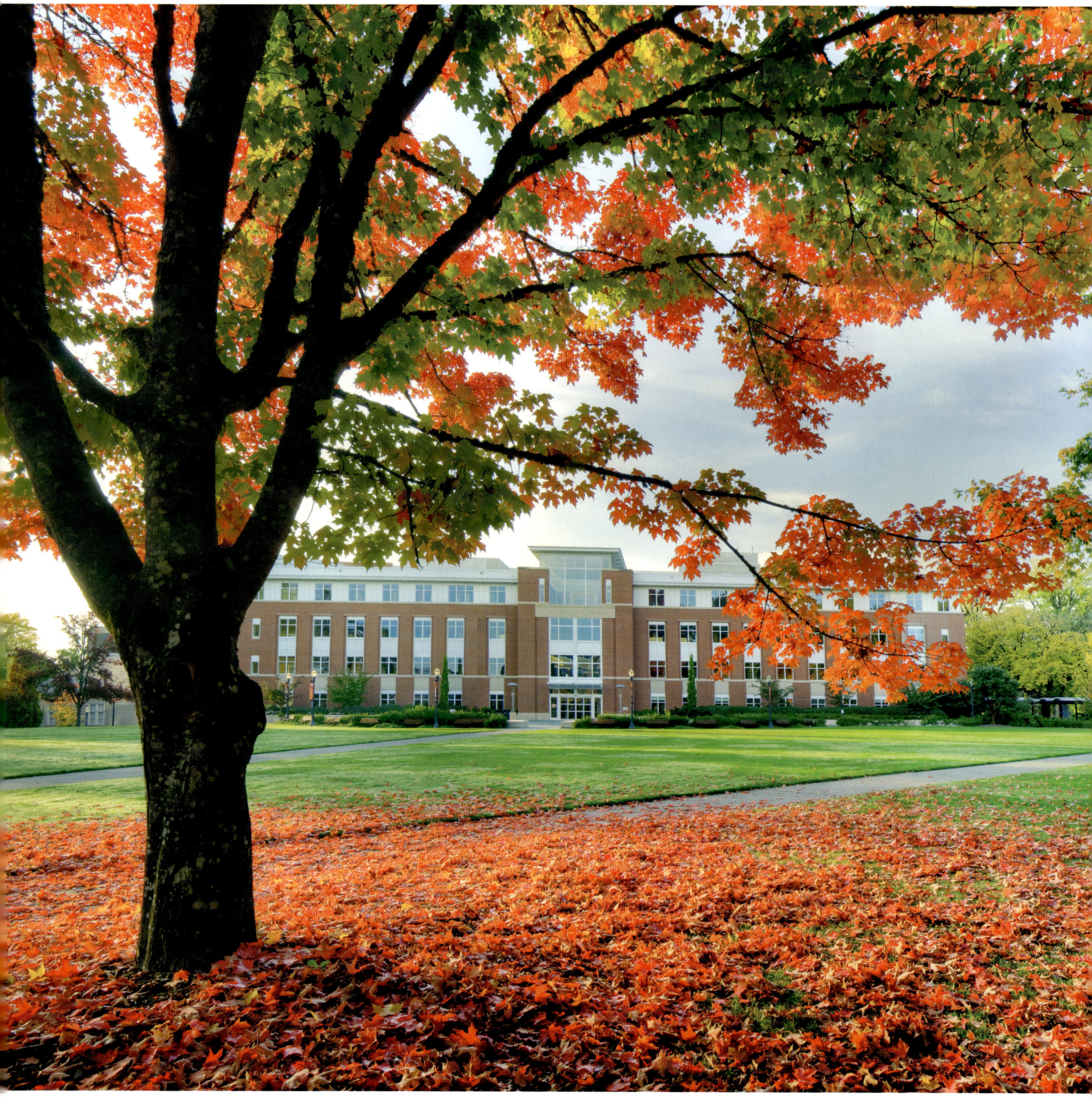

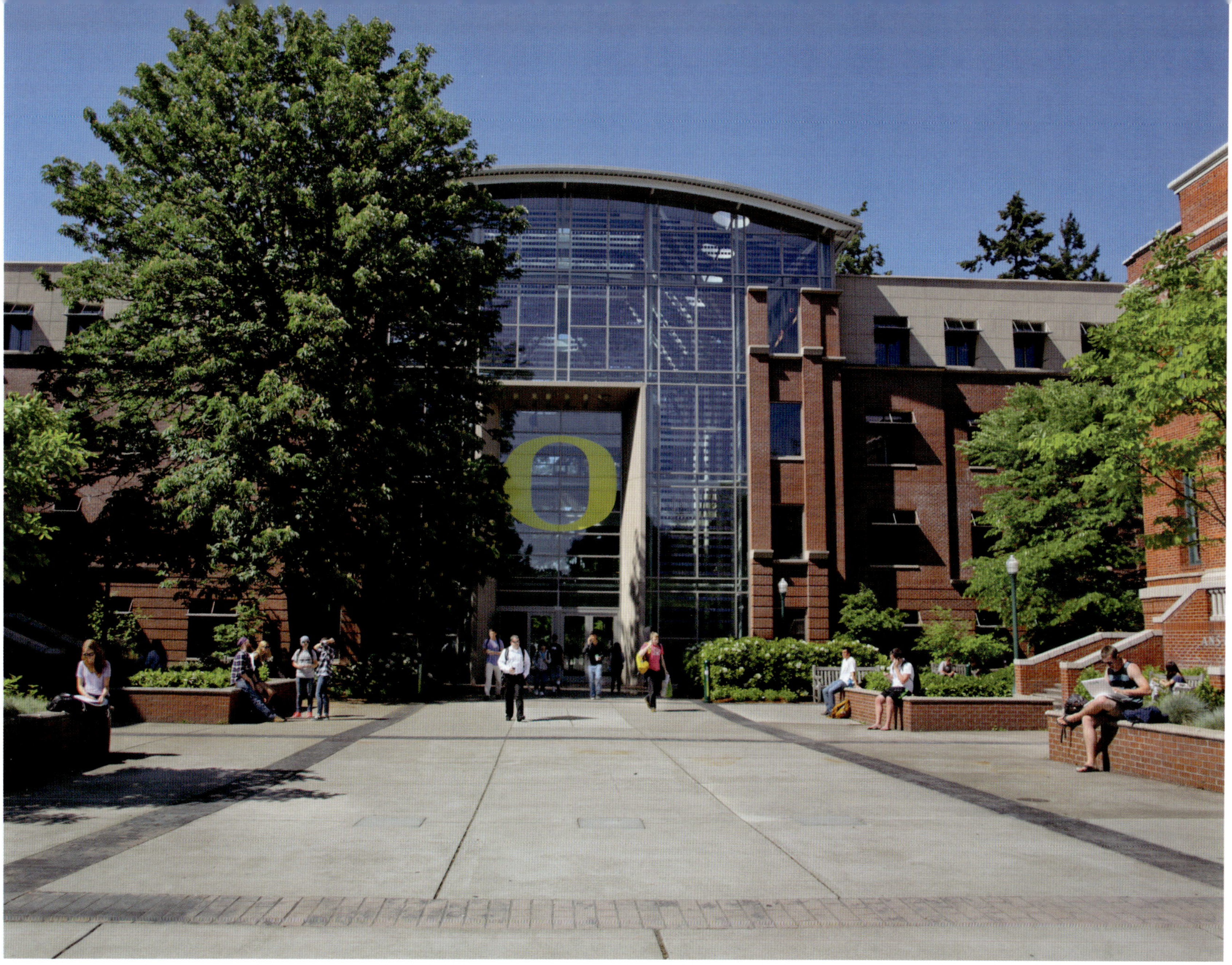

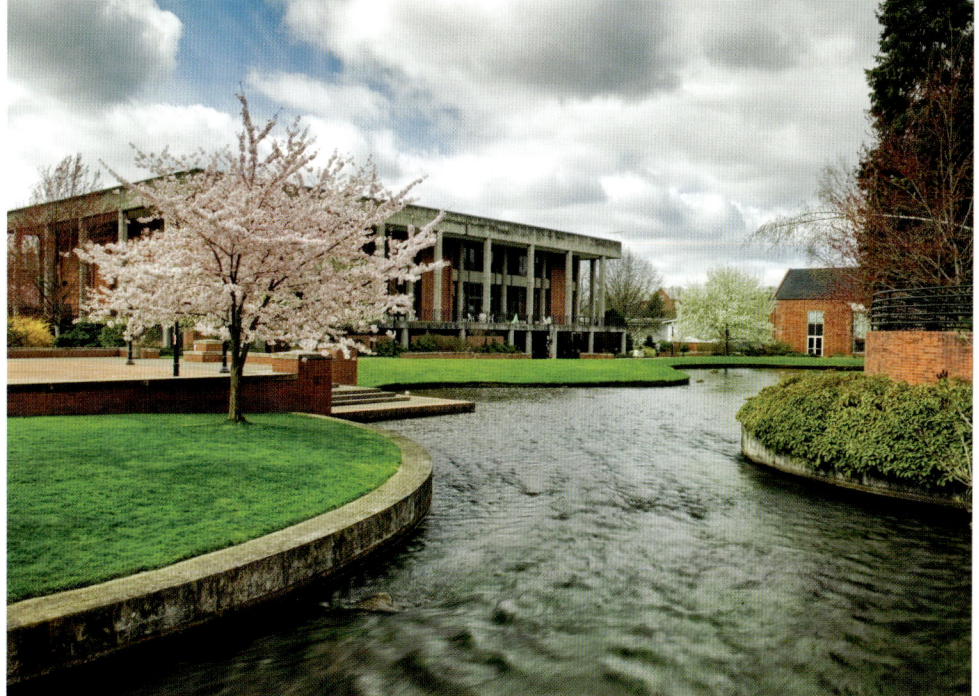

Above: With one of the largest solar power installations in the Northwest, the Lillis Business Complex at the University of Oregon sets new standards for environmentally friendly design and sustainability.
PHOTO COURTESY OF THE UNIVERSITY OF OREGON

Left: Mill Stream is a popular campus gathering place and study spot for students at Willamette University. The Salem institution of higher learning is the oldest in the state.
PHOTO COURTESY OF WILLAMETTE UNIVERSITY

Facing page: The Valley Library and quad stand at the heart of the 400-acre Oregon State University campus in Corvallis. The largest public research university in the state, OSU has a student body of over 25,000.

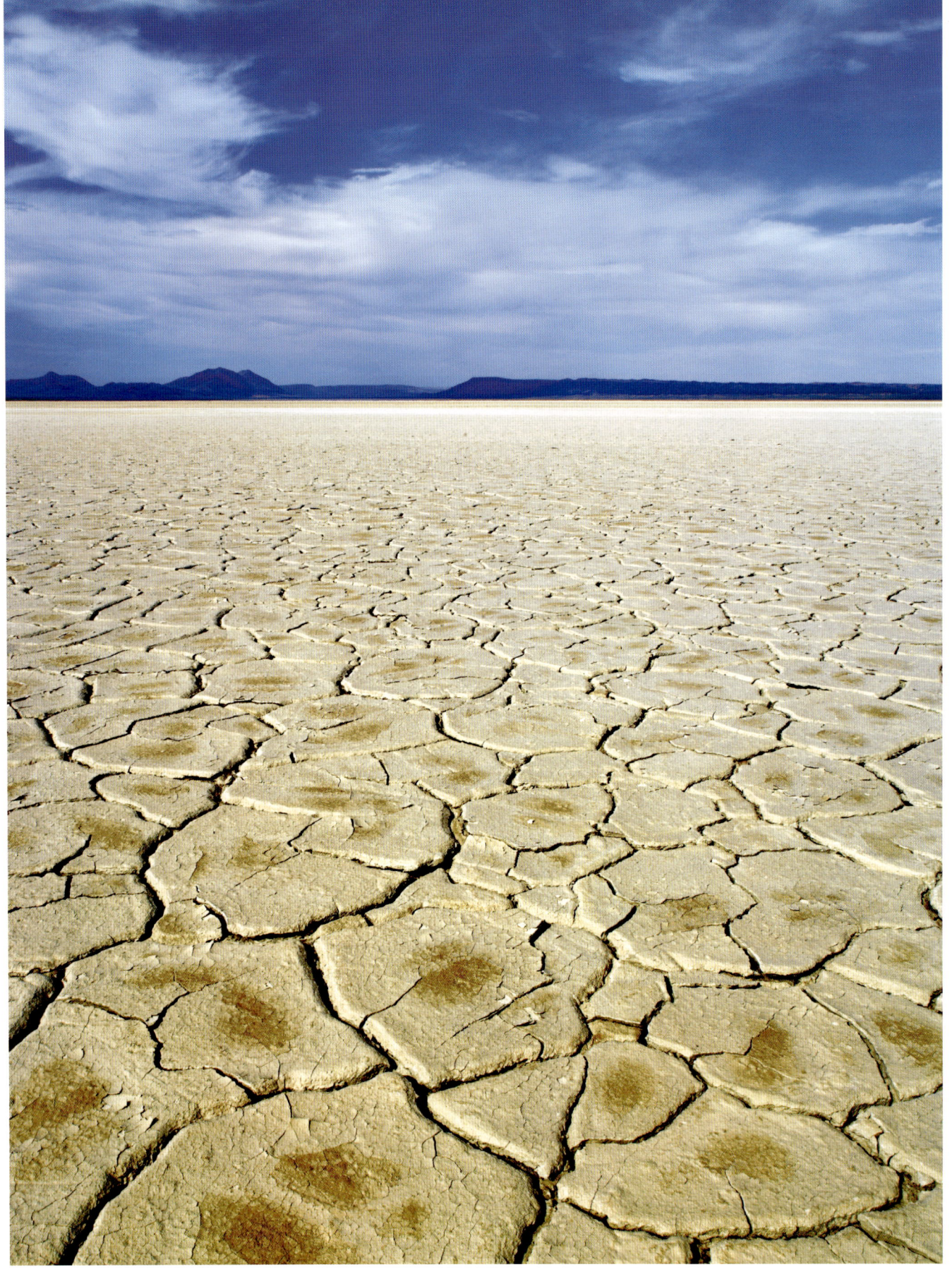

Above: At 6 miles wide and 11 miles long, the Alvord Desert playa is one of the largest in Oregon. These uninhabited salt flats east of Steens Mountain are a favorite site for land sailing and glider flying.

Right: World-class climbers head to Smith Rock State Park near Redmond to test their fingers and chalk on one of thousands of vertical routes up the golden rock. The River Trail, with its panoramic views of the Cascades, is a popular alternative for those who prefer a gentler gradient.

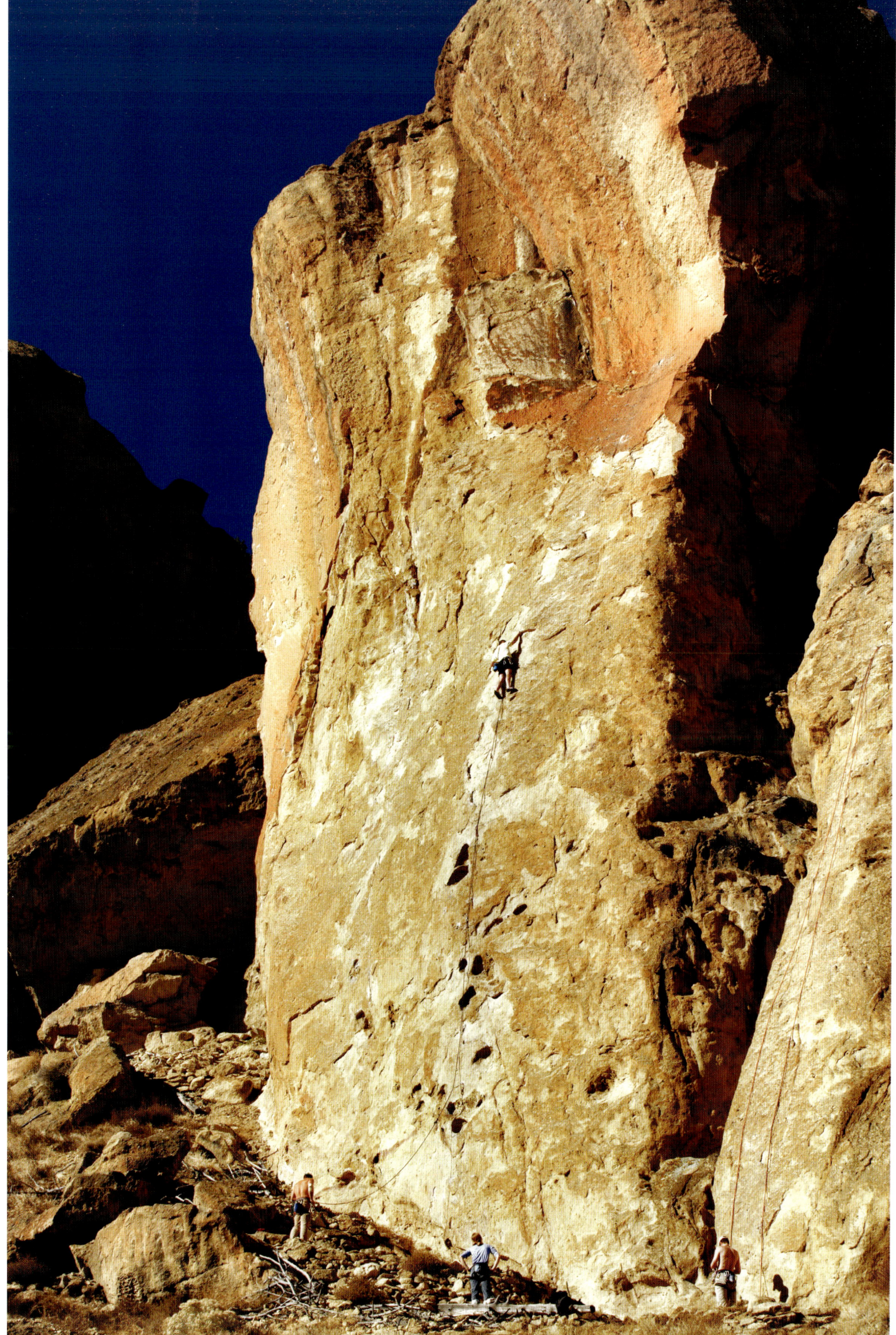

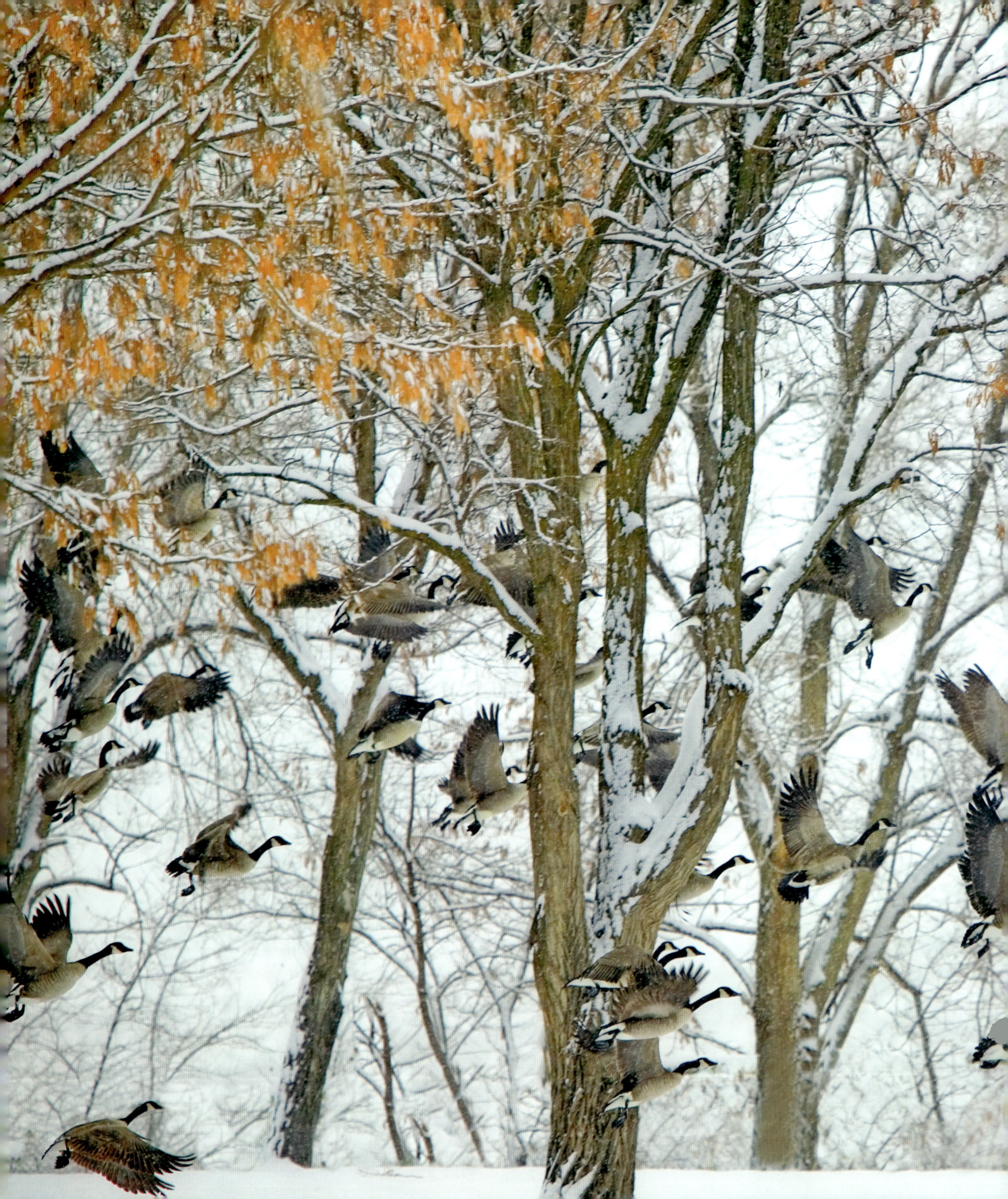

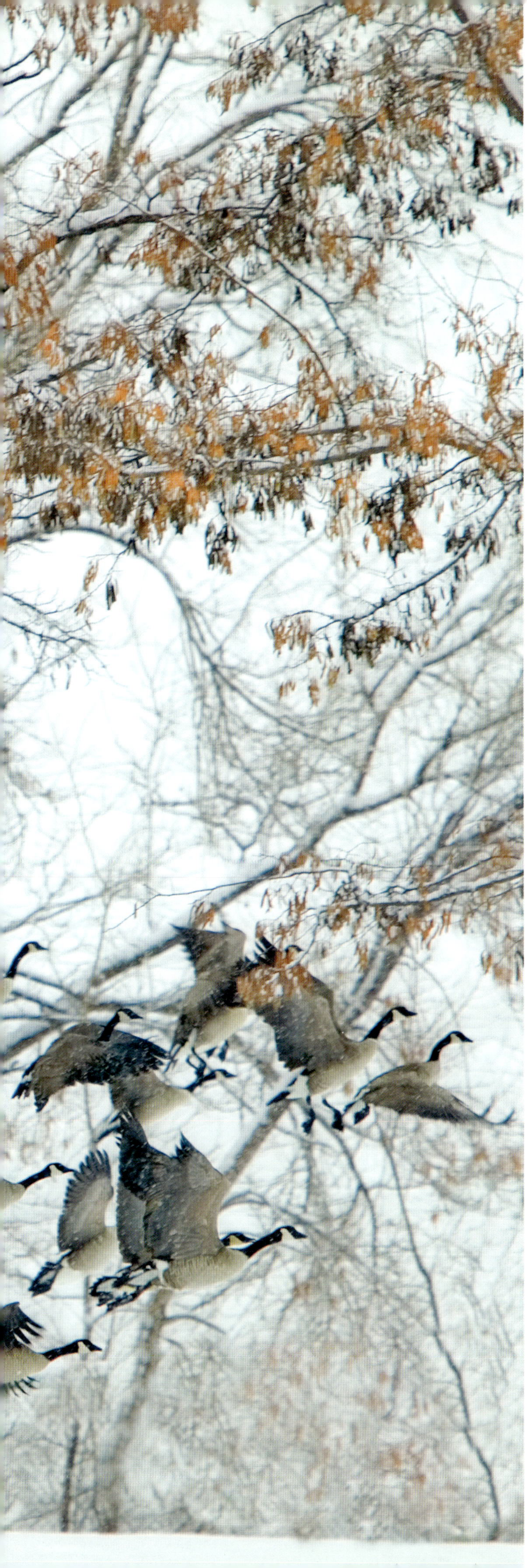

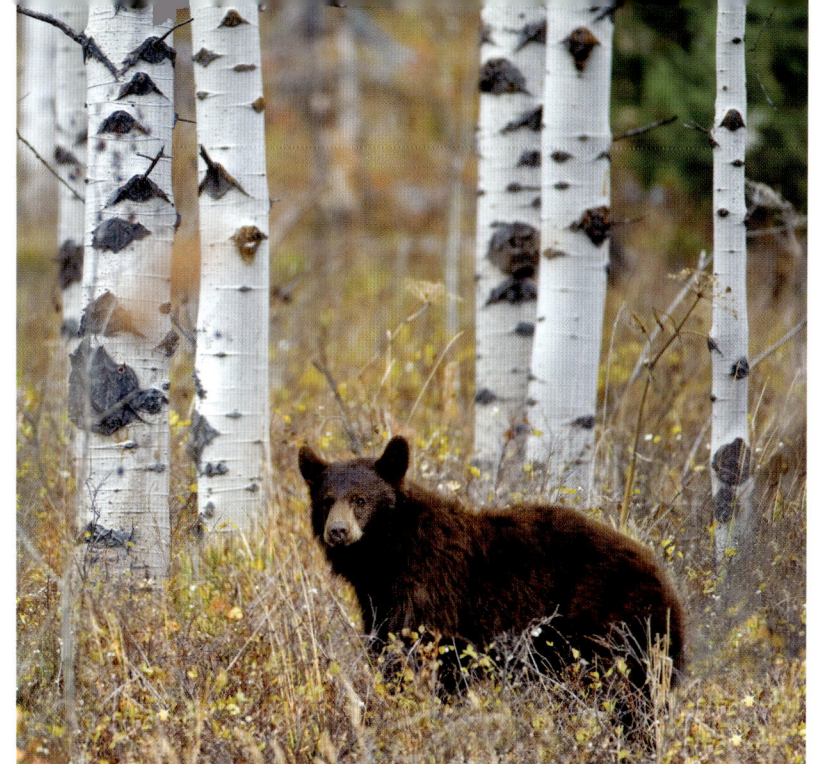

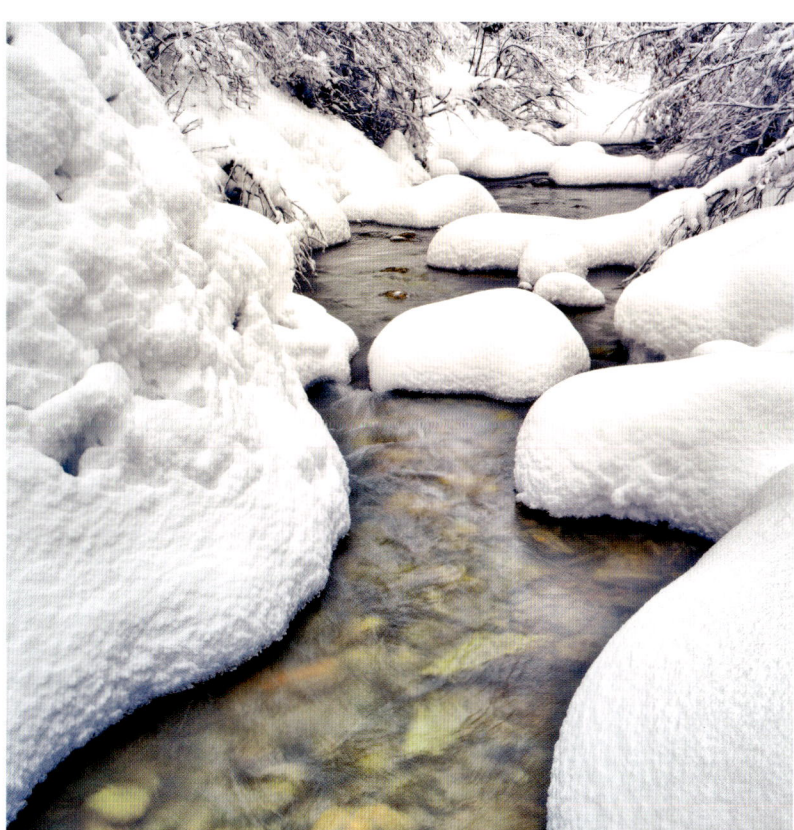

Above, top: Oregon is black bear country. North America's most common bear species, more than 25,000 black bears live in the state's berry-laden forests.

Above, bottom: Gold was discovered in Bull Run Creek in 1862, spurring a prospecting rush that lasted 80 years. The creek runs along a leg of the Elkhorn Drive National Scenic Byway west of Baker City, one of four nationally designated byways in Oregon.

Left: In the fall, geese and ducks follow ancient routes from their breeding grounds to warmer climates in search of food and habitat. Thousands of these migratory birds rest and feed in the wide-open spaces of Oregon's high desert on their journey south.

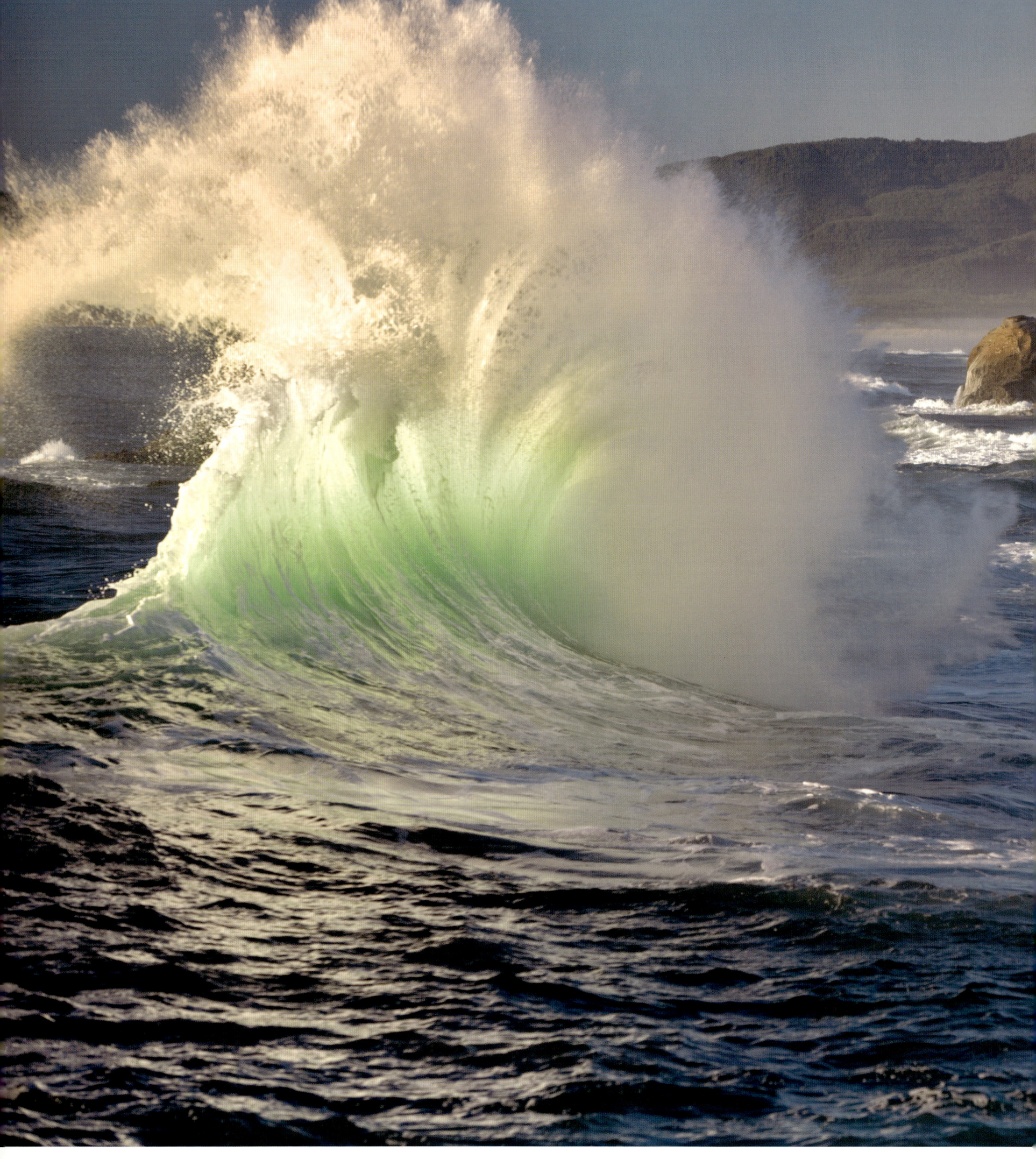

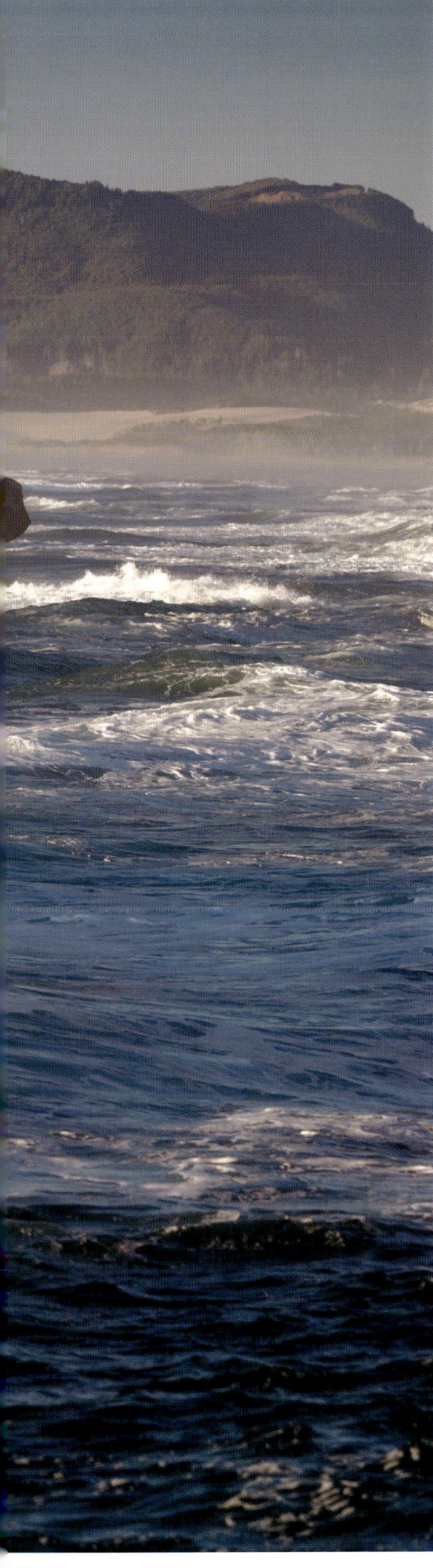

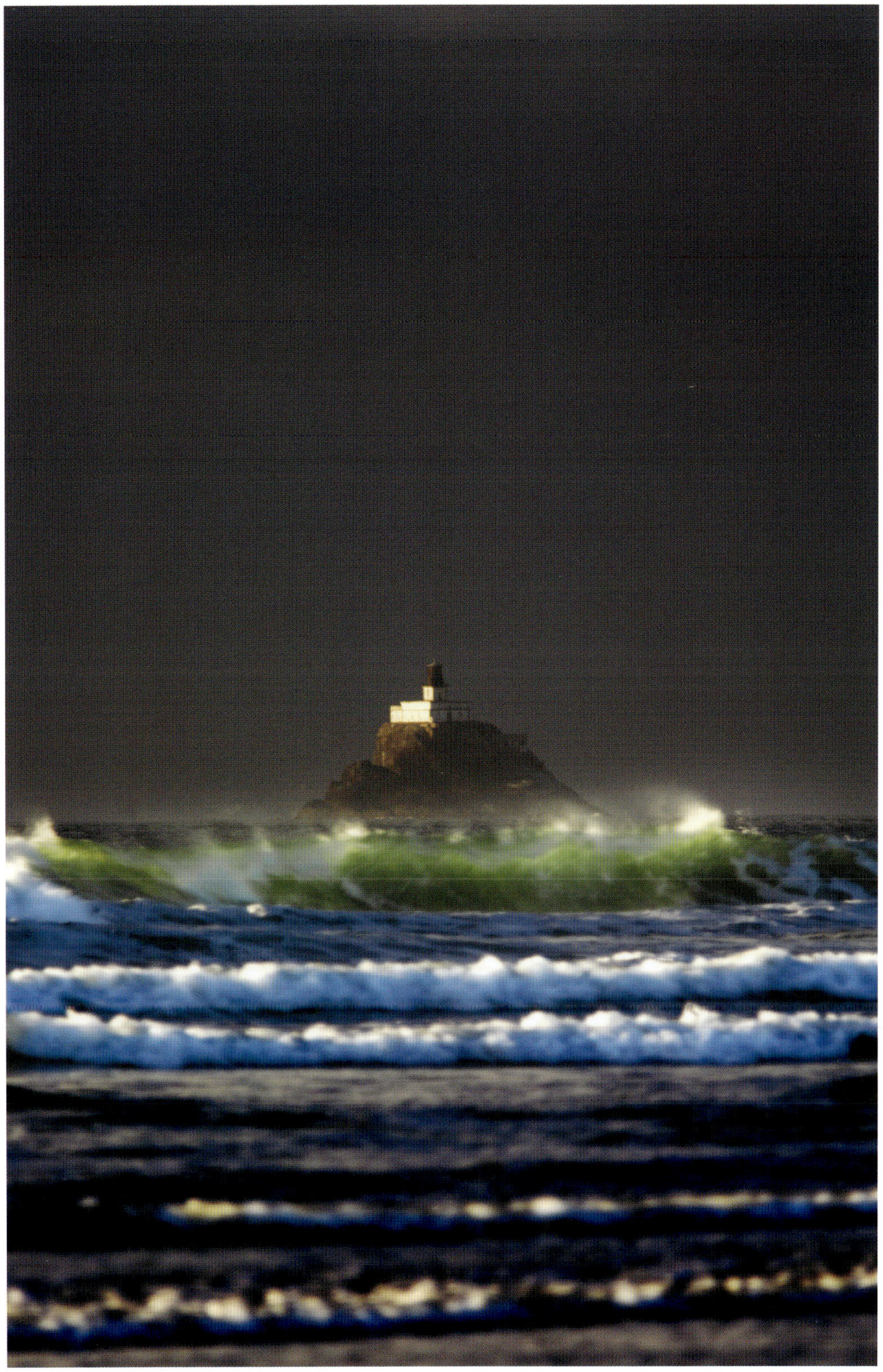

Above: Fierce winds and horizontal rain make storm watching on the Oregon Coast an exhilarating winter pastime. From 1881 to 1957, the 62-foot Tillamook Rock Lighthouse guided ships away from dangerous seas. The fortitude required of both the lighthouse and its crew earned it the name Terrible Tilly.

Left: Mighty North Pacific swells end their 5,000-mile journey in dramatic fashion as they rise to meet Oregon's sea stacks, headlands, and broad beaches.

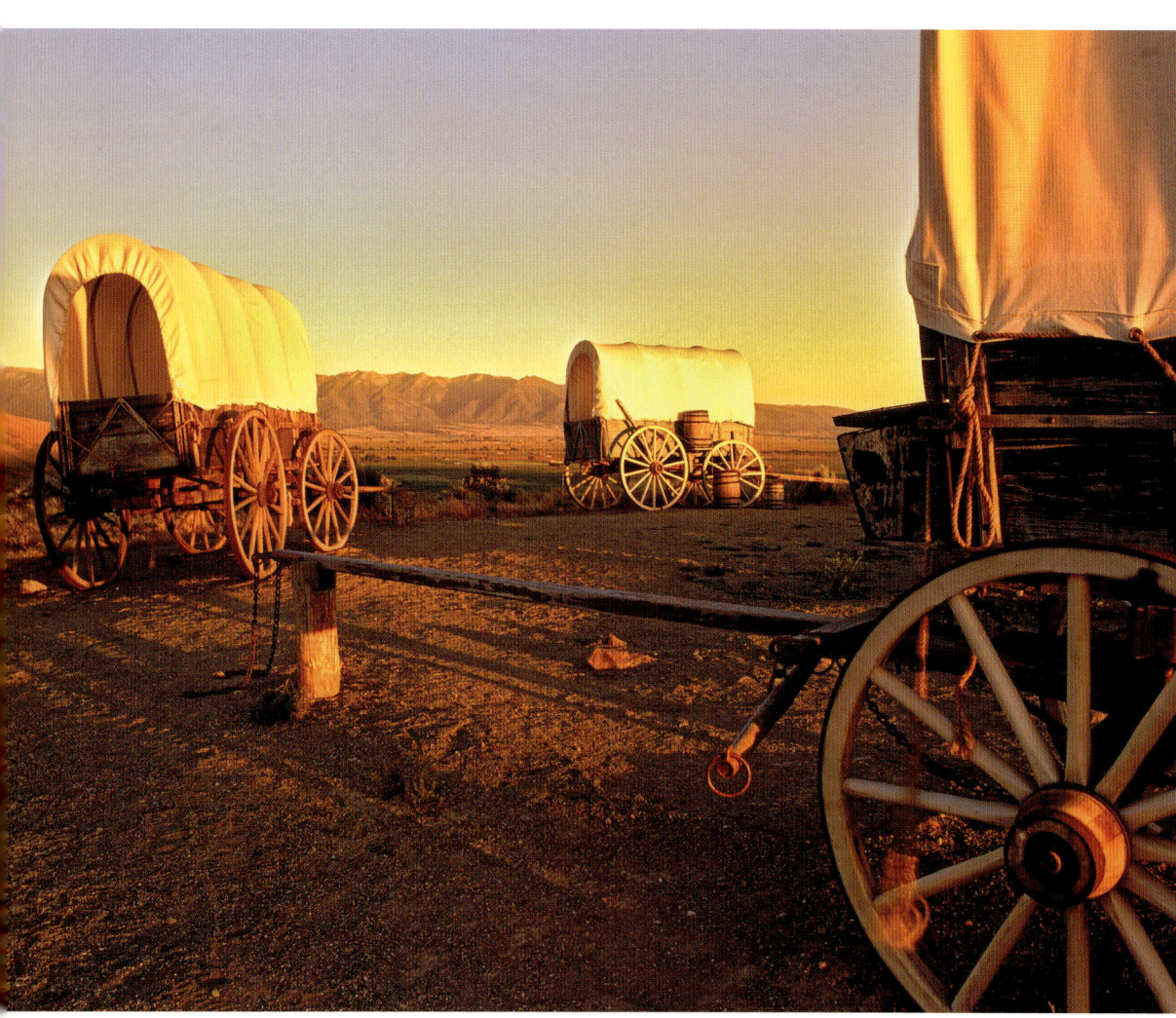

Above: History comes to life at the National Historic Oregon Trail Interpretive Center near Baker City, where costumed presenters tell it like it was during the 2,000-mile walk from St. Louis, Missouri. The replica wagon encampment and mining site are a short walk from a section of the original trail still rutted from thousands of wagon wheels.

Right: Mount Washington—along with its central Cascade neighbors North Sister and Three-Fingered Jack—is an example of an extinct broad-shield volcano.

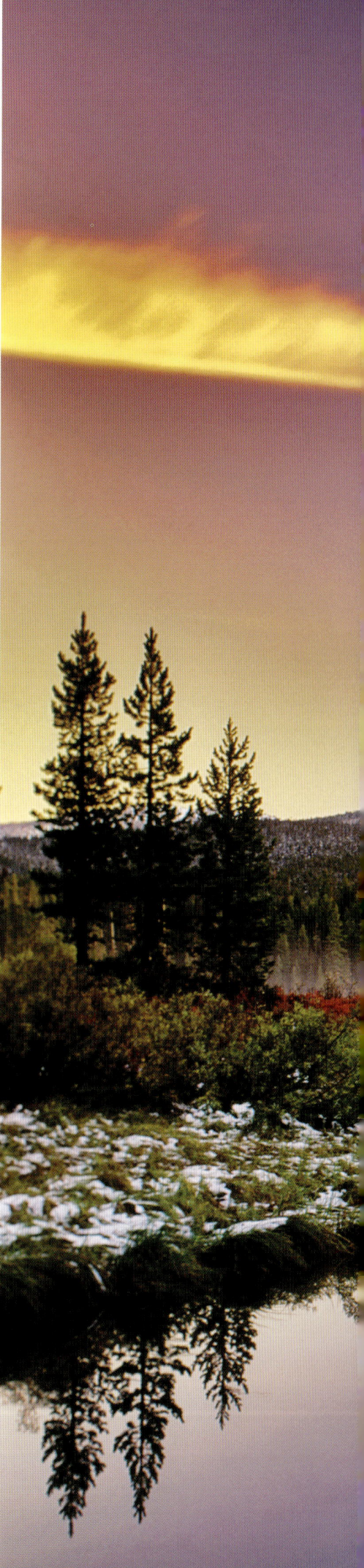

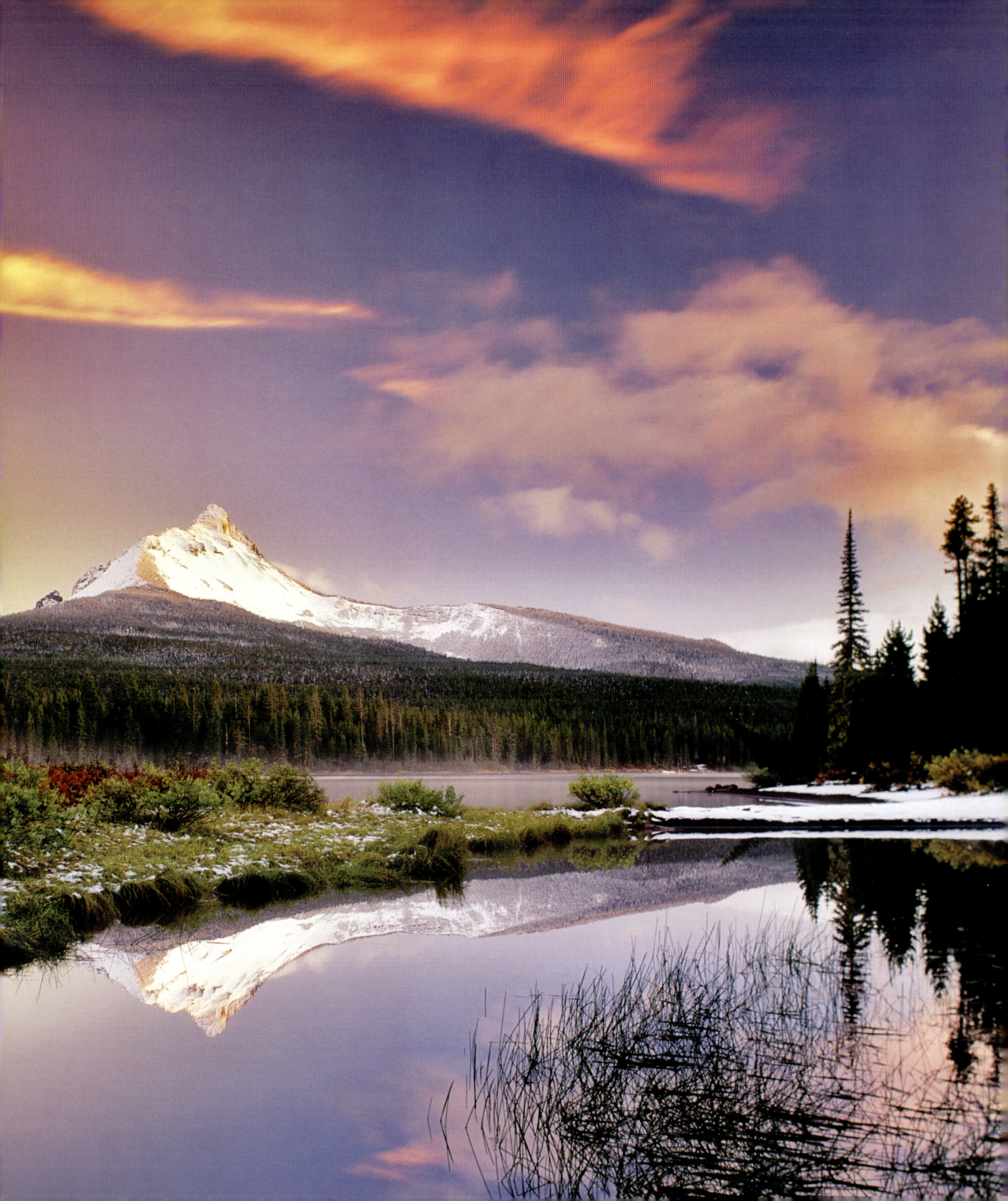

Right: At the Oregon Garden in the Willamette Valley, near Silverton, paths wind over 80 acres and through 20 specialty gardens that reveal the botanical diversity of the Pacific Northwest.

Below, top: Whether it is a short ride across town or the epic eight-day trek known as Cycle Oregon, biking is a passion for many Oregonians. Knobby-tired mountain bikers, sleek spandexed road racers, and country road cruisers have plenty of rides to choose from across the state.

Below, bottom: A display of colorful Indian headdresses at the High Desert Museum in Bend is part of the "Hand through Memory" exhibit, which details the history and present-day experience of the Columbia River Plateau Indian nations.

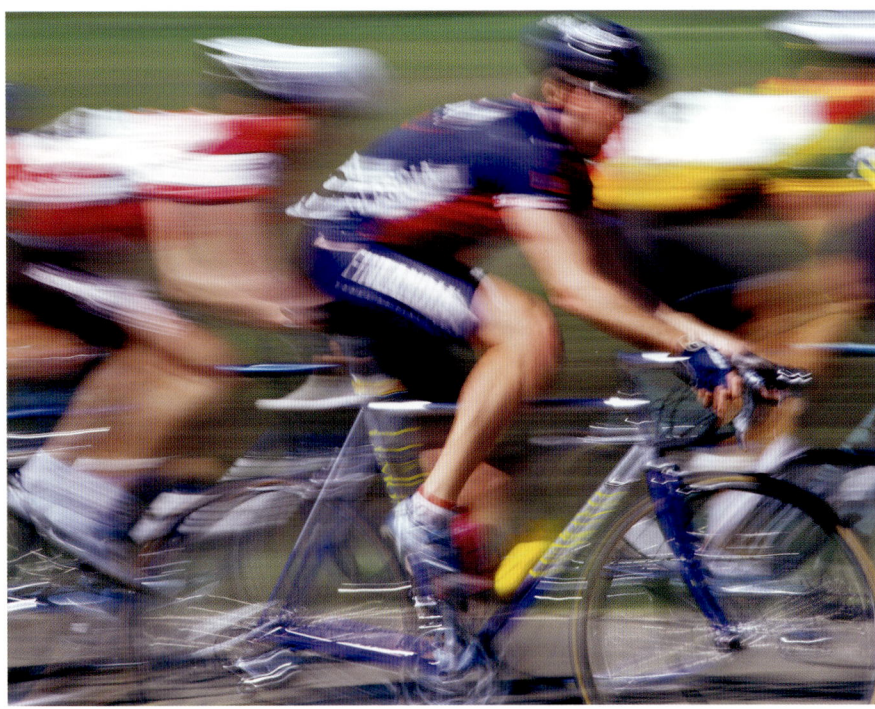

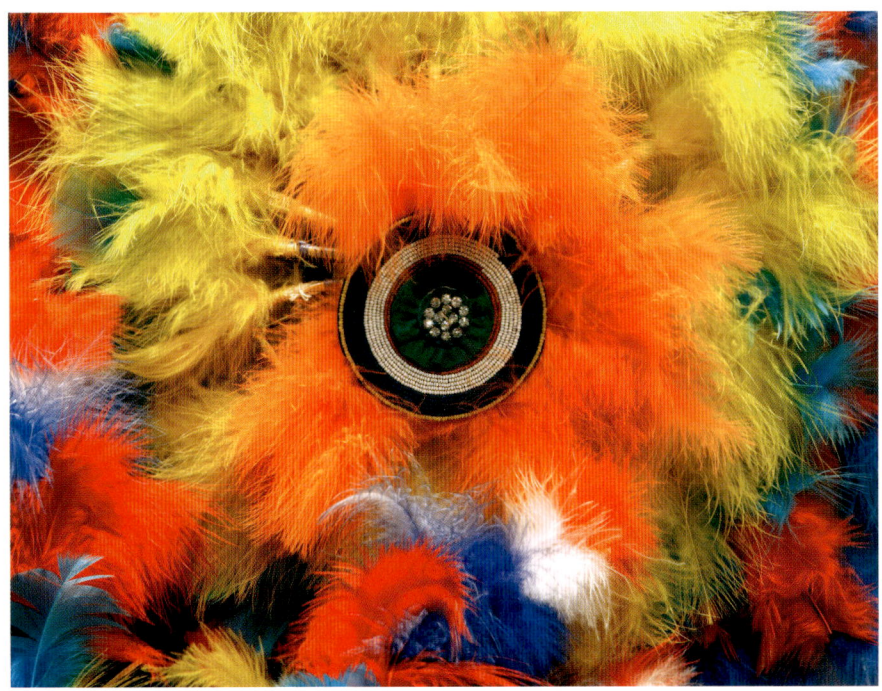

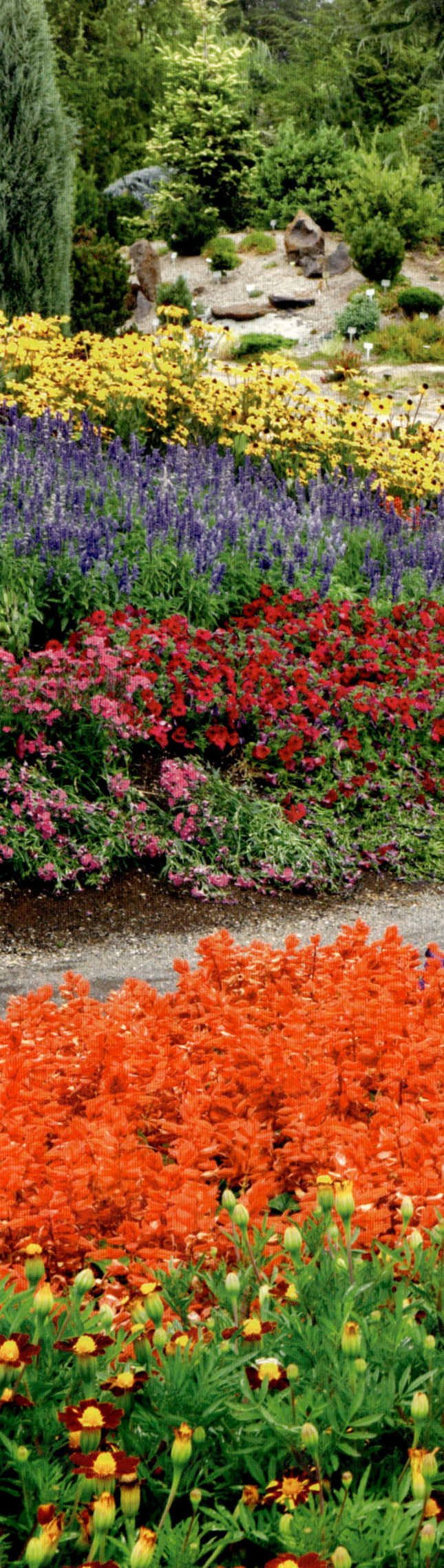

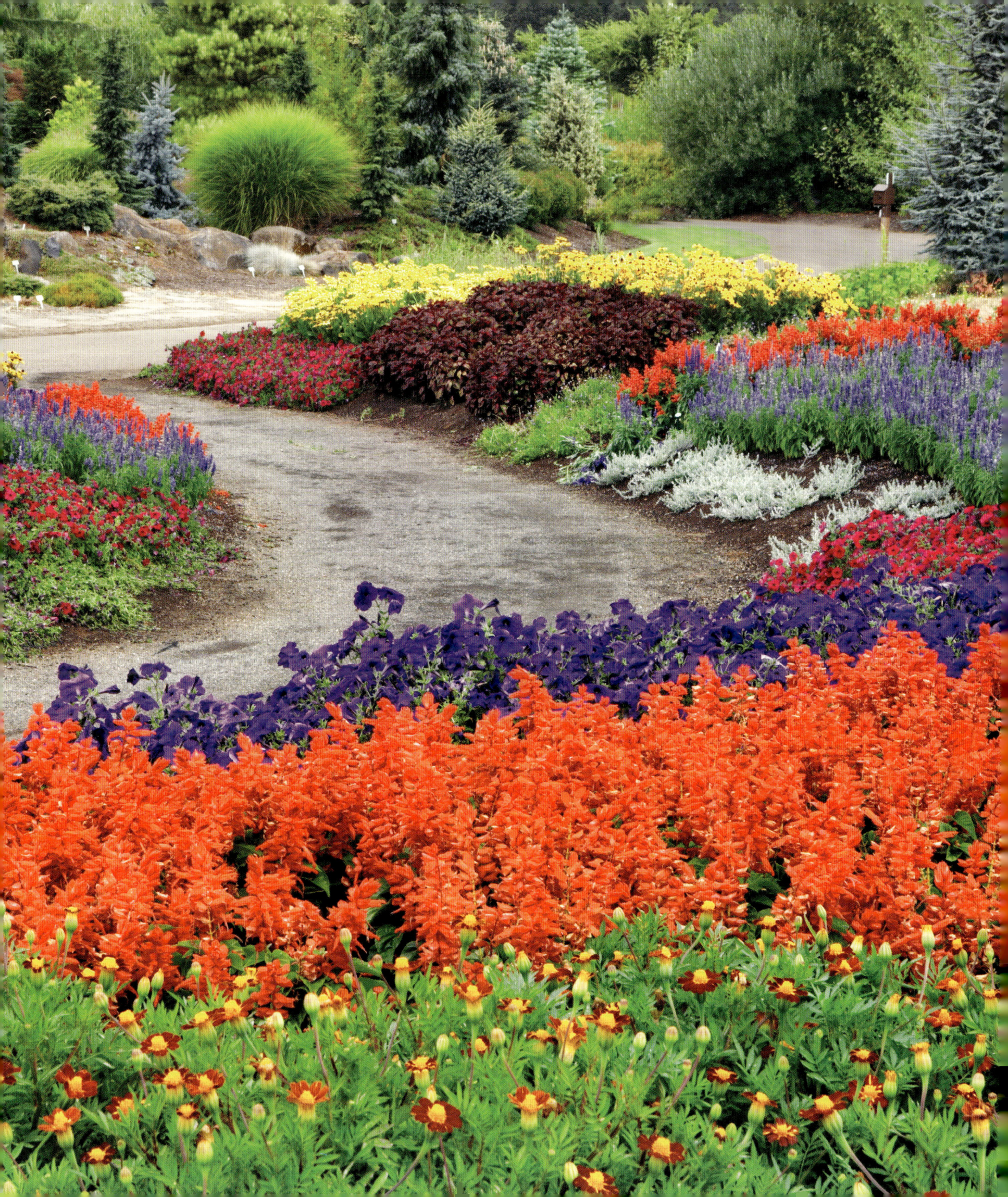

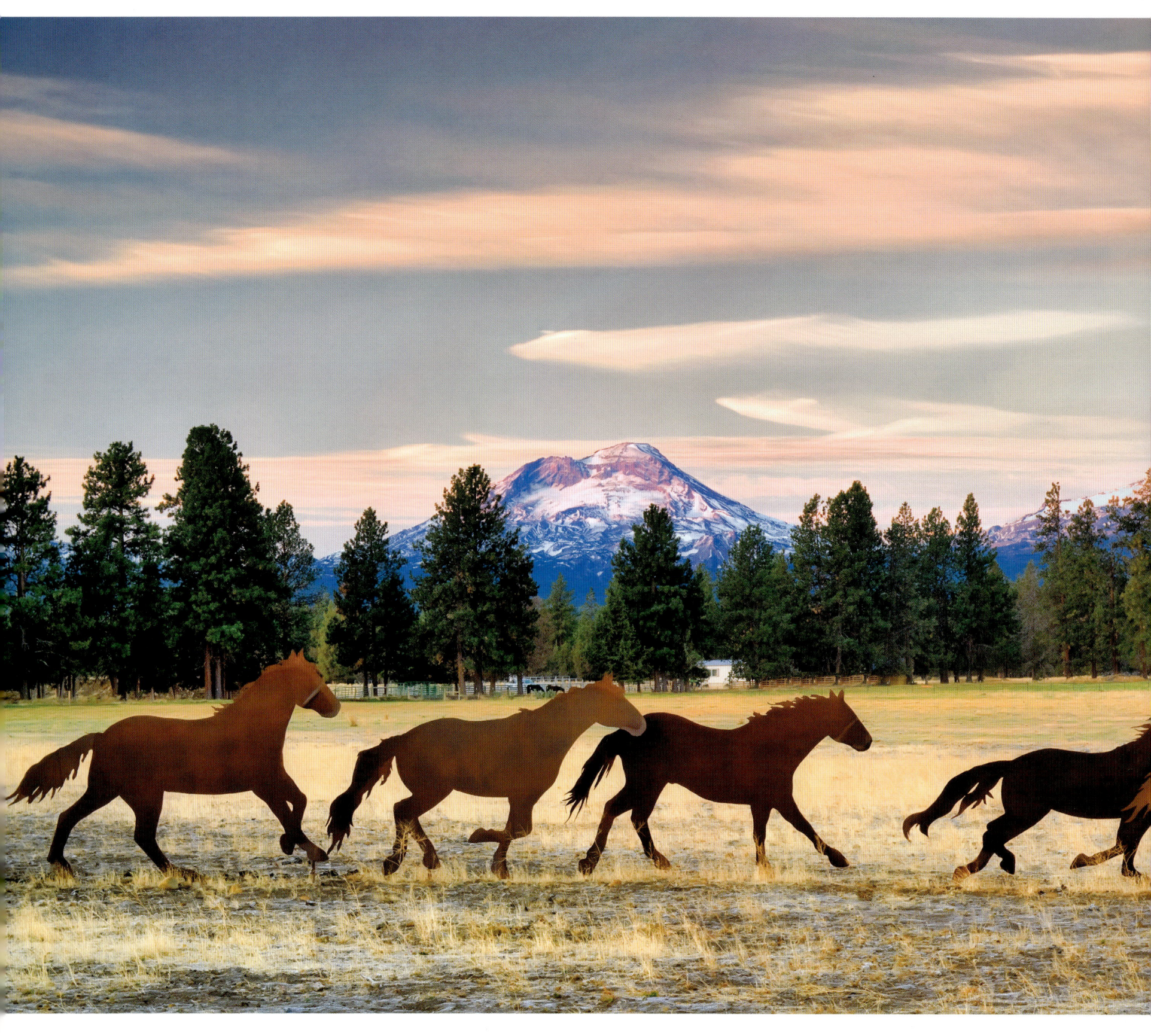

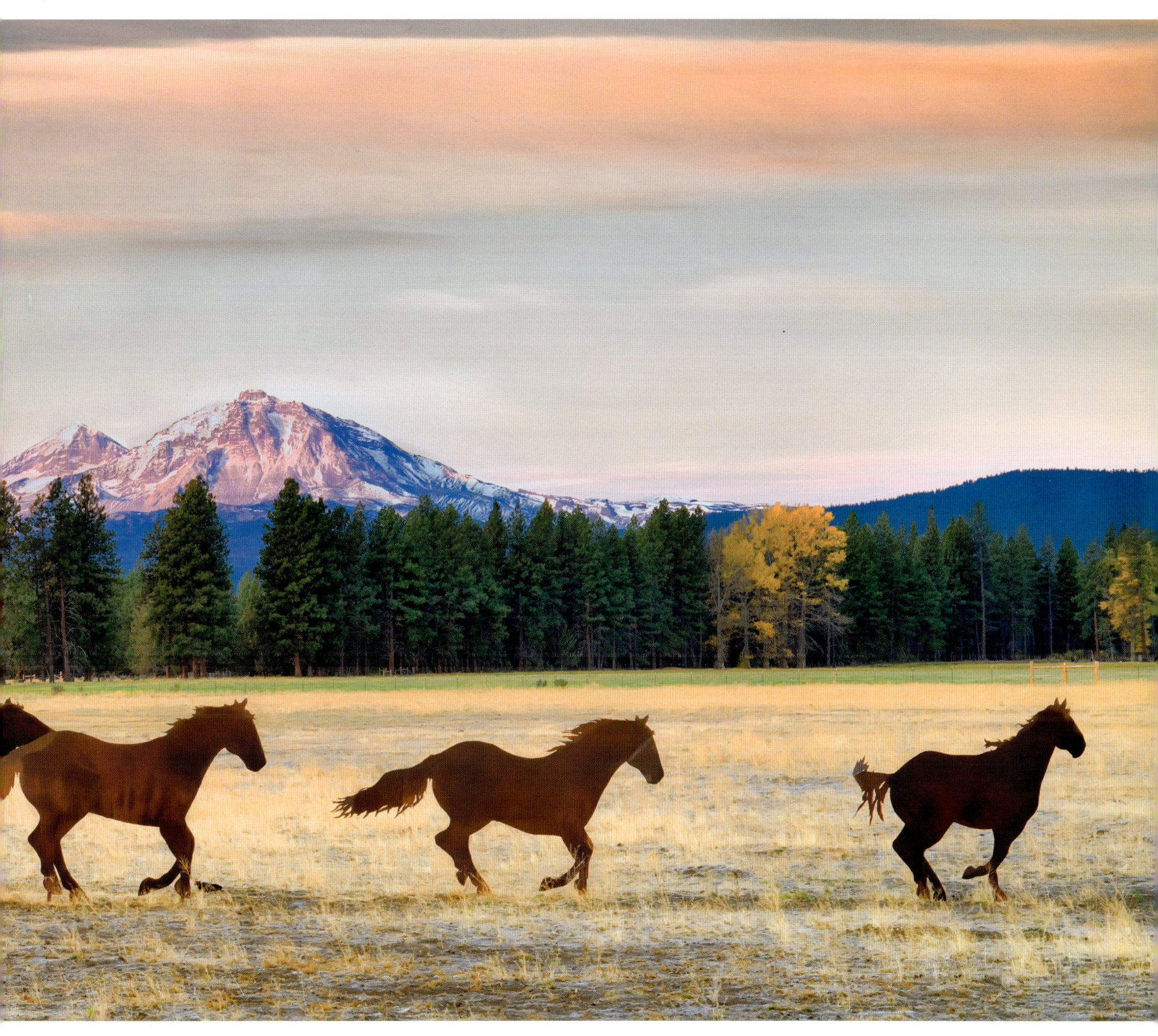

A herd of iron horses gallops across the pasture at the Lazy Z Ranch near Sisters. Sculptor Brian Bain modeled the steeds after horses from two local ranches.

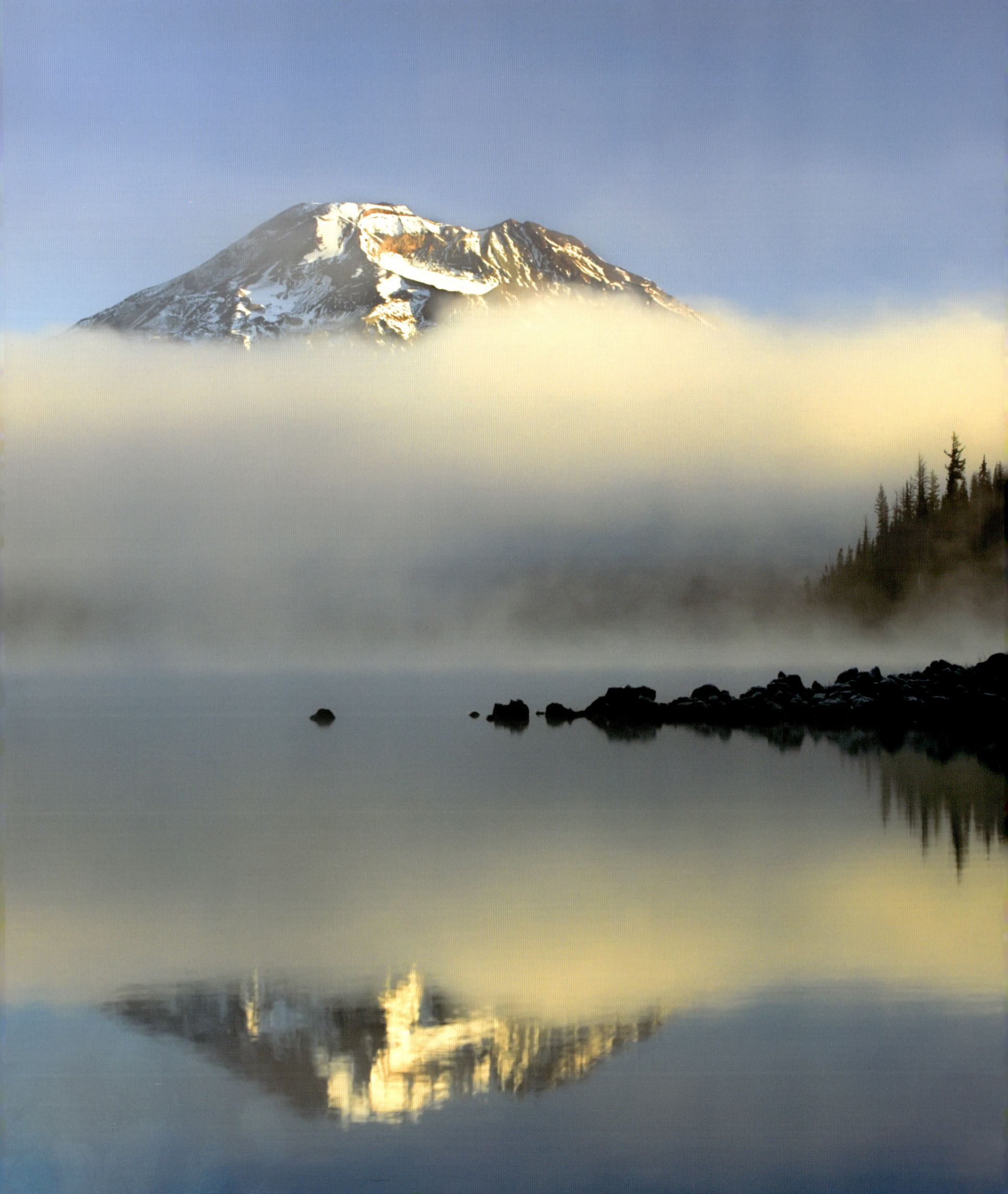

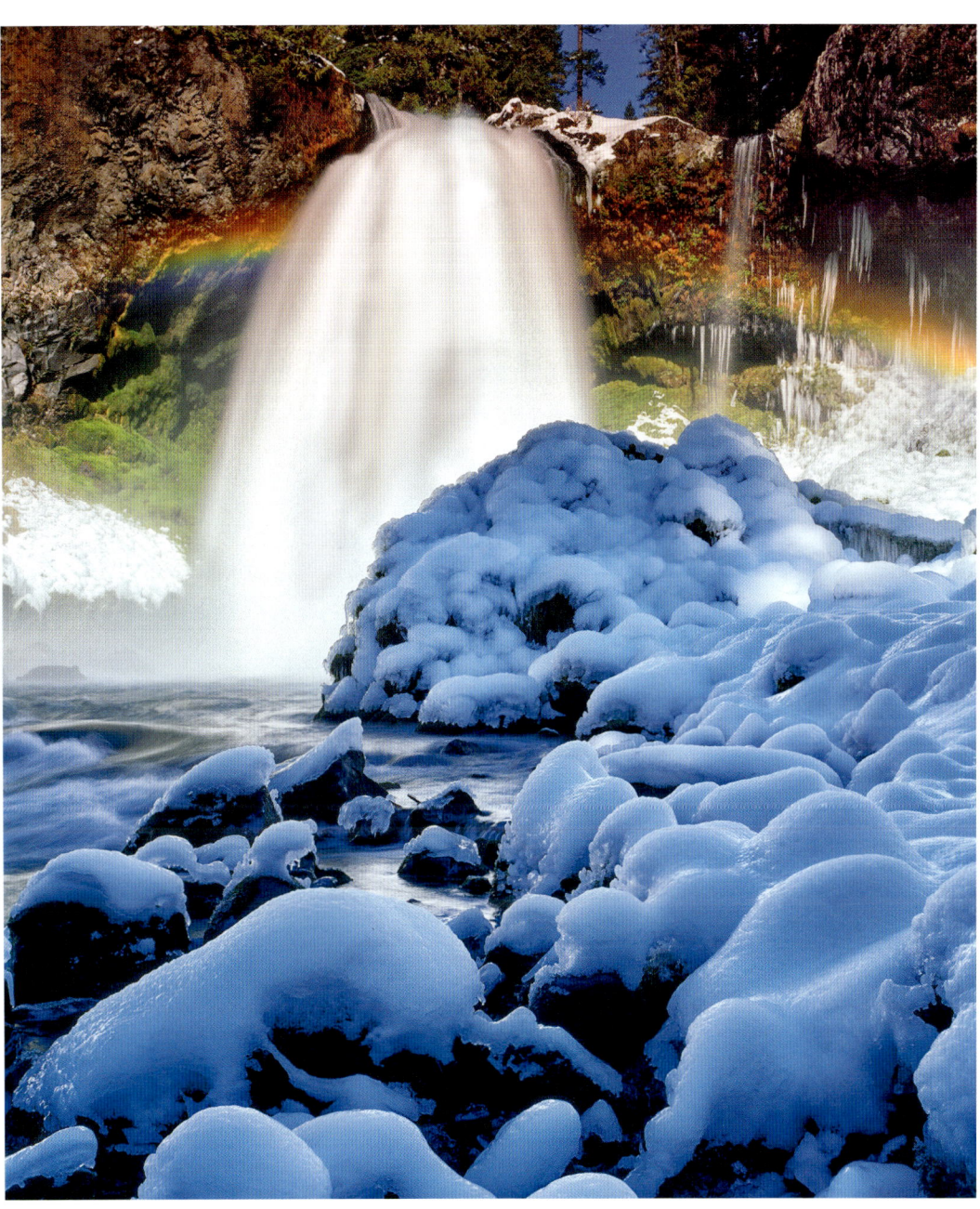

Above: Find the end of the rainbow along the McKenzie River Trail at Sahalee Falls. Take in the long view from the overlook, or head down the Waterfall Loop Trail for a close-up look at both sides of the falls.

Left: South Sister Mountain provides a stunning backdrop to Elk Lake and other stops along the Cascade Lakes Highway outside of Bend. In the 1960s, Apollo astronauts trained on lava beds near here prior to their trip to the moon.

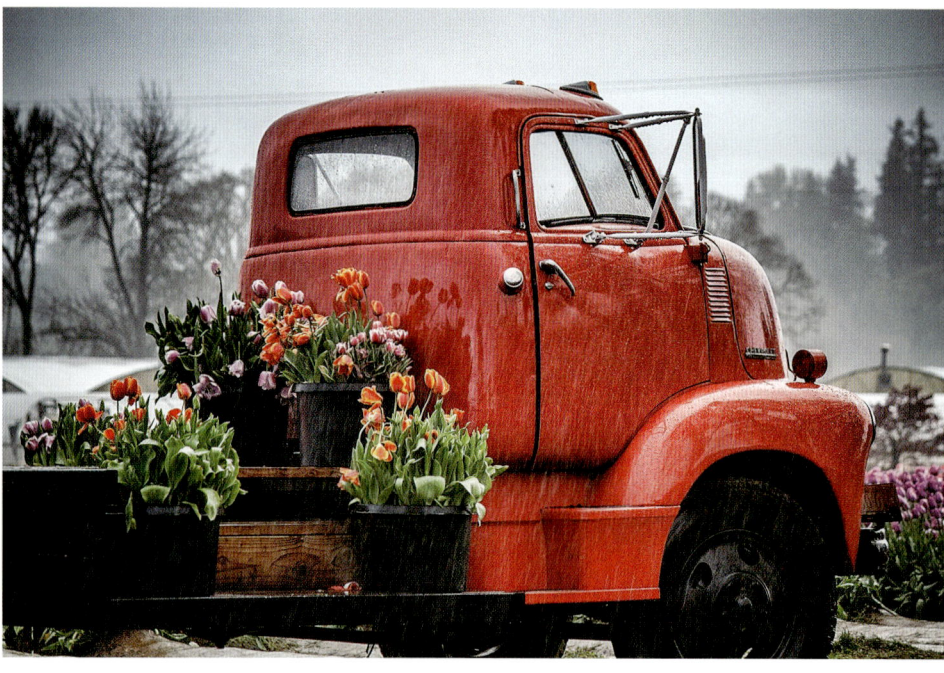

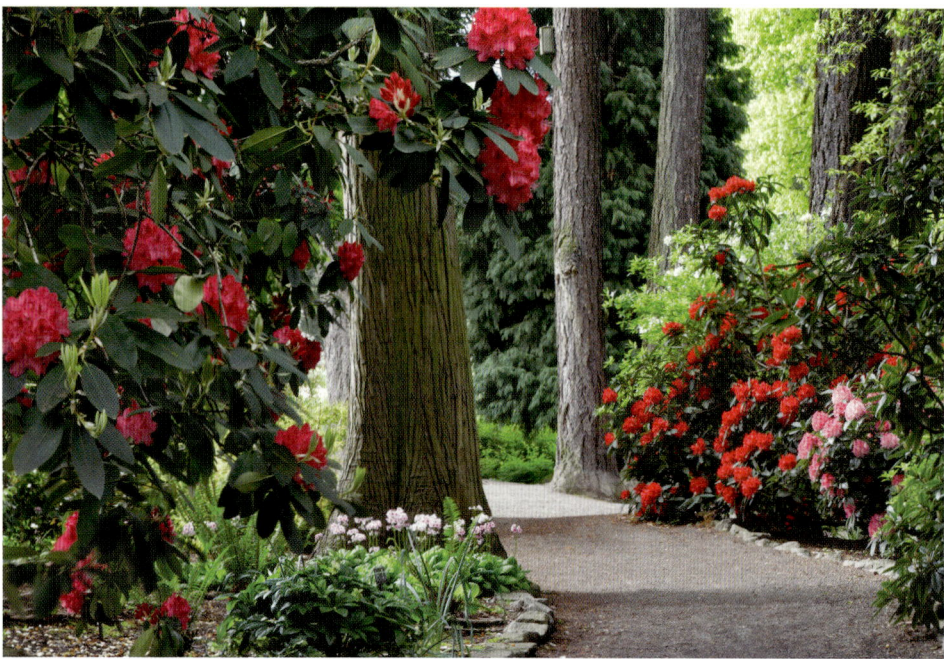

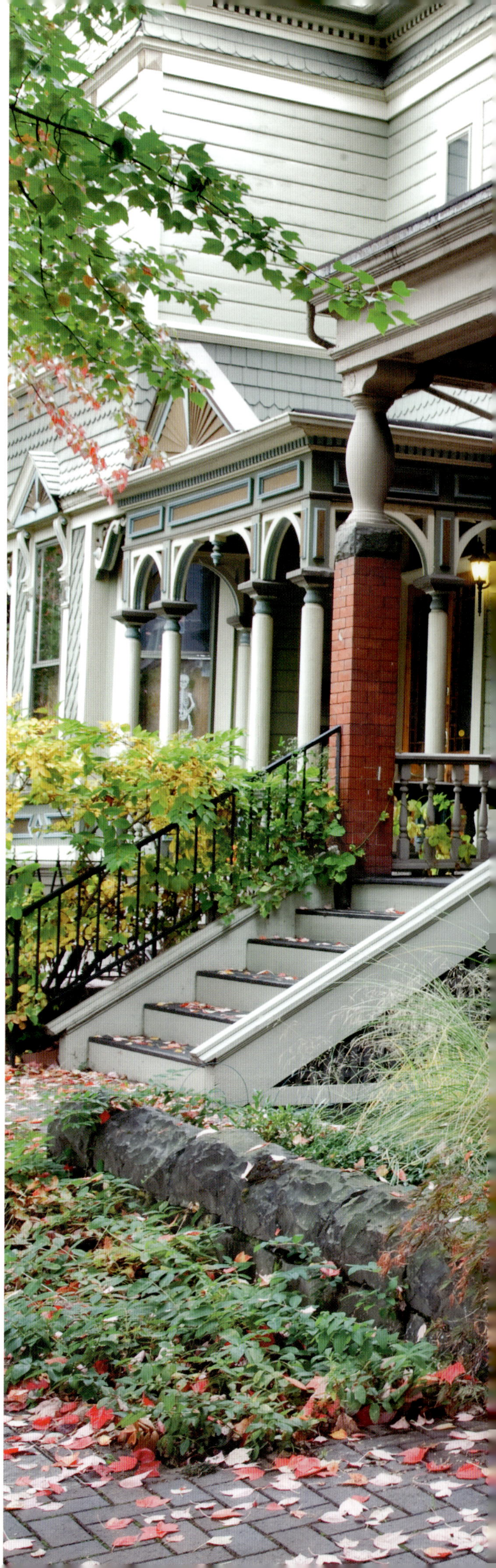

Above, top: Rain or shine, Woodburn welcomes spring with the Wooden Shoe Tulip Festival. Guests can view tulip and daffodil fields and enjoy wooden shoe making demonstrations during the weeklong event. PHOTO COURTESY OF MARK STALCUP

Above, bottom: The Crystal Springs Rhododendron Garden is a must-see in spring when more than 2,500 rhododendrons and azaleas light the place with color. The garden has flourished since the 1950s, when volunteers reclaimed the land from overgrown brush.

Facing page: From Hawthorne to the Pearl, St. Johns to Sellwood, Portland is a city of diverse neighborhoods. With over two million people in its greater metro area, the city has cultivated a reputation for its proud, simple life: bicycles, local beer, and fresh music.

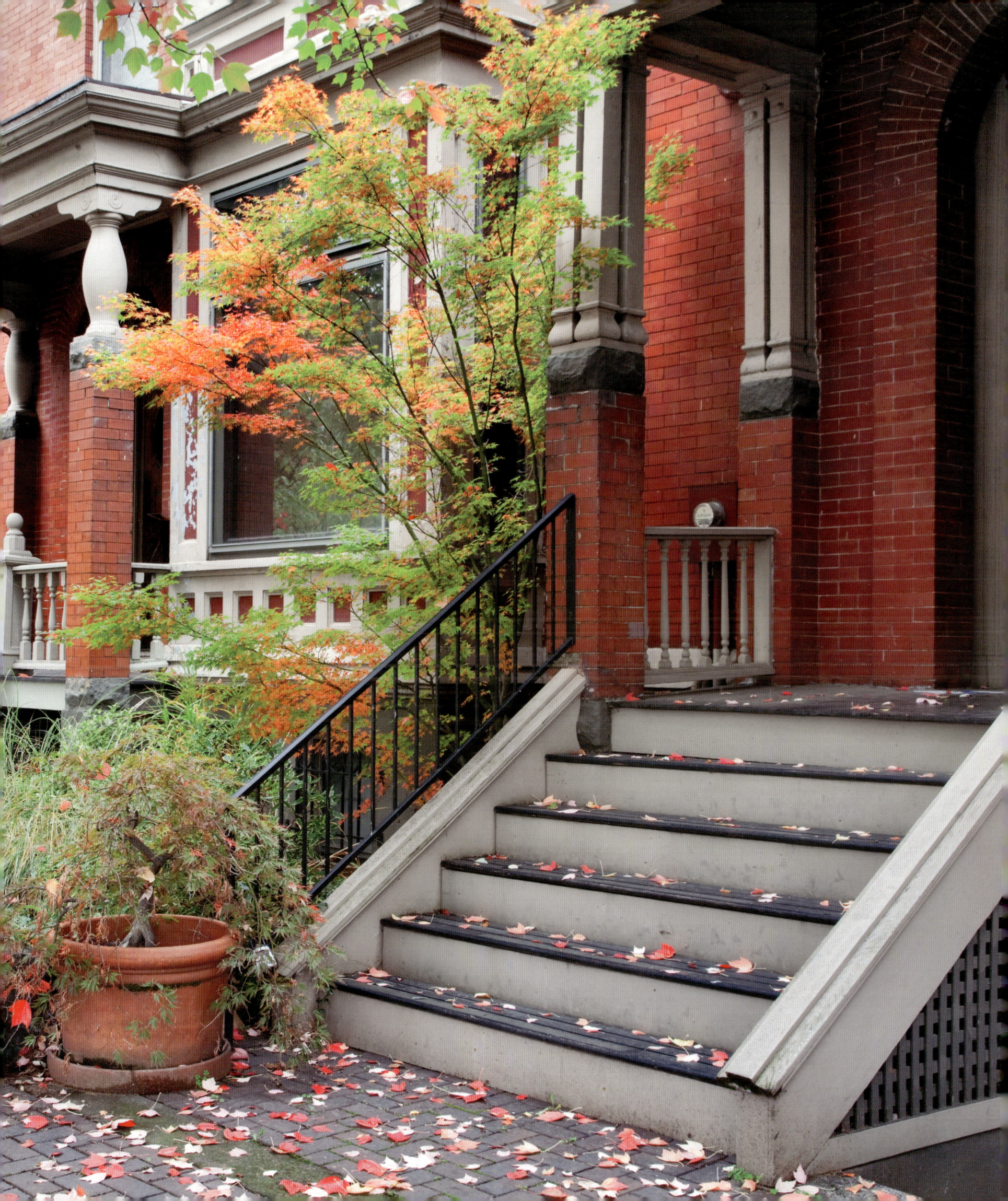

Right: From December to May, one of the nation's largest herds of Rocky Mountain elk claims the Bridge Creek Wildlife Area as its wintering ground. The majestic creatures come down from higher elevations in the Blue Mountains to avoid deep snow.

Far right: First carved into the basalt walls in 1917, the Historic Columbia River Highway formerly extended 88 miles along the south side of the Columbia from Troutdale to The Dalles. Once dubbed "America's Greatest Highway" for its stunning scenery and stonework, the original roadway has been replaced by Interstate 84, but is preserved in sections. The Rowena Loops west of The Dalles are a favorite with cyclists who are greeted with 180 degree views of the river as they summit the hill.

Below: In the remote Imnaha Canyon in Hells Canyon National Recreation Area, the only neighbors for miles are black bear, deer, and elk.

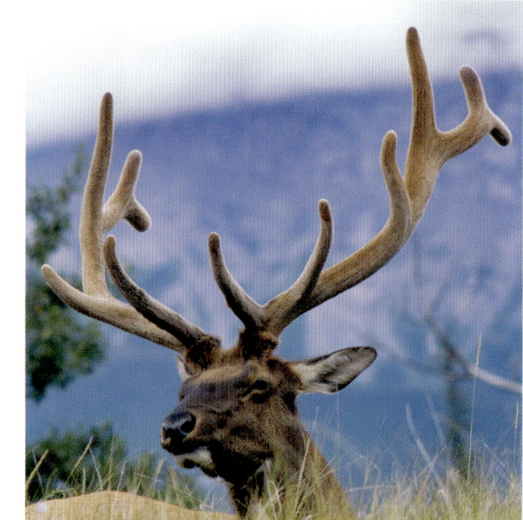

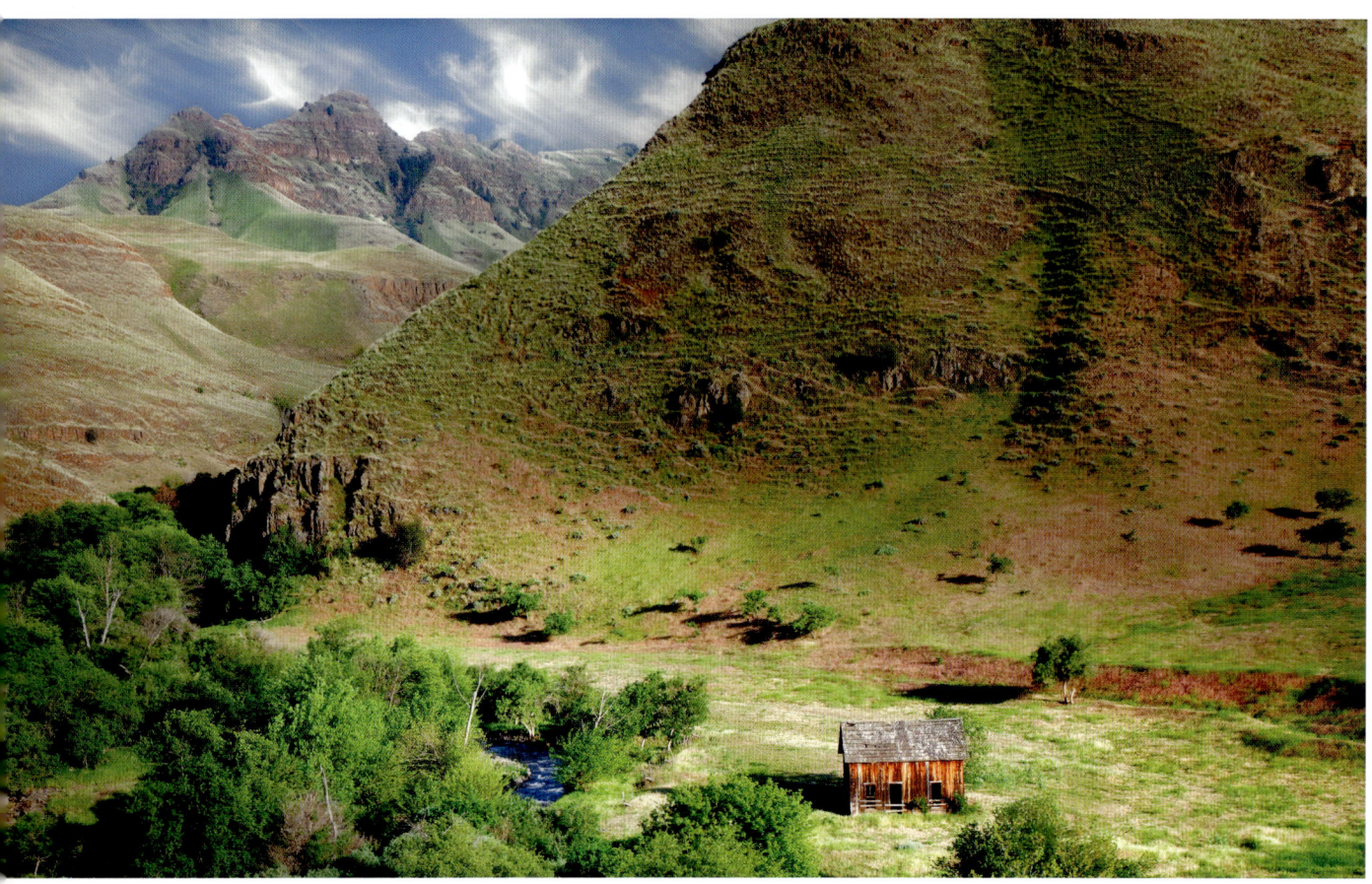

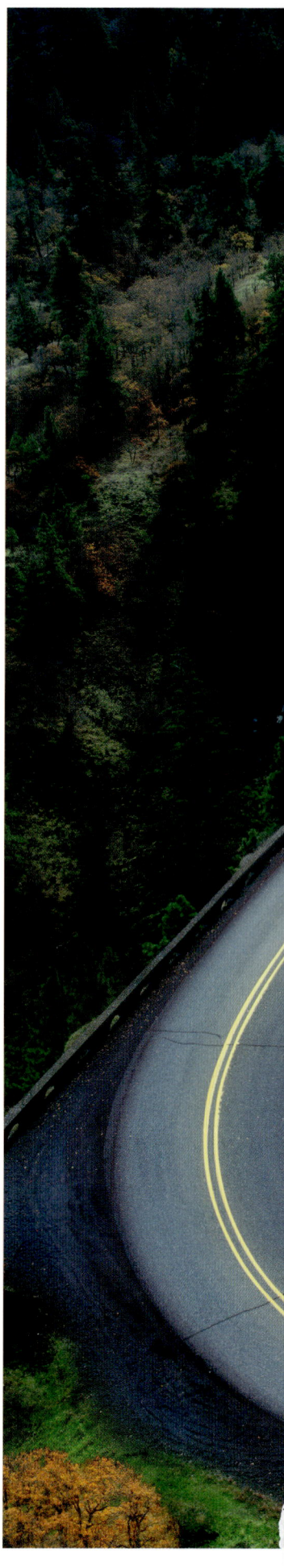

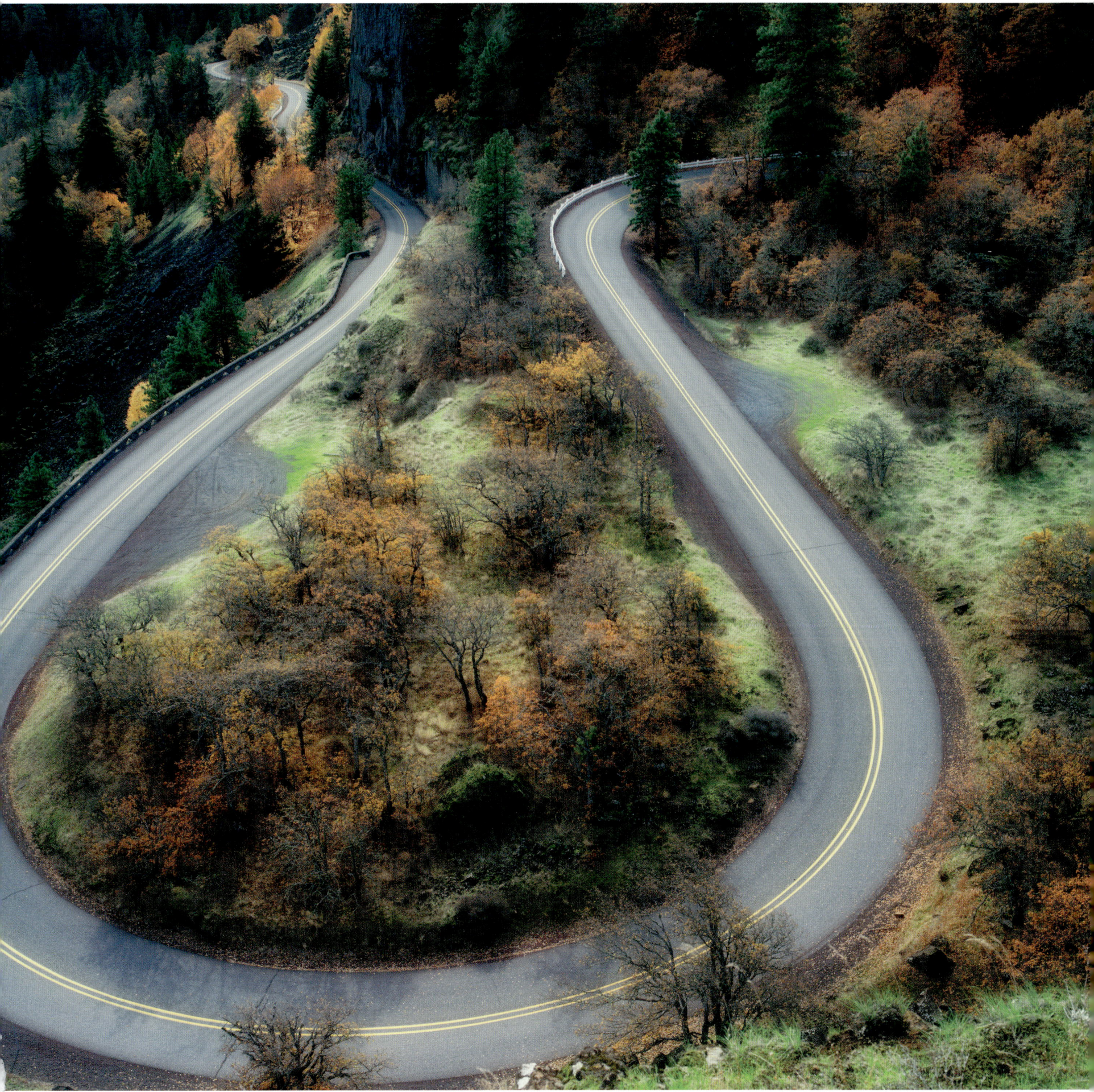

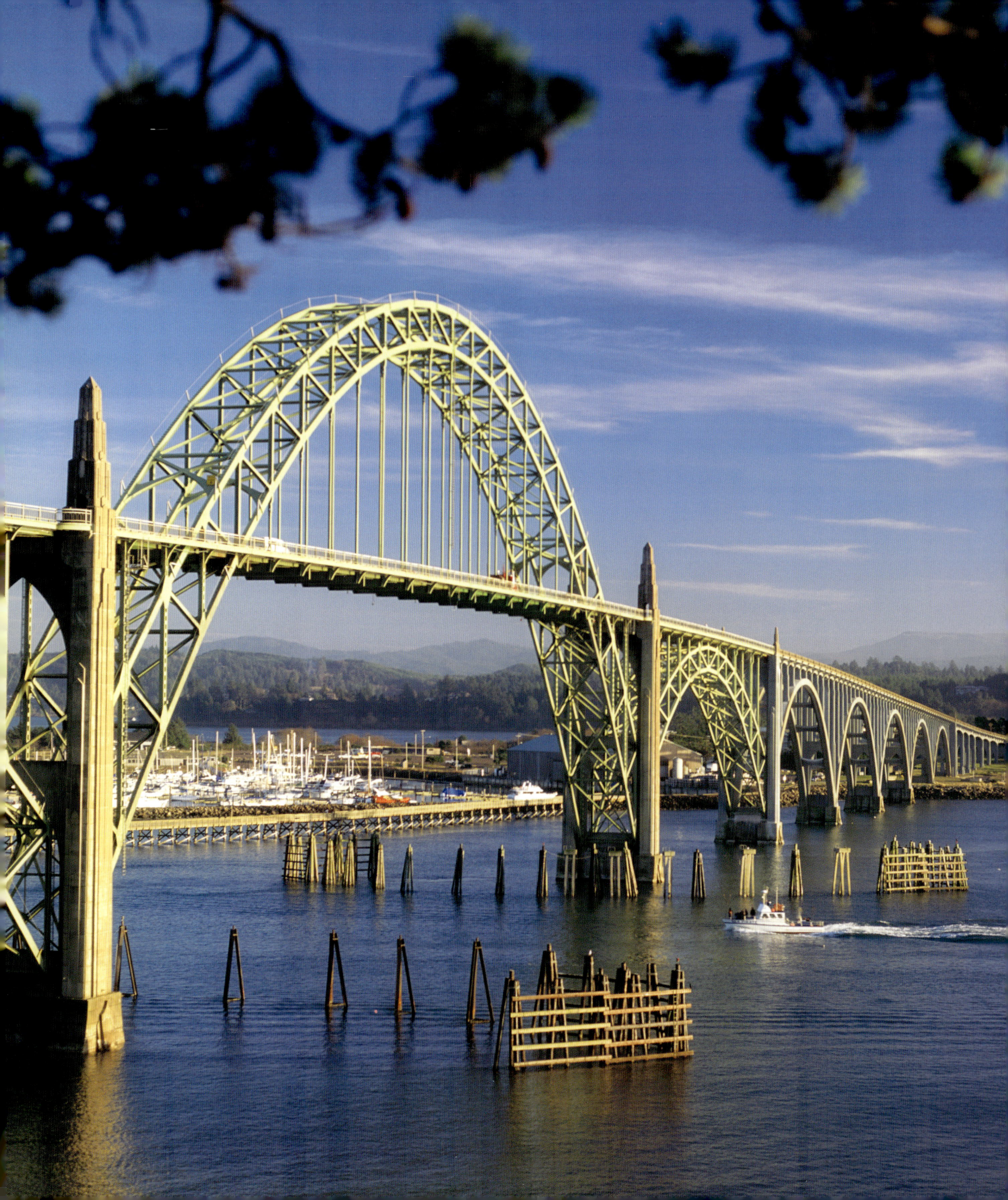

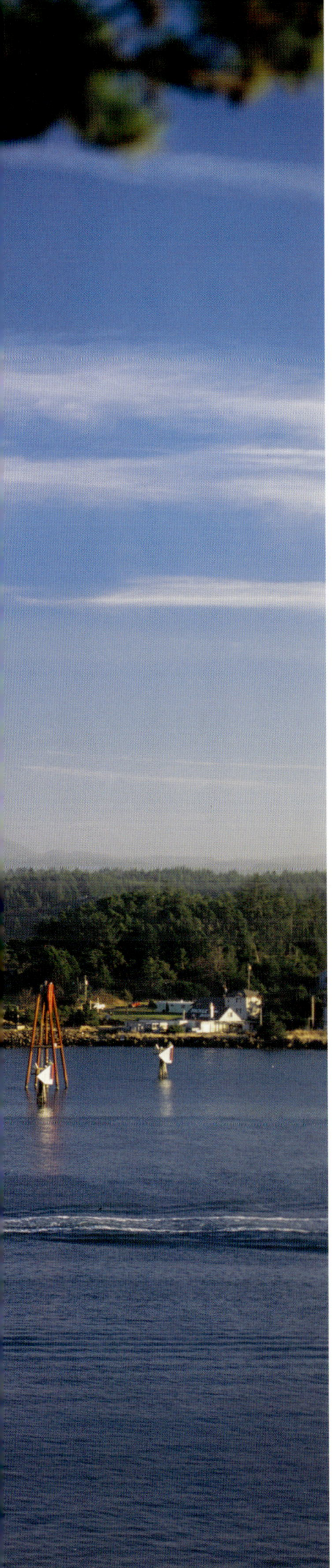

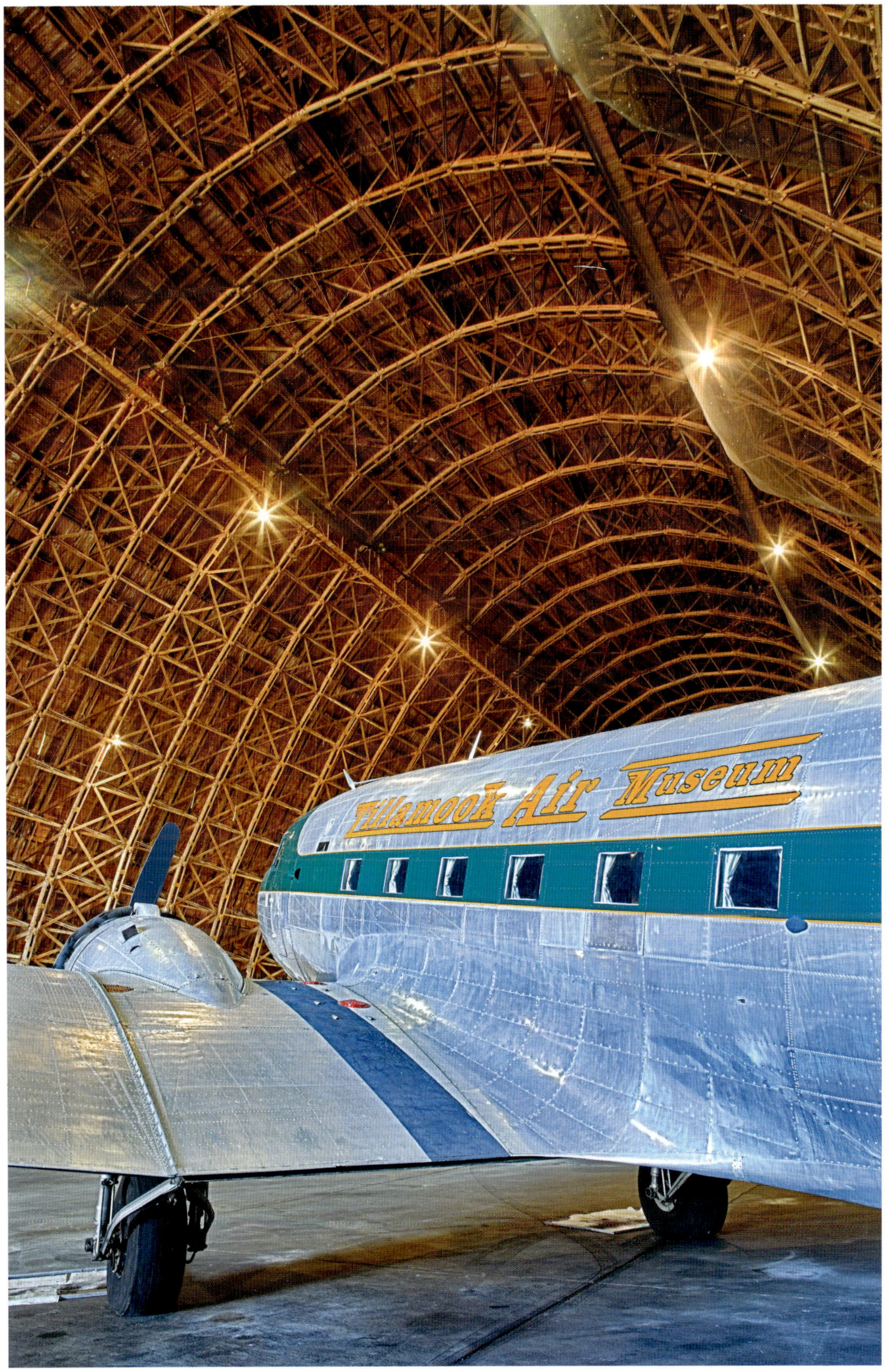

Above: This mighty Douglas DC-3 is one of more than 30 restored airplanes housed in a World War II blimp hangar at the Tillamook Air Museum.

Left: The Yaquina Bay Bridge stands as a landmark for sport and commercial fisherman headed home to Newport Harbor.

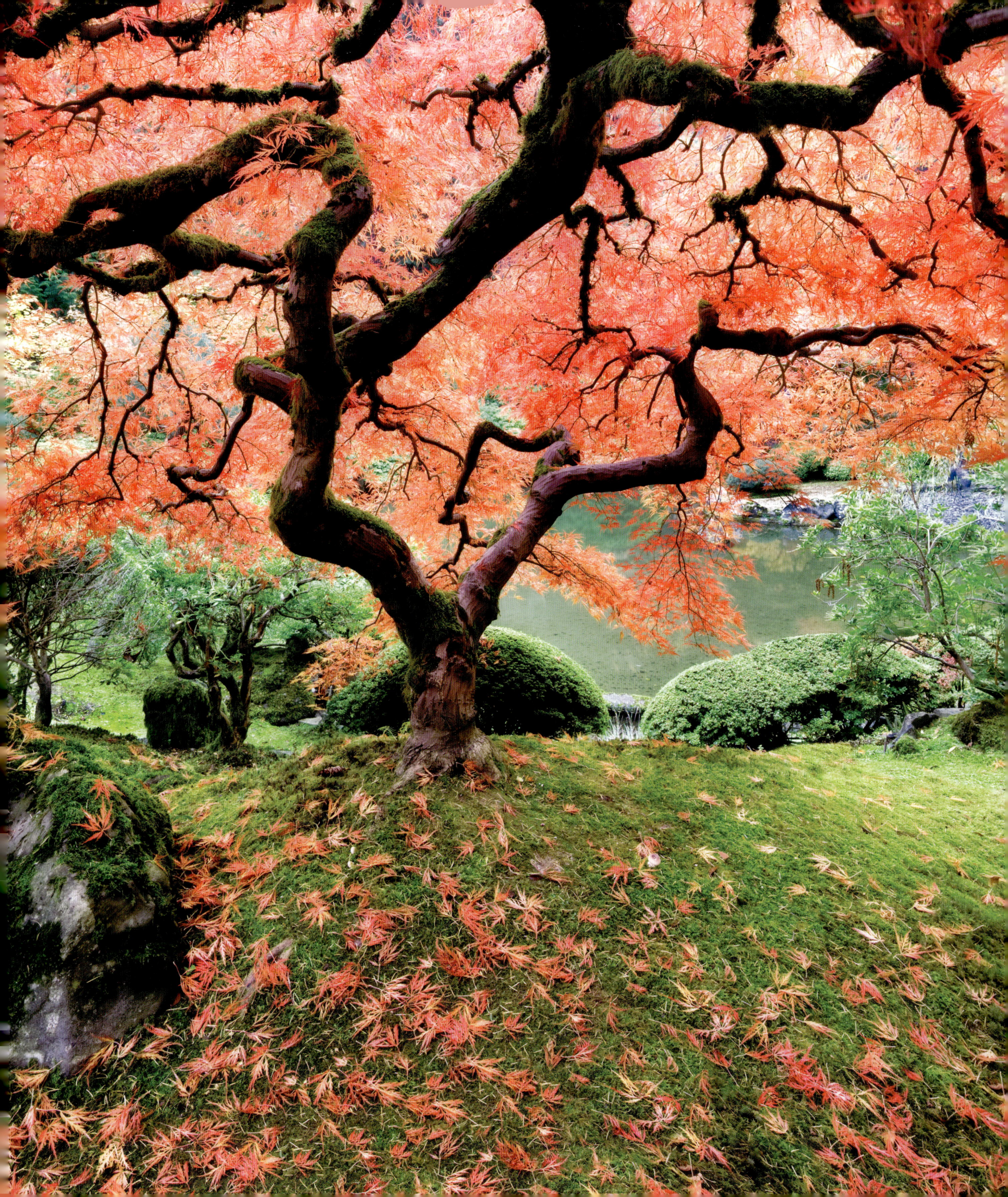

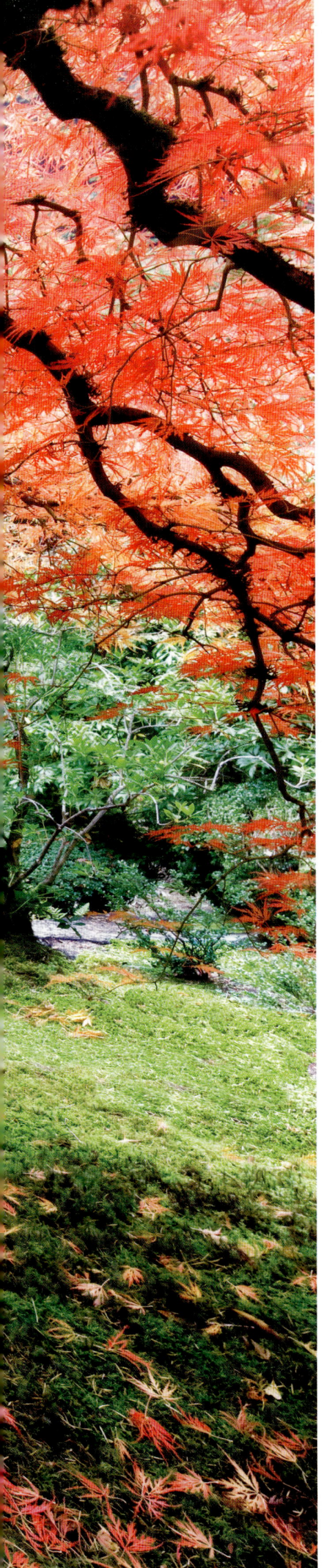
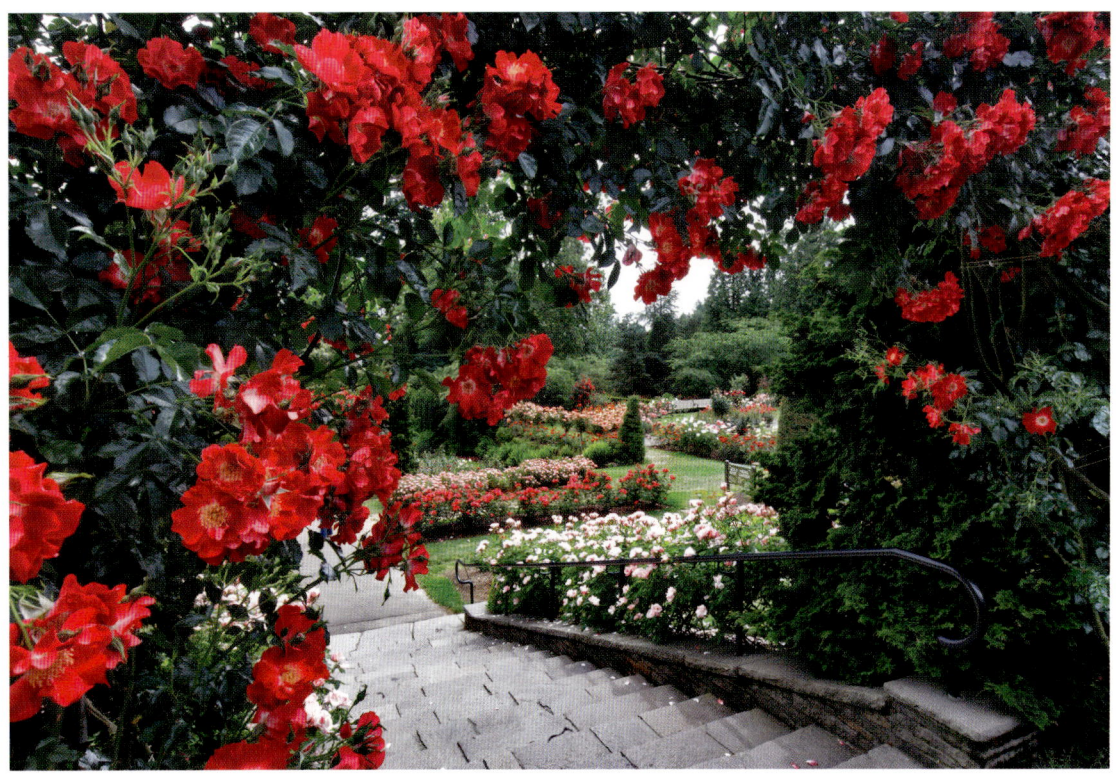
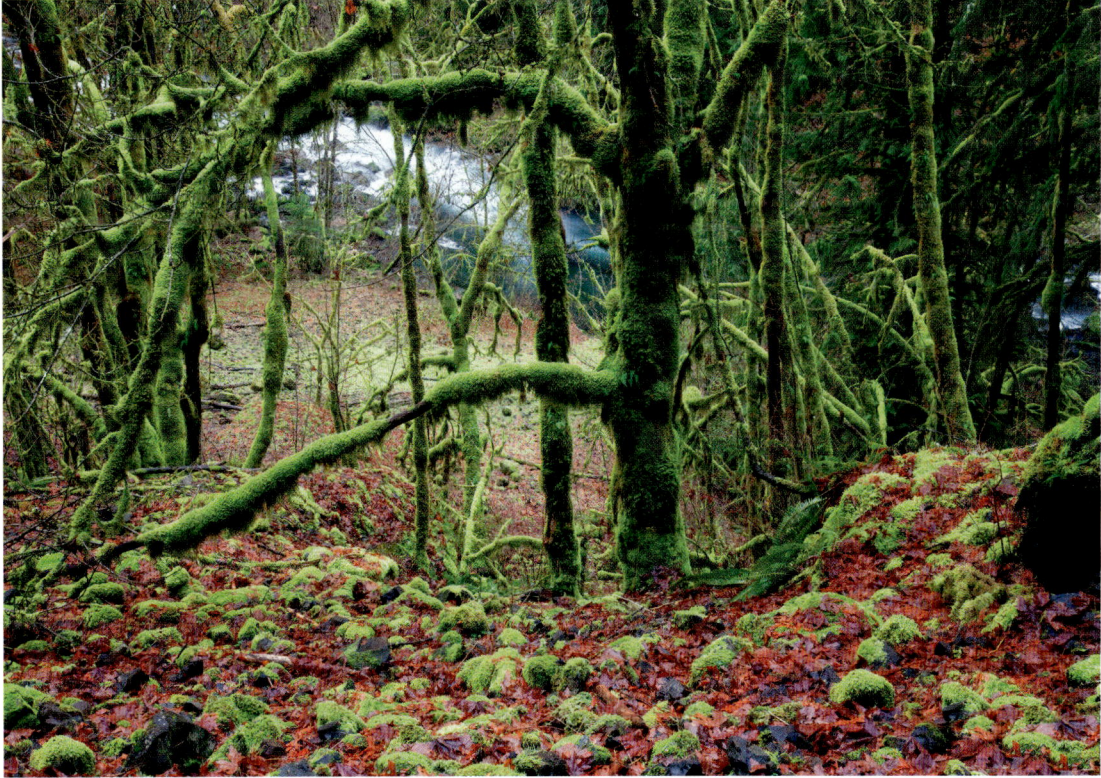

Above, top: A rose arch and stone steps lead to the Portland International Rose Test Garden, where new varieties have been tested since 1919. The City of Roses keeps the garden open free of charge to visitors.

Above, bottom: Moss clings to trees and rocks along the Eagle Creek Trail in the Columbia River Gorge National Scenic Area. The popular path winds past several major waterfalls.

Left: In autumn, it is the Japanese maples' turn to shine at the Portland Japanese Garden.

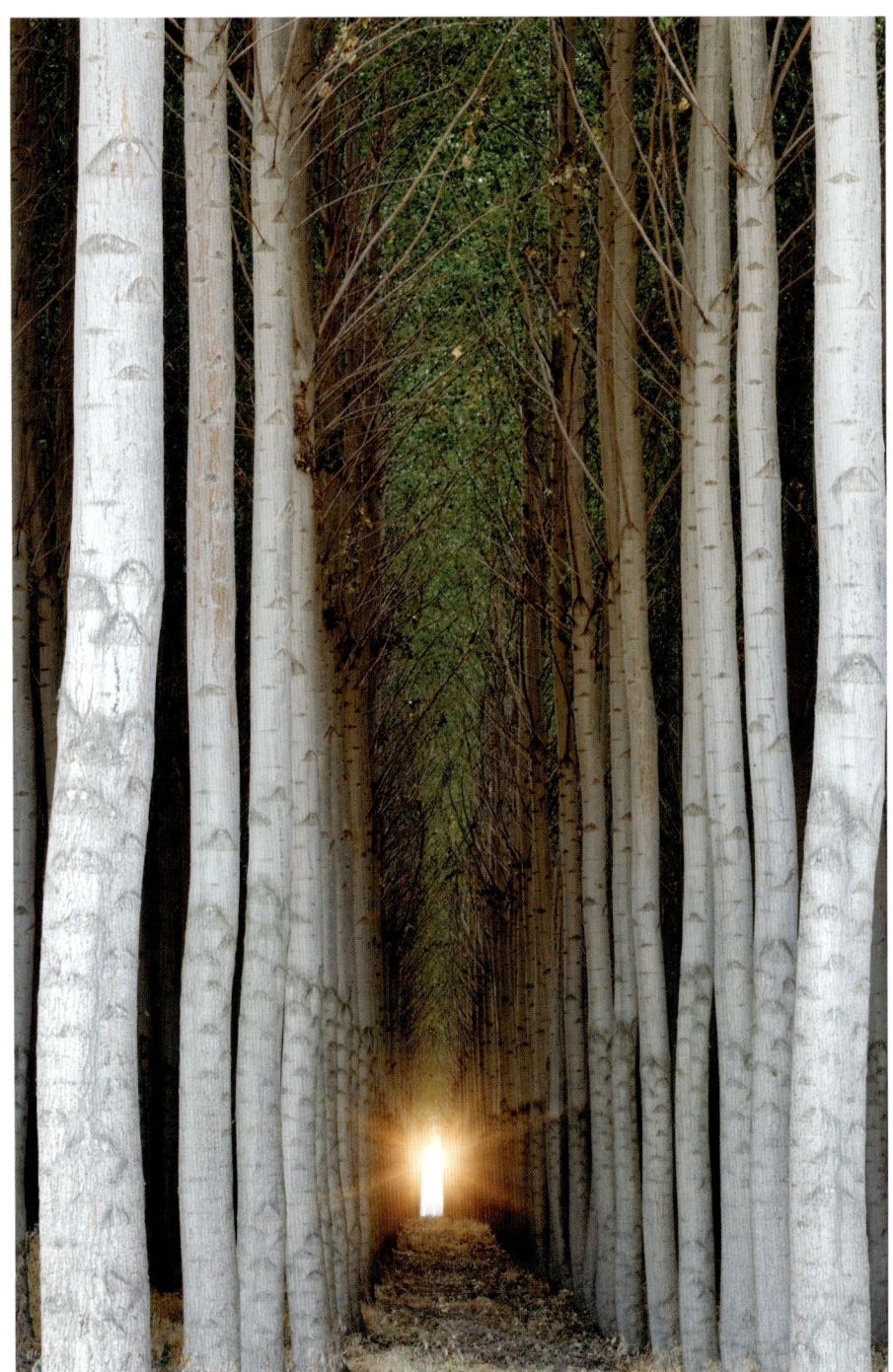

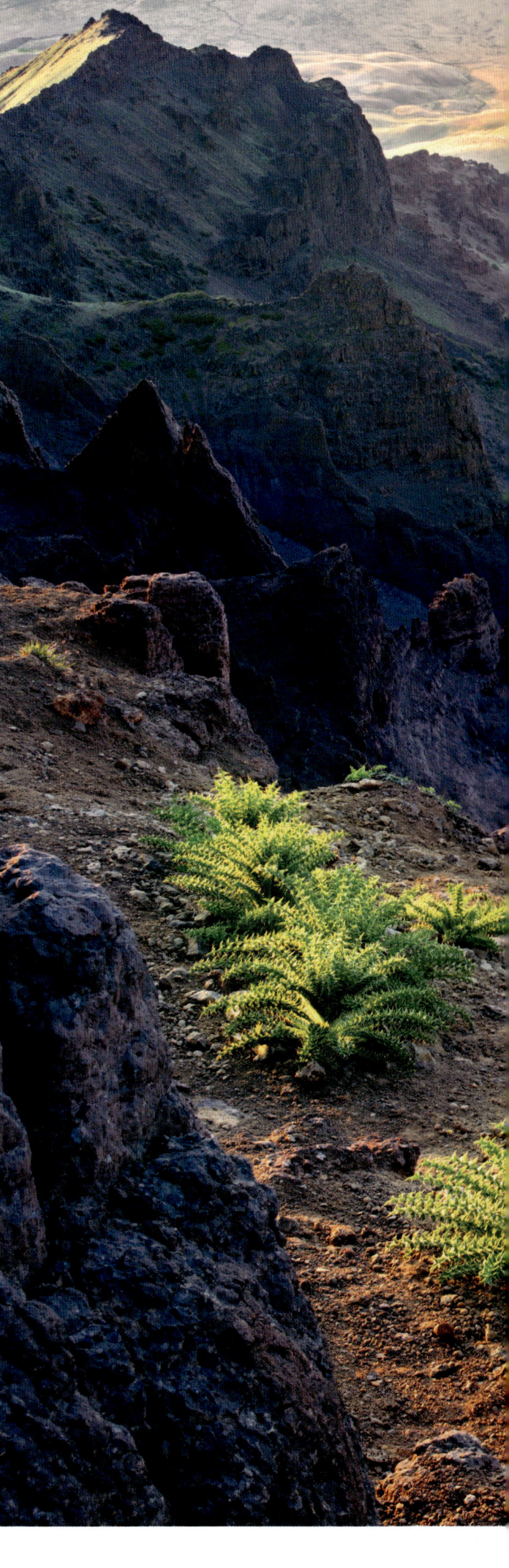

Above: Pacific albus trees grow on a tree plantation in the high desert along the Columbia River near Boardman. The hybrid poplar is prized for its fast growth—six to ten feet per year. The hardwood is used for millwork, furniture, landscape timbers, and other products.

Right: East Rim Overlook at Steens Mountain offers a long look down—more than one vertical mile—onto the Alvord Desert below. This fault-block mountain formed when tremendous internal pressure forced the east edge of a continental plate upward along a fault line. The mountain was then further sculpted by glacial erosion.

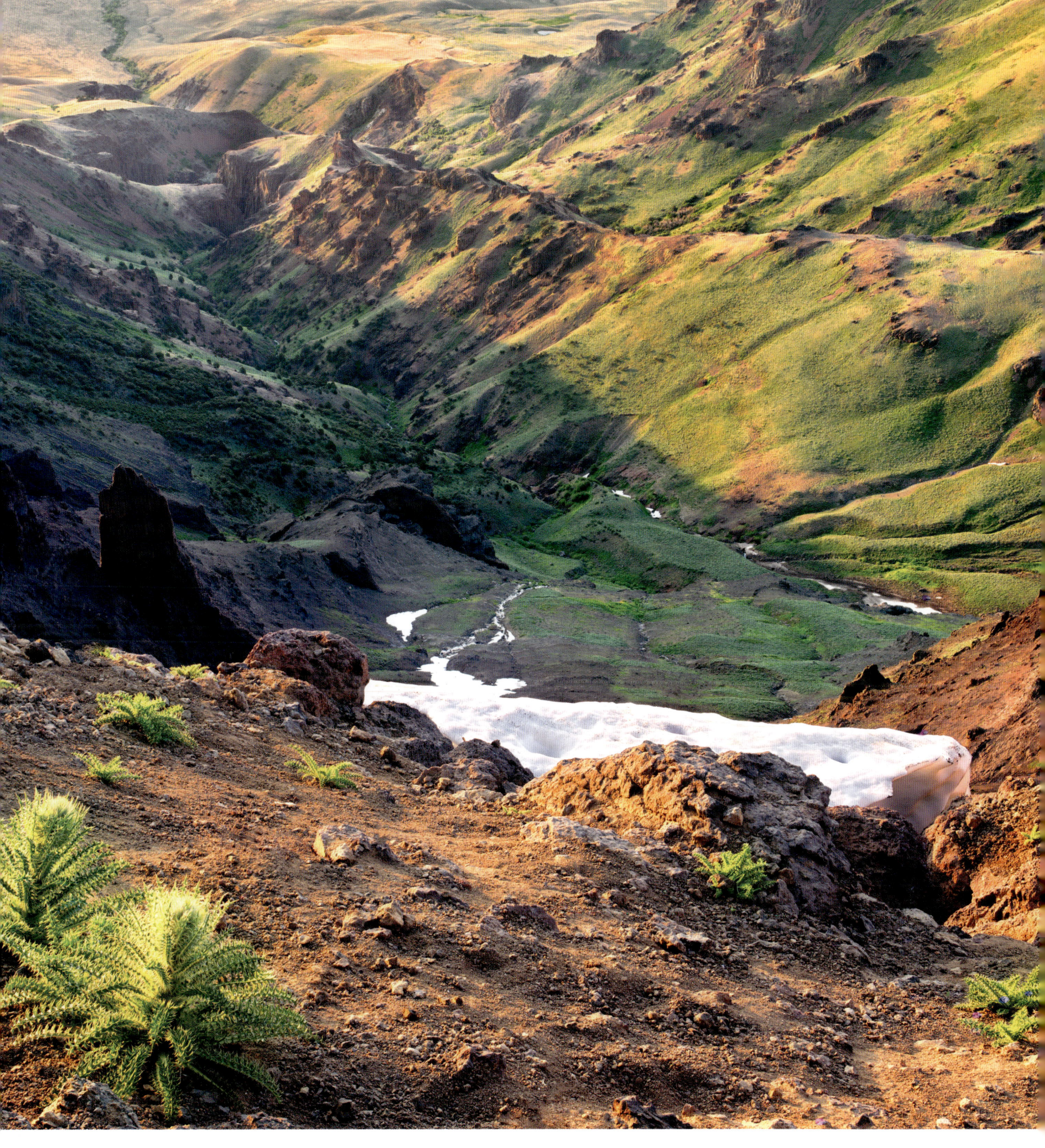

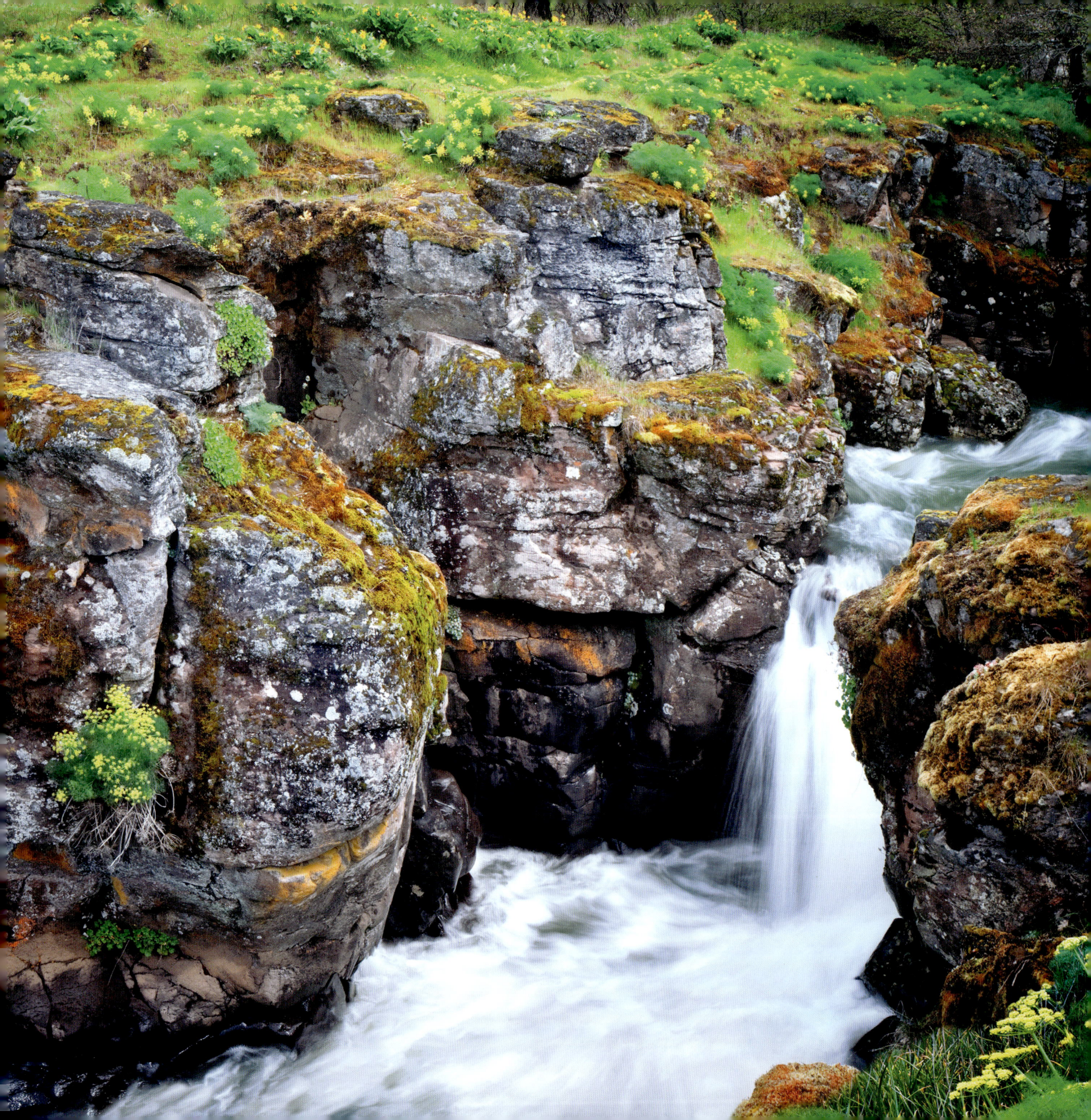

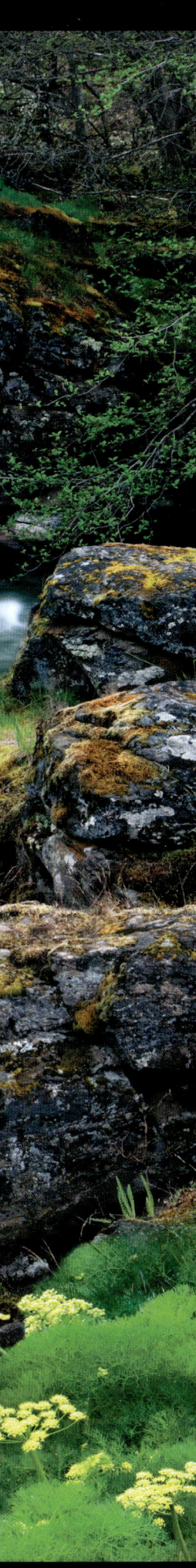

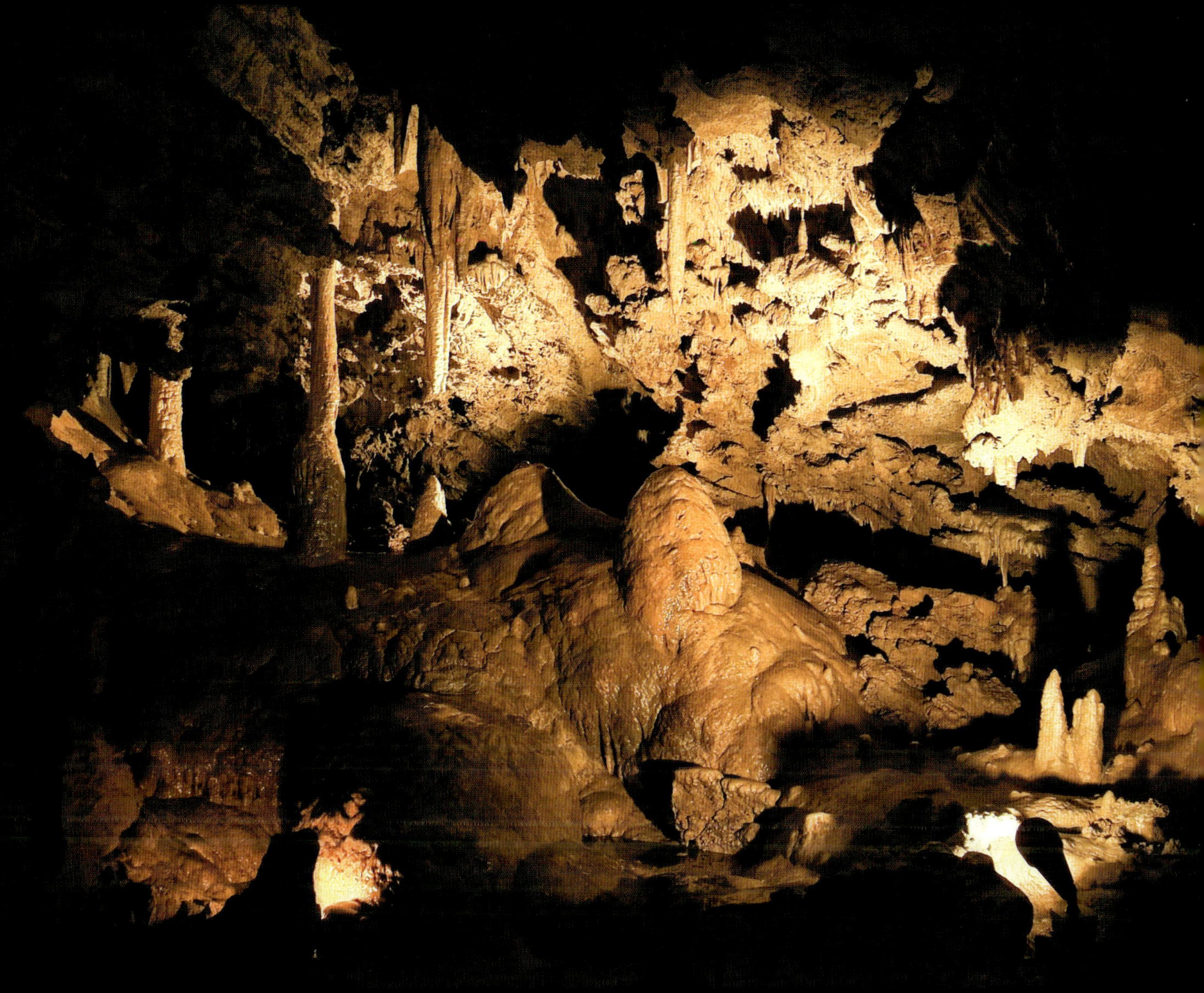

Above: Untold eons ago, flowing water hollowed out marble and limestone in the Siskiyou Mountains, creating one of the most dramatic cavern systems in the Northwest. Joaquin Miller's Chapel—named after the "Poet of the Sierras," who lobbied for protection of the caves—is one of the natural wonders on the Oregon Caves National Monument tour.
PHOTO COURTESY OF OREGON CAVES NATIONAL MONUMENT

Left: The bright yellow, tightly clustered flowers of desert parsley emerge in the early spring along the dry, rocky slopes and flats of the Columbia River Gorge National Scenic Area.

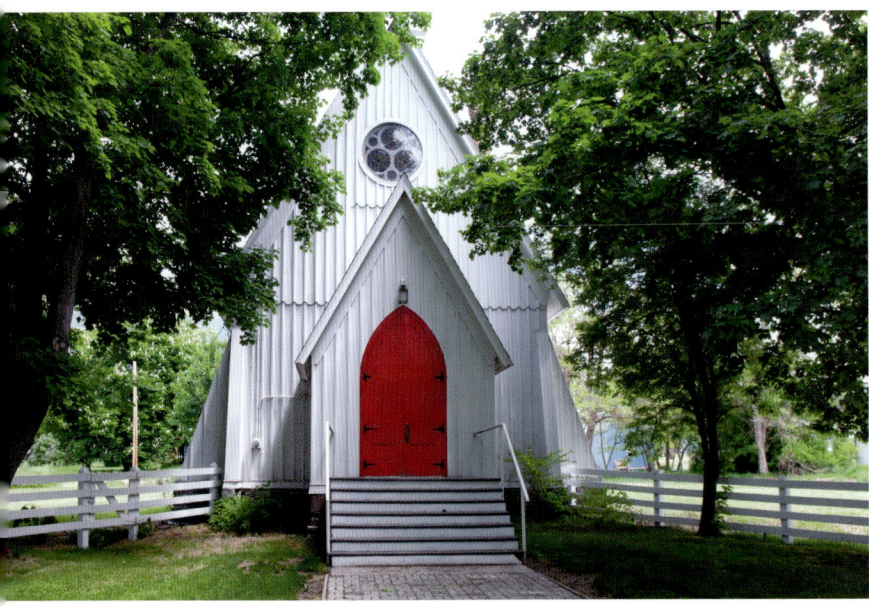

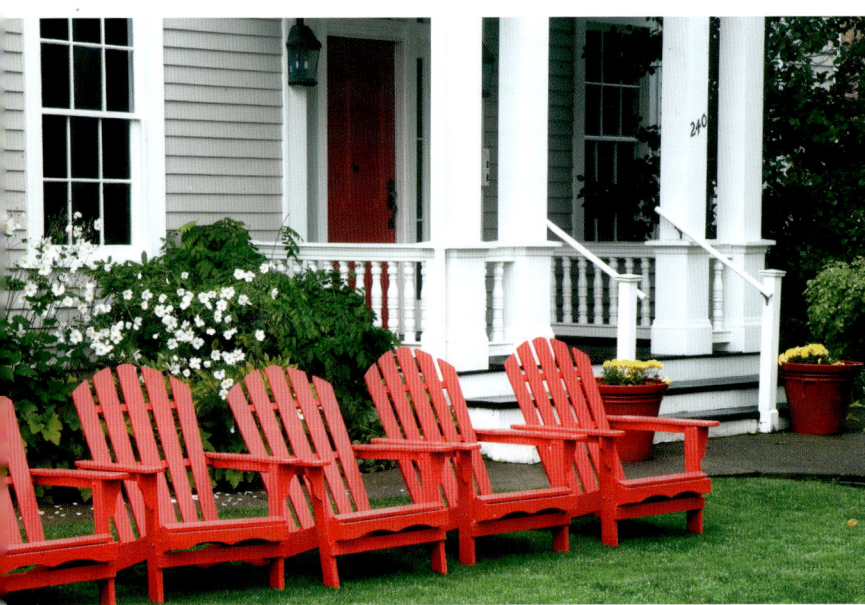

Above, top: Built in the late 1800s, the Ascension Chapel in the rural community of Cove is still in use. The little Episcopal church and its accompanying rectory are on the National Register of Historic Places.

Above, bottom: The entire town of Jacksonville was declared a National Historic District in 1966. It is home to the Britt Festival, a world-class outdoor concert series, and also romantic lodgings like the McCall House Inn.

Right: The bright blooms of the red-flowering currant stand out against the pale bark of alder trees along the banks of Quartzville Creek Wild and Scenic River. Praised as one of the most beautiful flowering shrubs, this currant's fruit tastes unpleasant to people, but the showy flower is a favorite food source for hummingbirds.

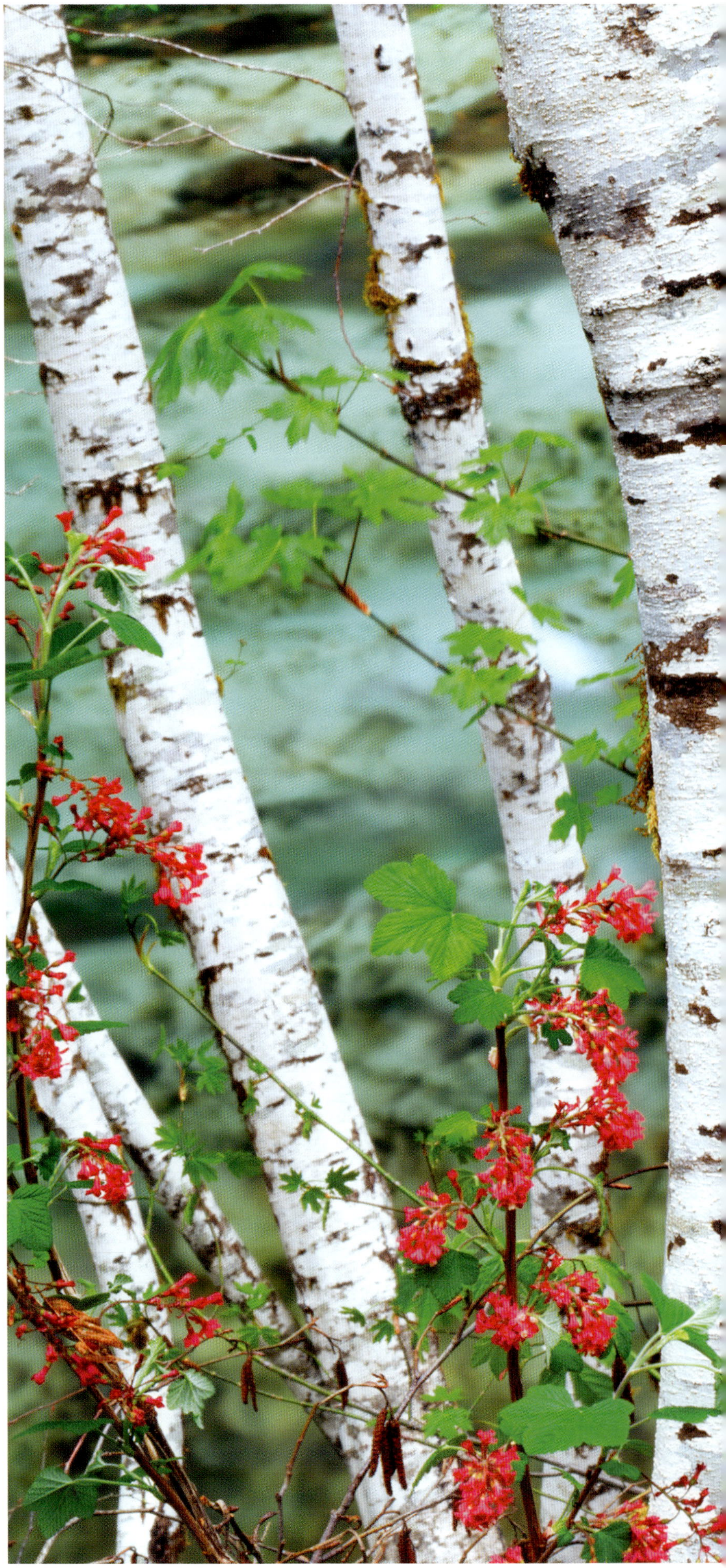

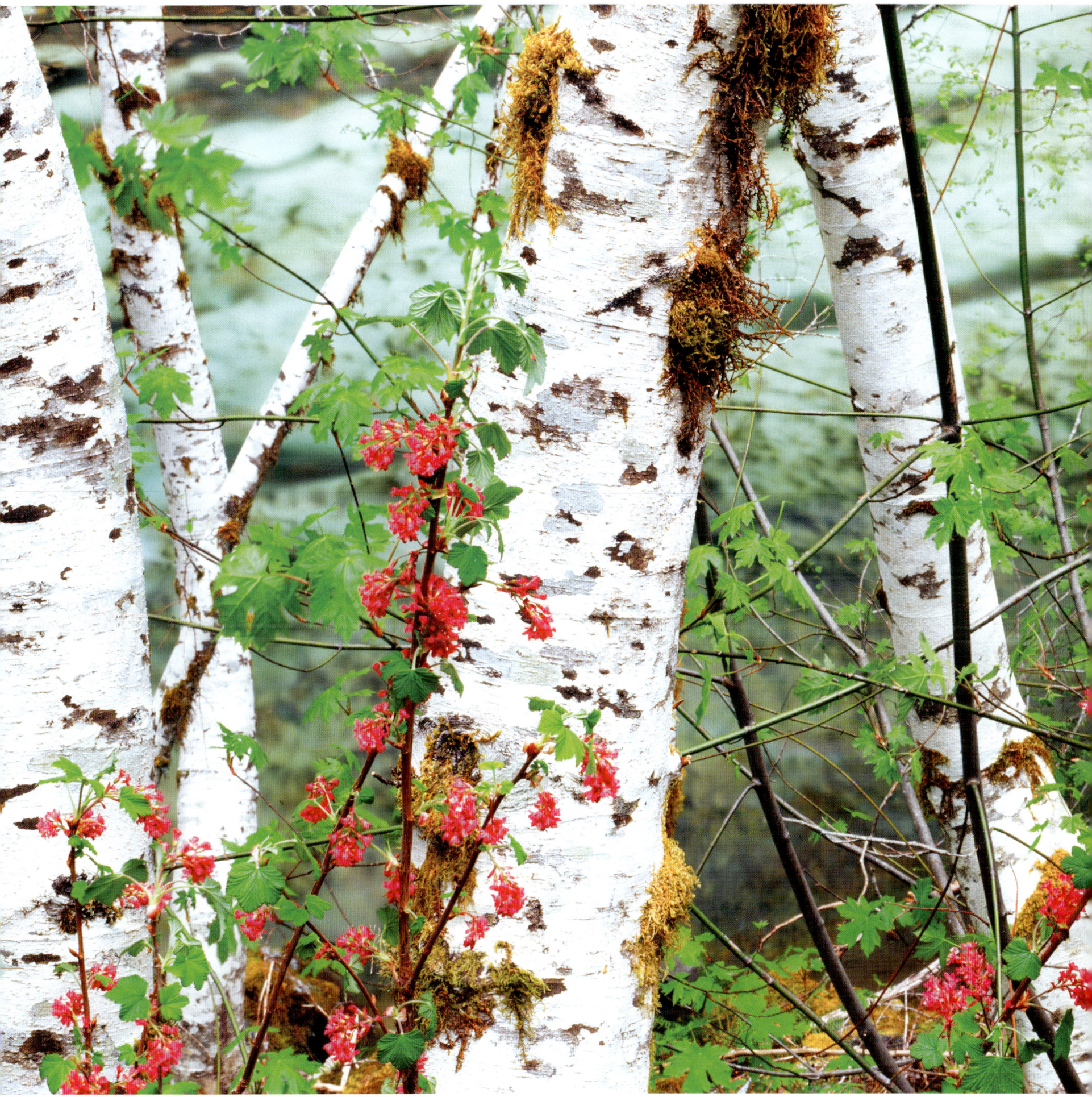

Right: A sport fishing boat at Garibaldi Marina on Tillamook Bay stands at the ready for its next ocean trip in search of salmon, lingcod, halibut, and albacore tuna.

Facing page: At Harris Beach State Park, sandy beaches intermingle with rocky outcroppings rich with tidal marine life. Visitors may see gray whales as they pass by on their winter and spring migrations.

Below: At Smelt Sands State Recreation Site, the water comes alive every spring when smelt, a small fish, make their way back to the streams of their birth to breed. Catch sight of the annual smelt run through the viewing telescope or just sit back and enjoy the sunset.

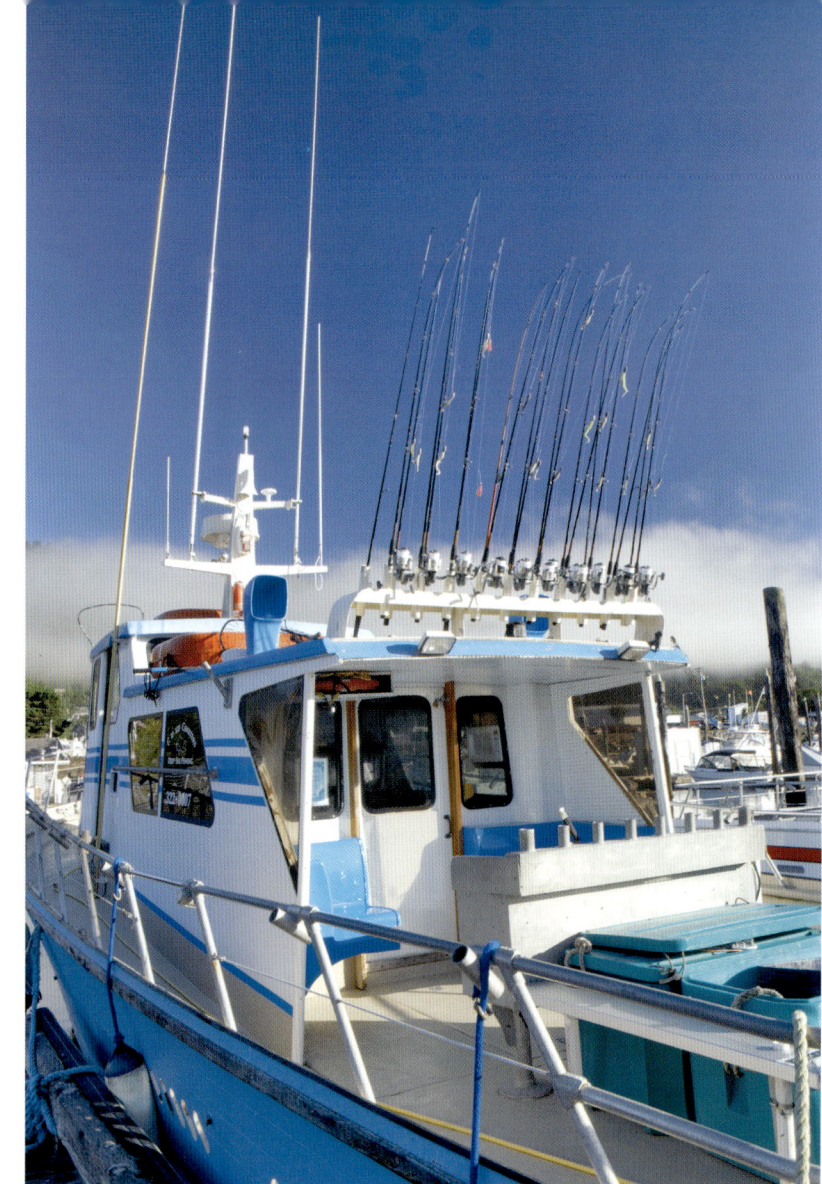

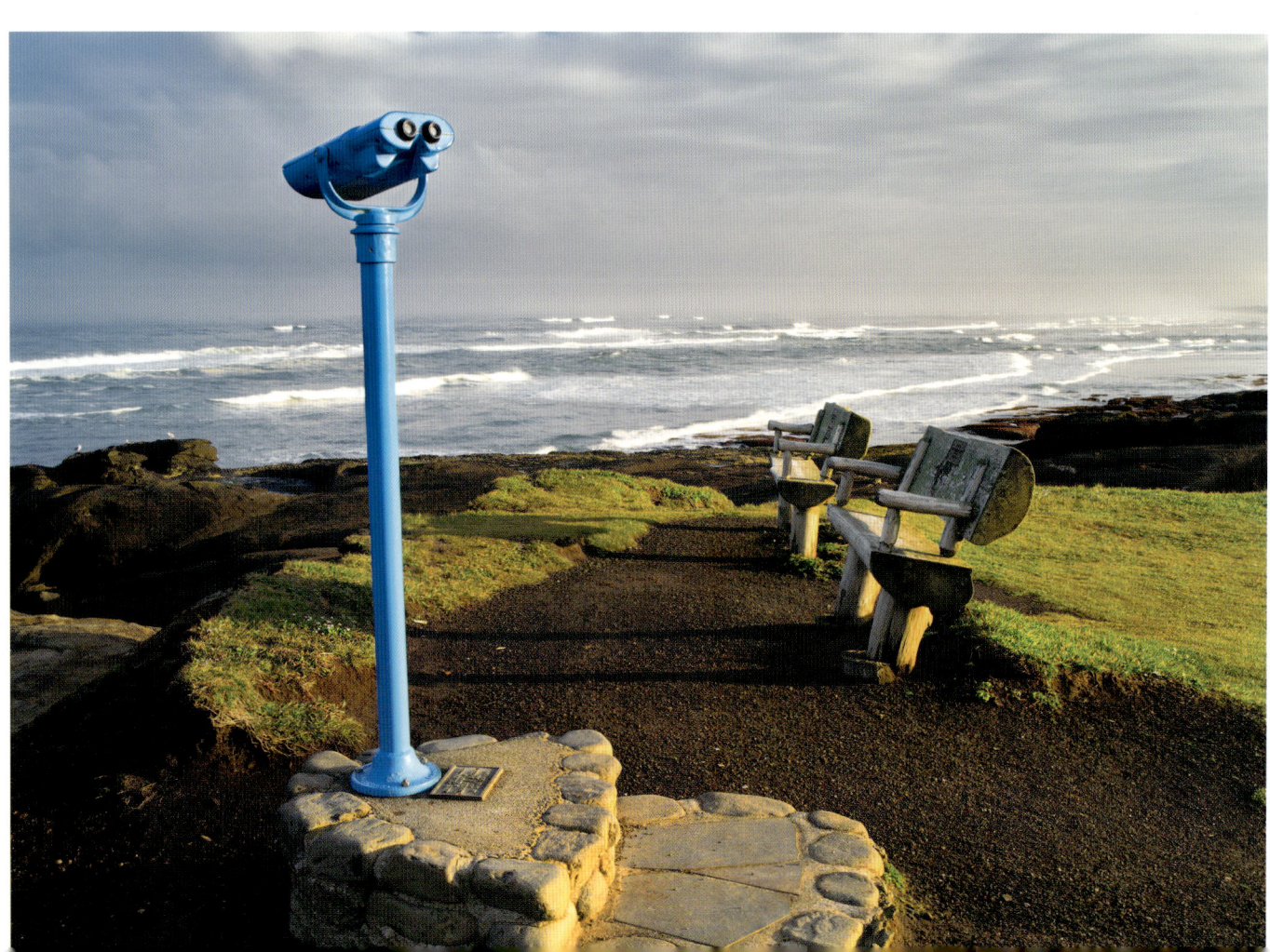

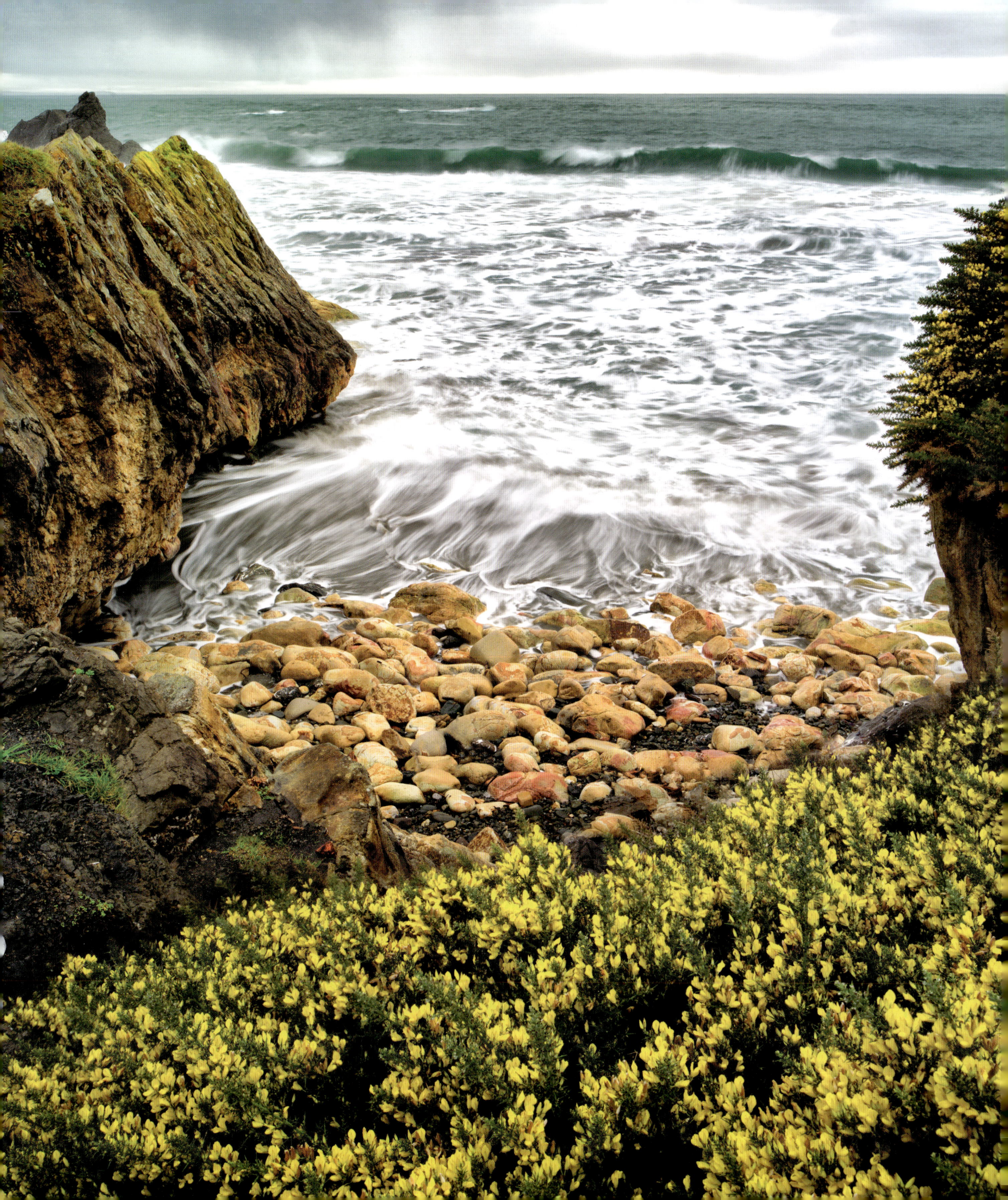

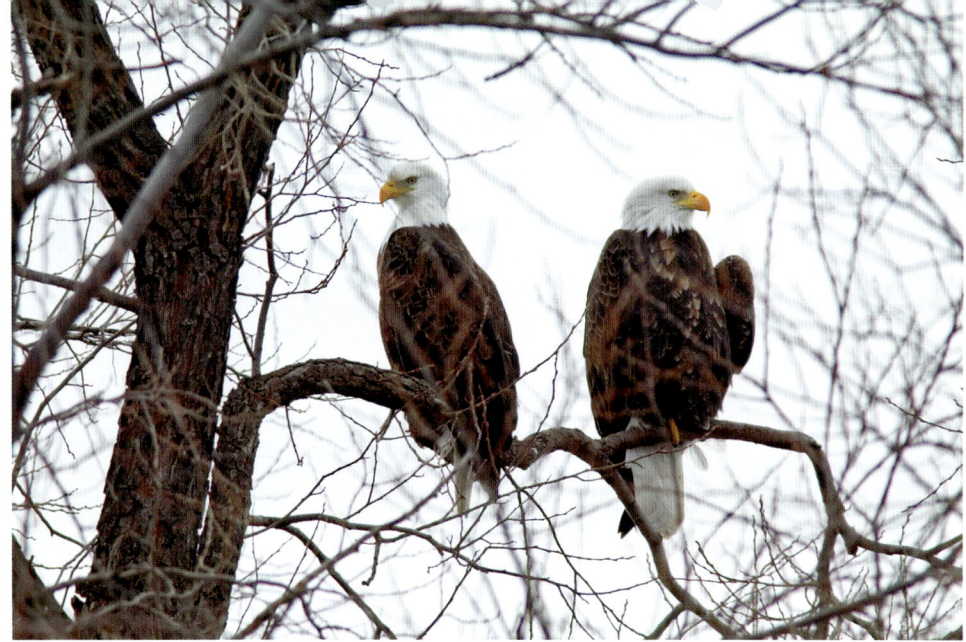

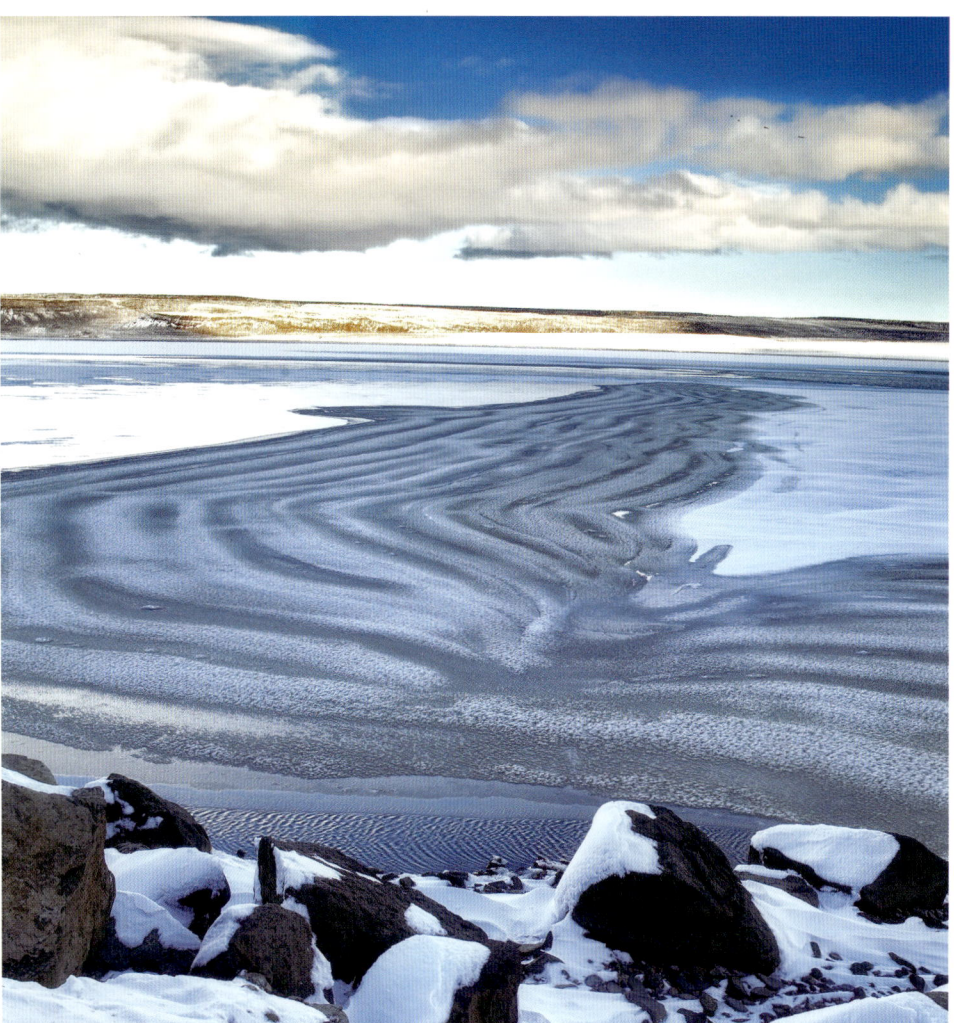

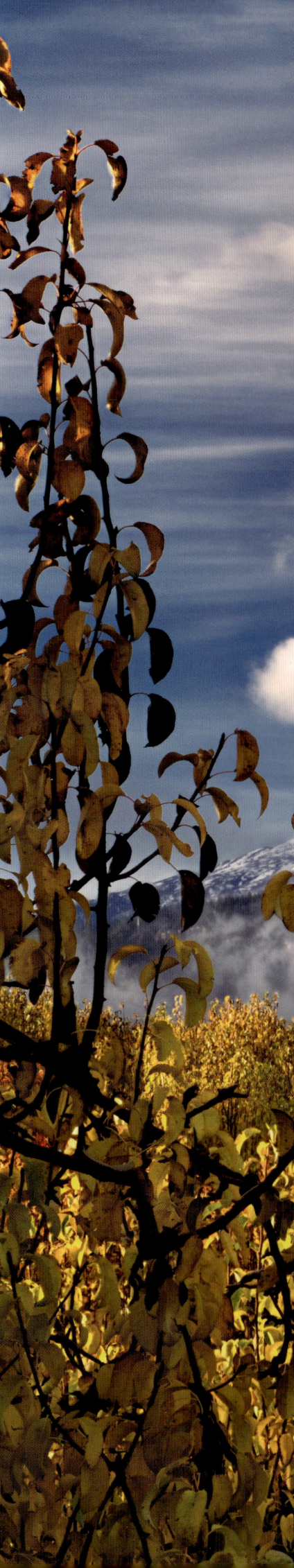

Above, top: January and February are the best months to observe America's national bird in its wintering grounds at the Lower Klamath National Wildlife Refuge. As many as 500 bald eagles vie for fish and waterfowl in the marshes of the basin.

Above, bottom: Ice formations create a textured pattern on the surface of Crump Lake in south-central Oregon's Warner Valley.

Right: The largest pear-growing region in the United States, the Hood River Valley is world-renowned for its fruit. Autumn is the perfect time to drive the back roads and sample Comice, Anjou, Bosc, and Bartlett varieties while enjoying scrumptious views of Mt. Hood.

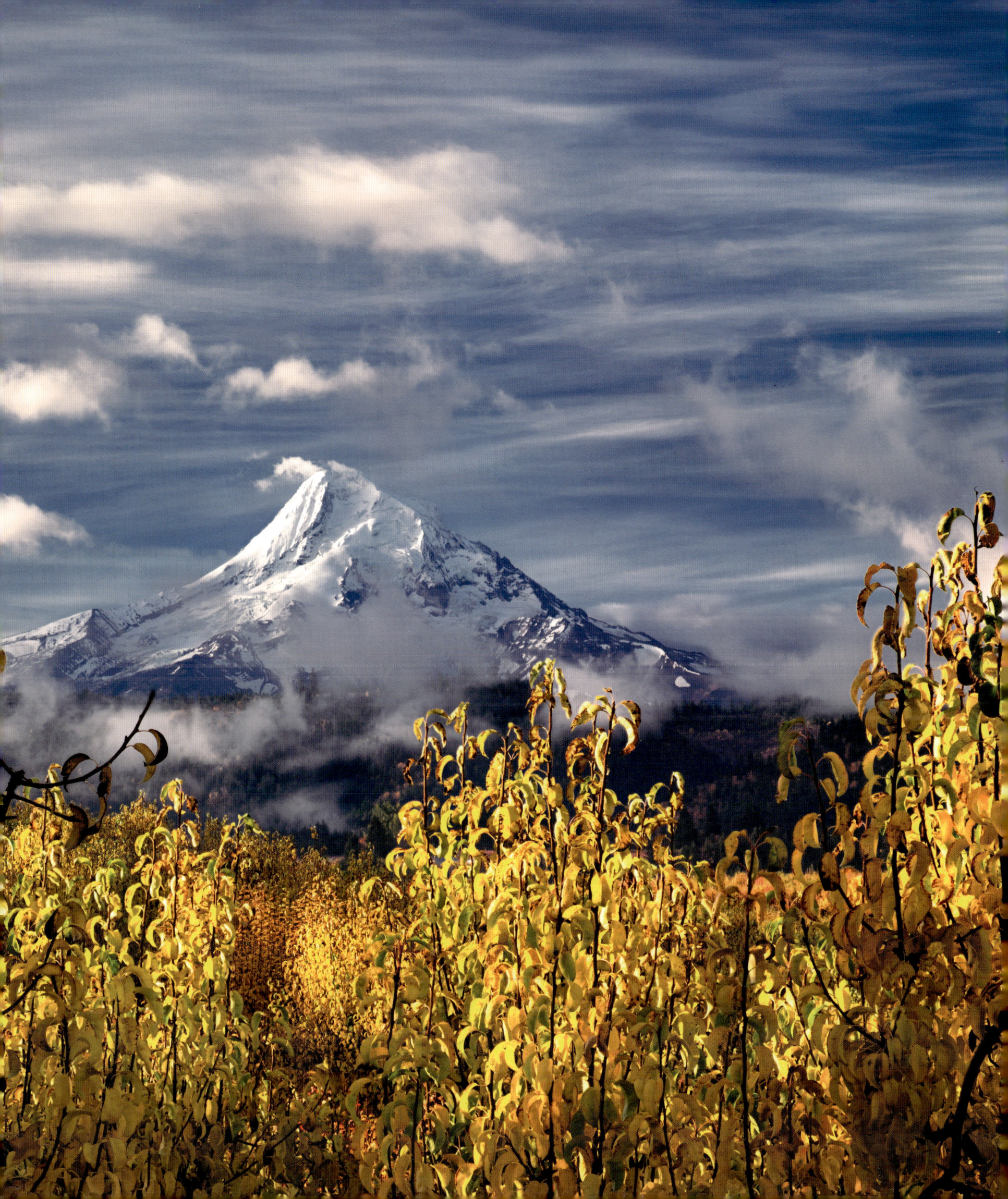

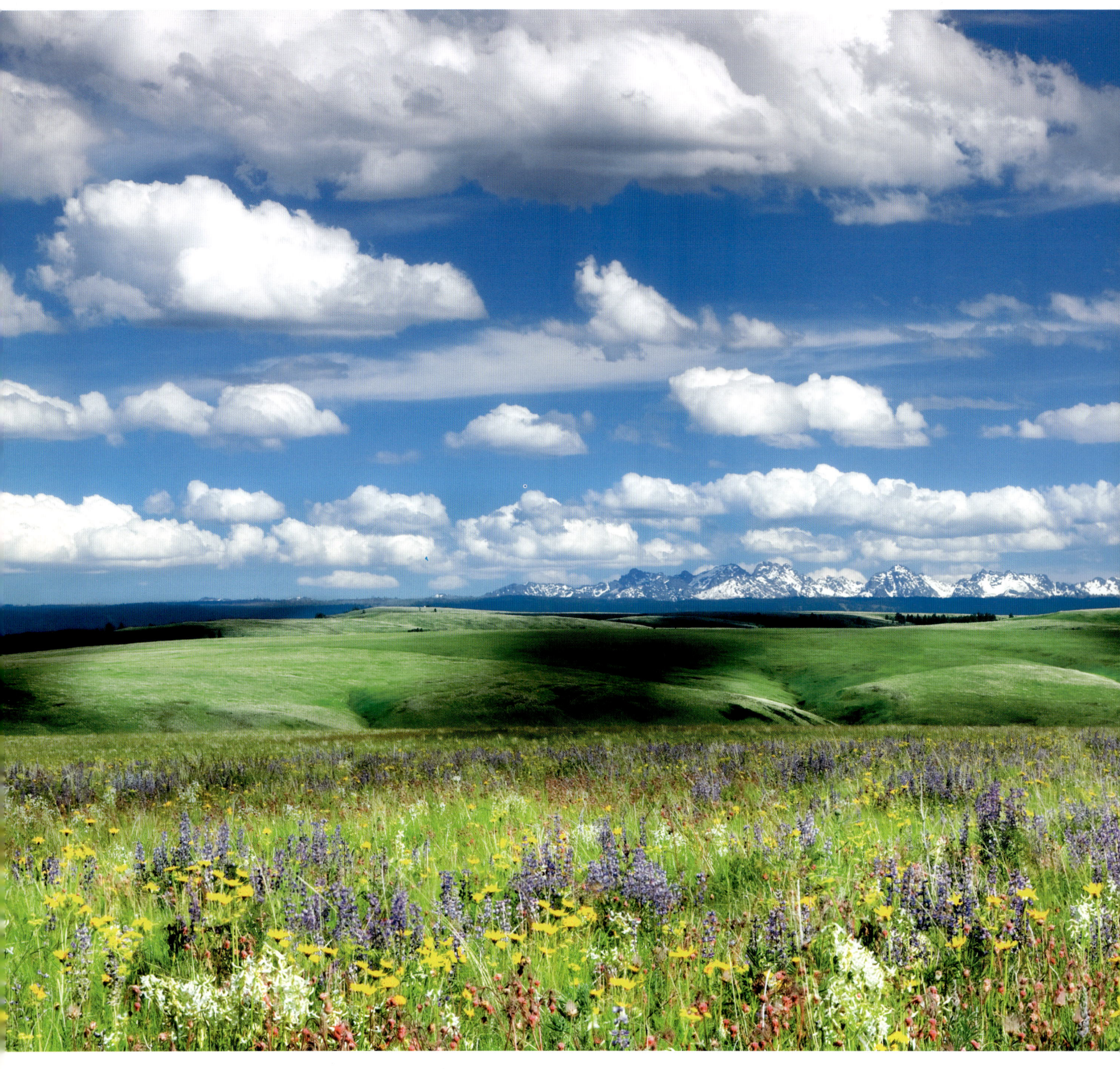

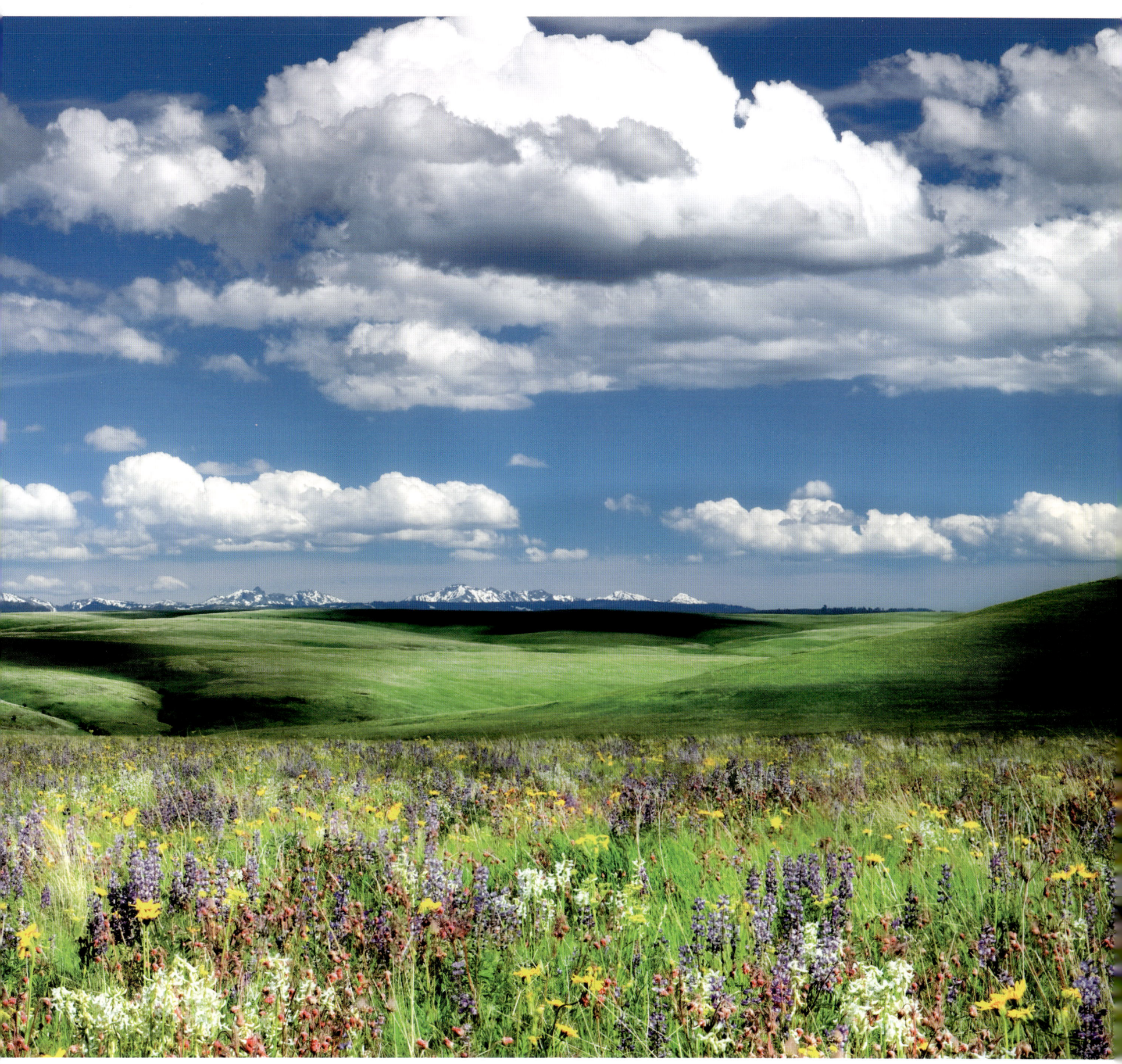

Wildflowers, bunchgrass, and over 90 species of native bees thrive on the Zumwalt Prairie Preserve in Wallowa County. The 51-square mile private nature sanctuary protects the largest undisturbed plateau grassland in the Northwest.

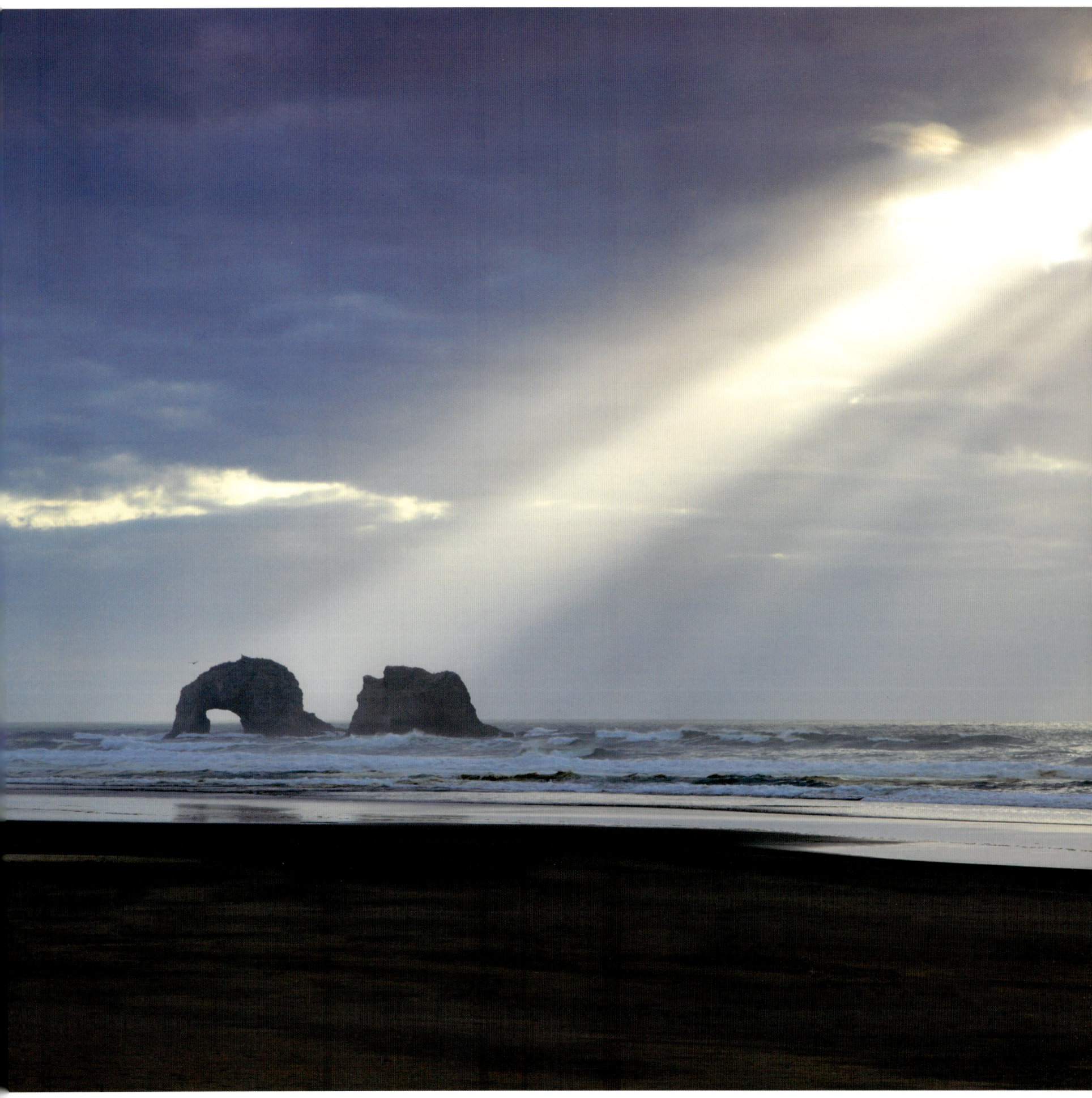

Left: Far from the bustling tourist towns, sunlight breaks through the coastal gray clouds spotlighting the two sea stacks known as Twin Rocks at Rockaway Beach.

Below: American avocets feed along the shallow waters and mudflats of Summer Lake Wildlife Refuge. The blue-legged shorebirds are among hundreds of species that visit the basin refuge, along with blue herons, tundra swans, and snow geese.

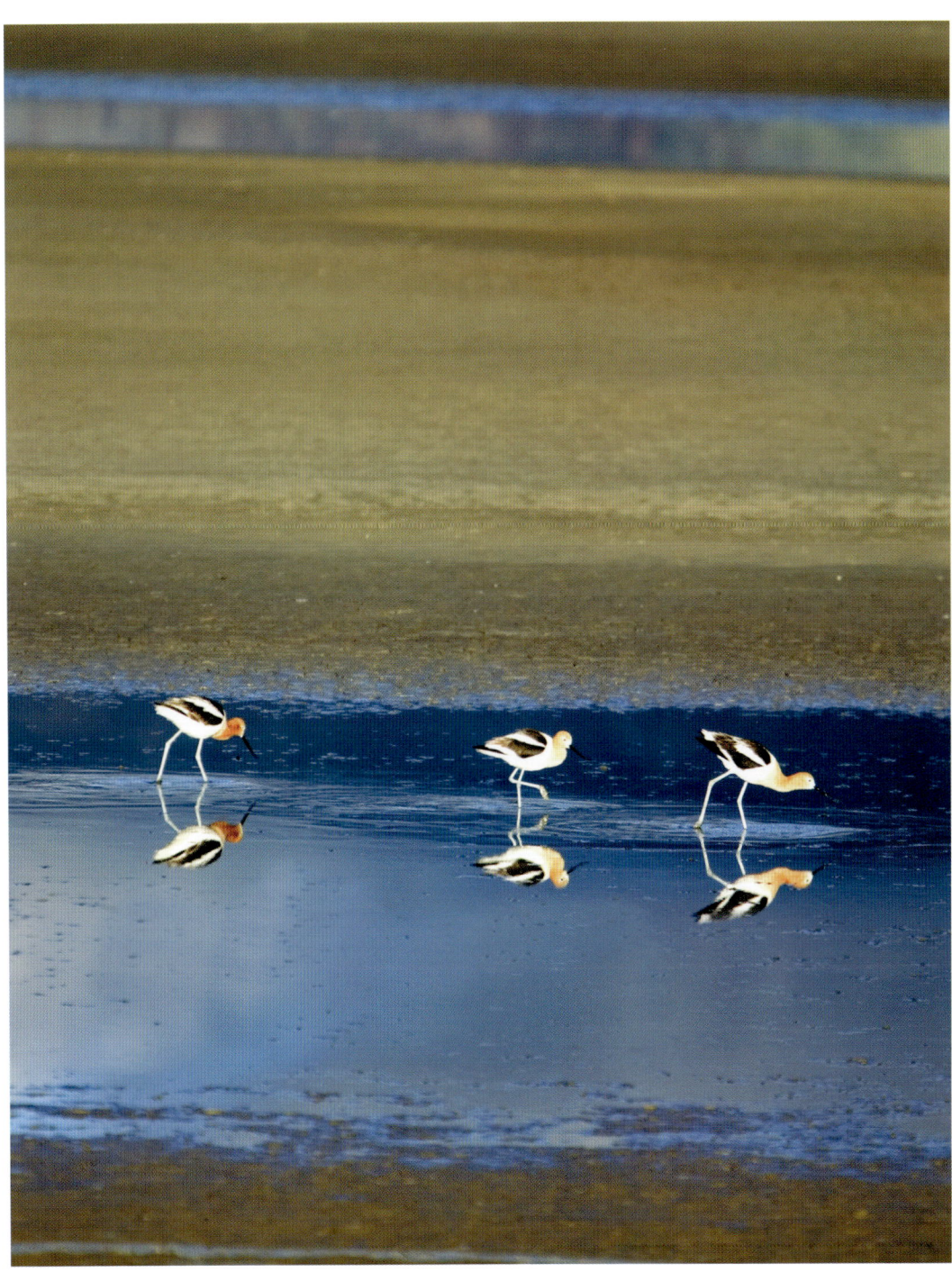

Facing page: Tumbling from the eastern slopes of the Cascades, the spring-fed Metolius River is home to kokanee salmon, rainbow trout, whitefish, bull trout, and brown trout.

Below: Malheur National Wildlife Refuge draws thousands of migratory birds to the Harney Basin of southeast Oregon. Located on the Pacific Flyway, the refuge boasts a checklist of more than 300 avian species.

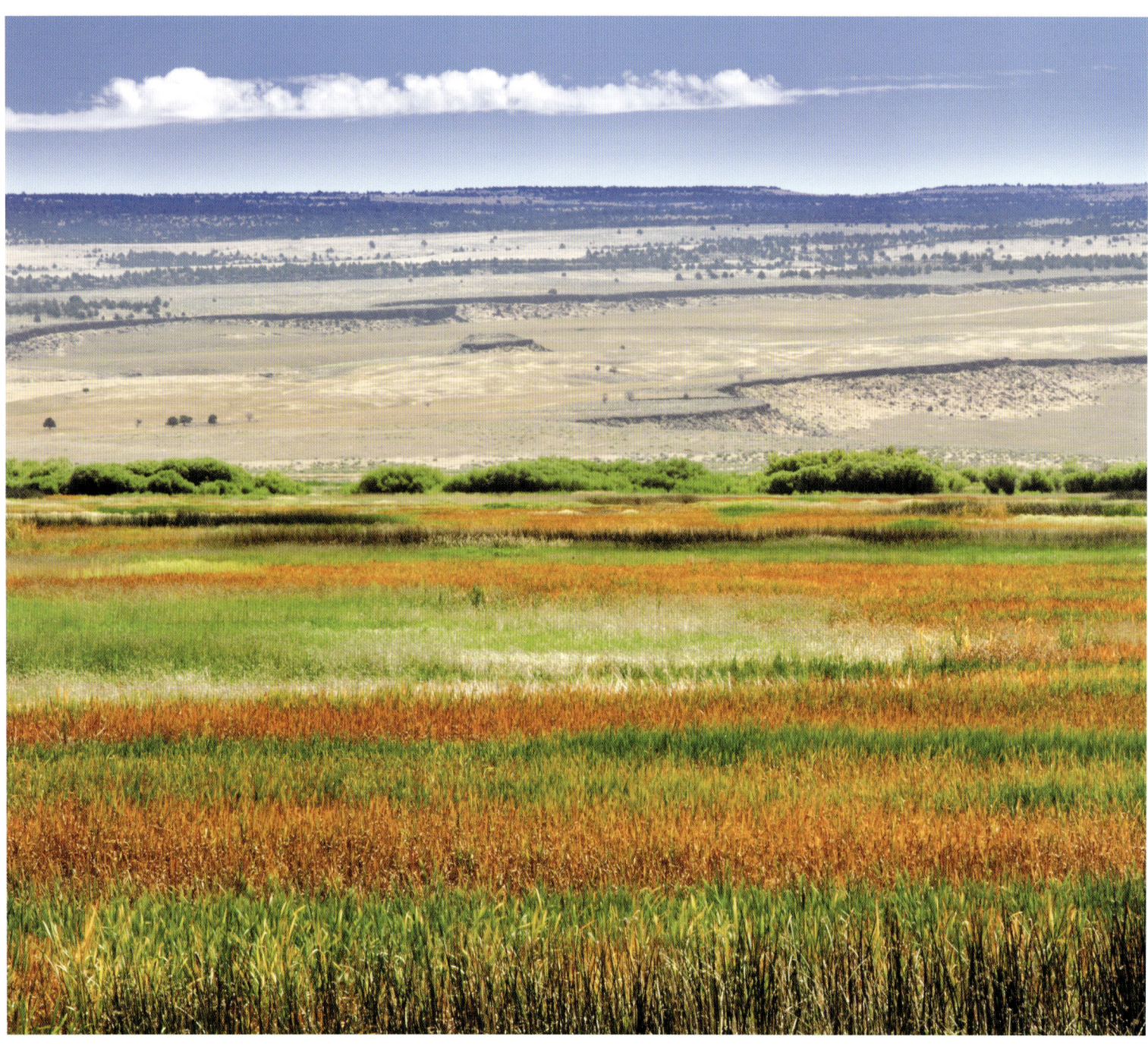

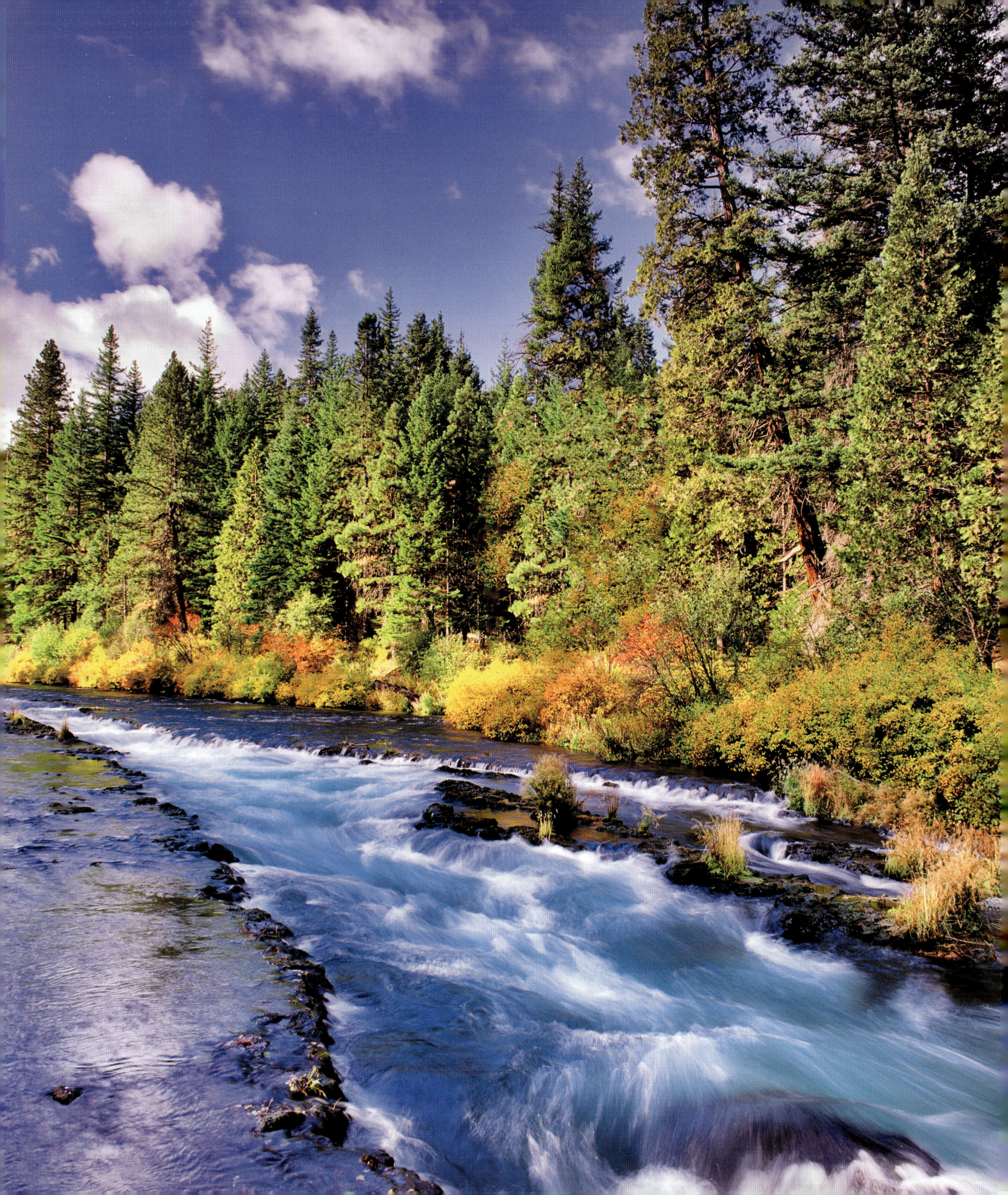

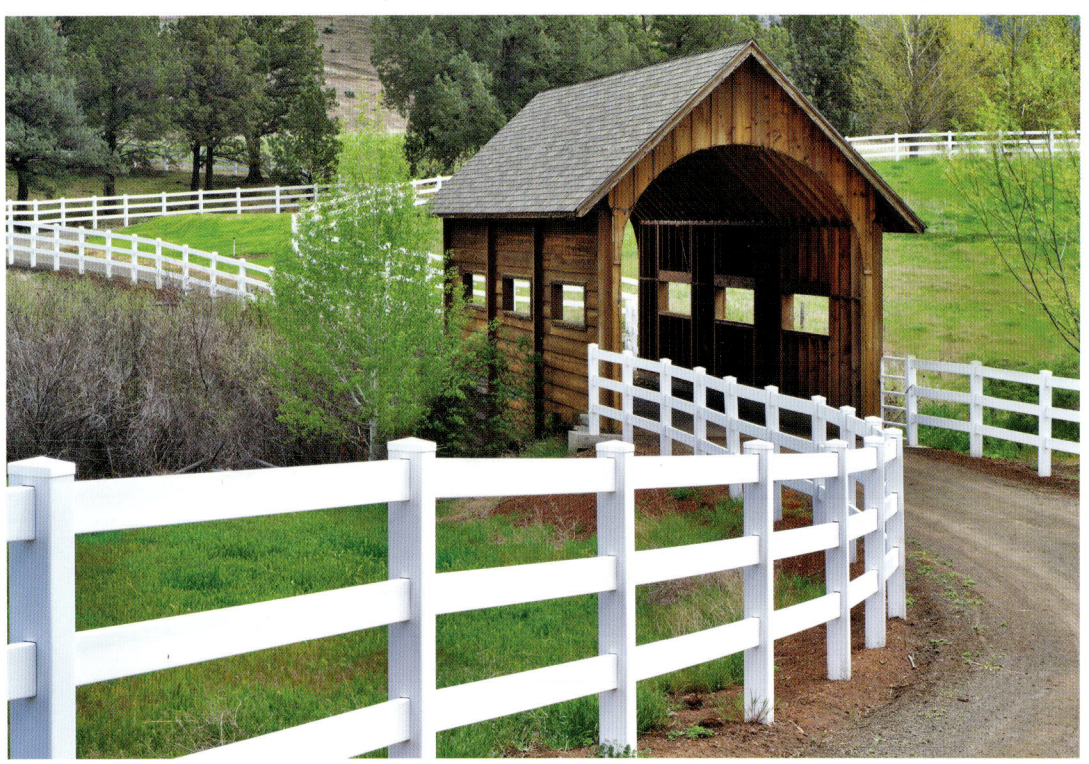

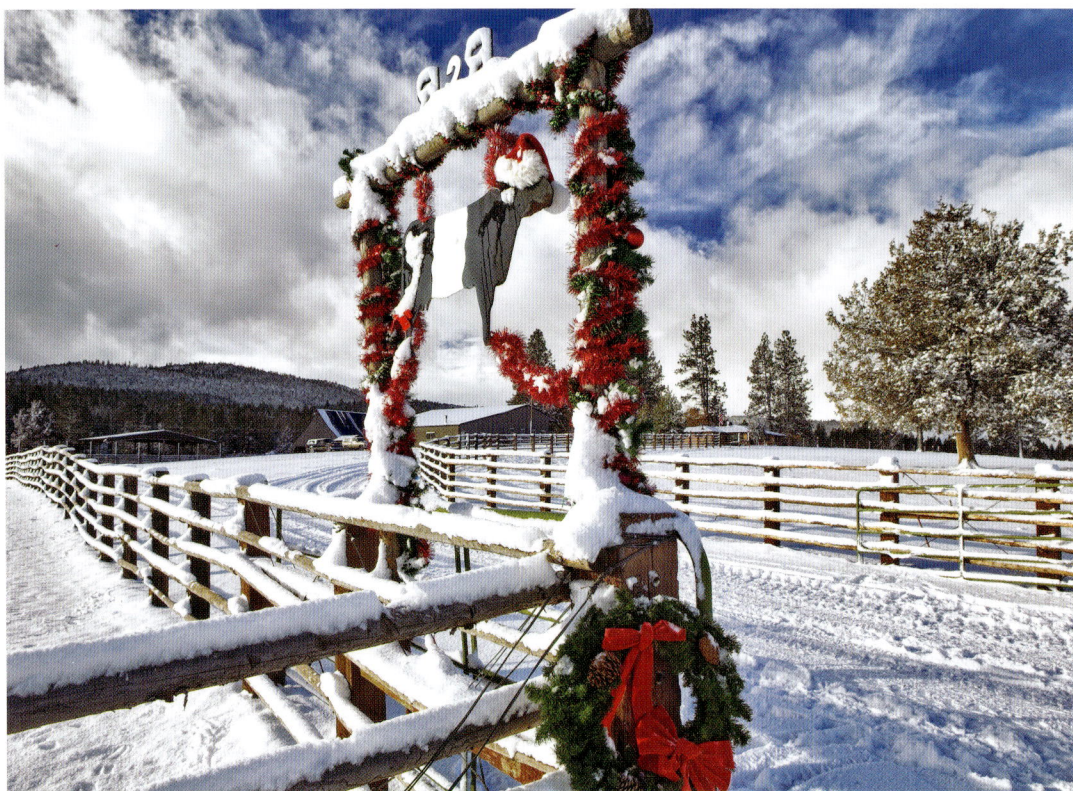

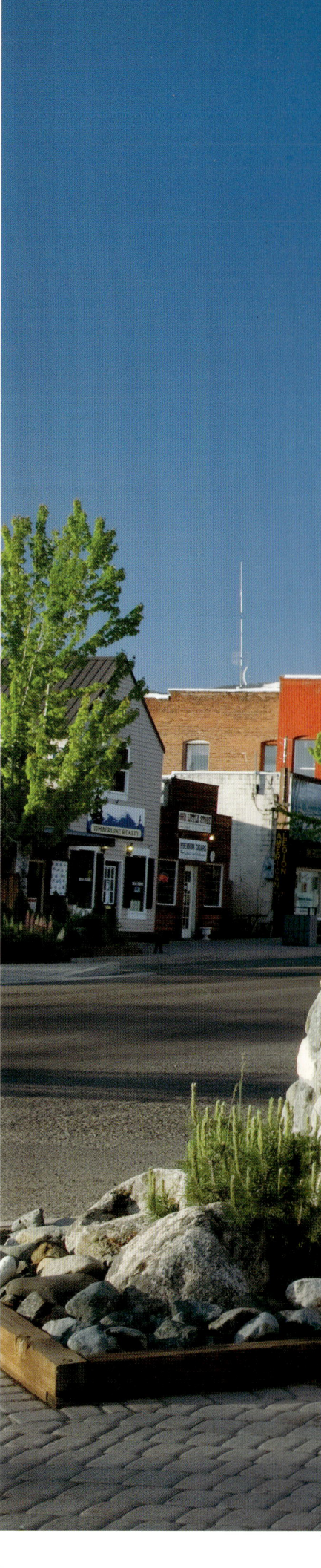

Above, top: During their heyday in the early 1900s, nearly 450 covered bridges graced Oregon's back roads. Today, the state's 50 remaining covered bridges, including this classic beauty near Mitchell, are the largest collection in the West.

Above, bottom: Holiday garlands take a new twist on a ranch near Lakeview, the seat of Lake County. The county is known for its sheep and cattle ranches, but more recently, the tongue-in-cheek Umpteenth Annual Festival of Free Flight has attracted hang gliders and paragliders.

Right: It may be referred to as the "Little Switzerland of the West," but the small city of Joseph knows how to get its cowboy on. The annual Chief Joseph Days celebration begins with the Bucking Horse Stampede through town.

Following page: The full moon rises at the end of another day in Oregon—unforgettable.

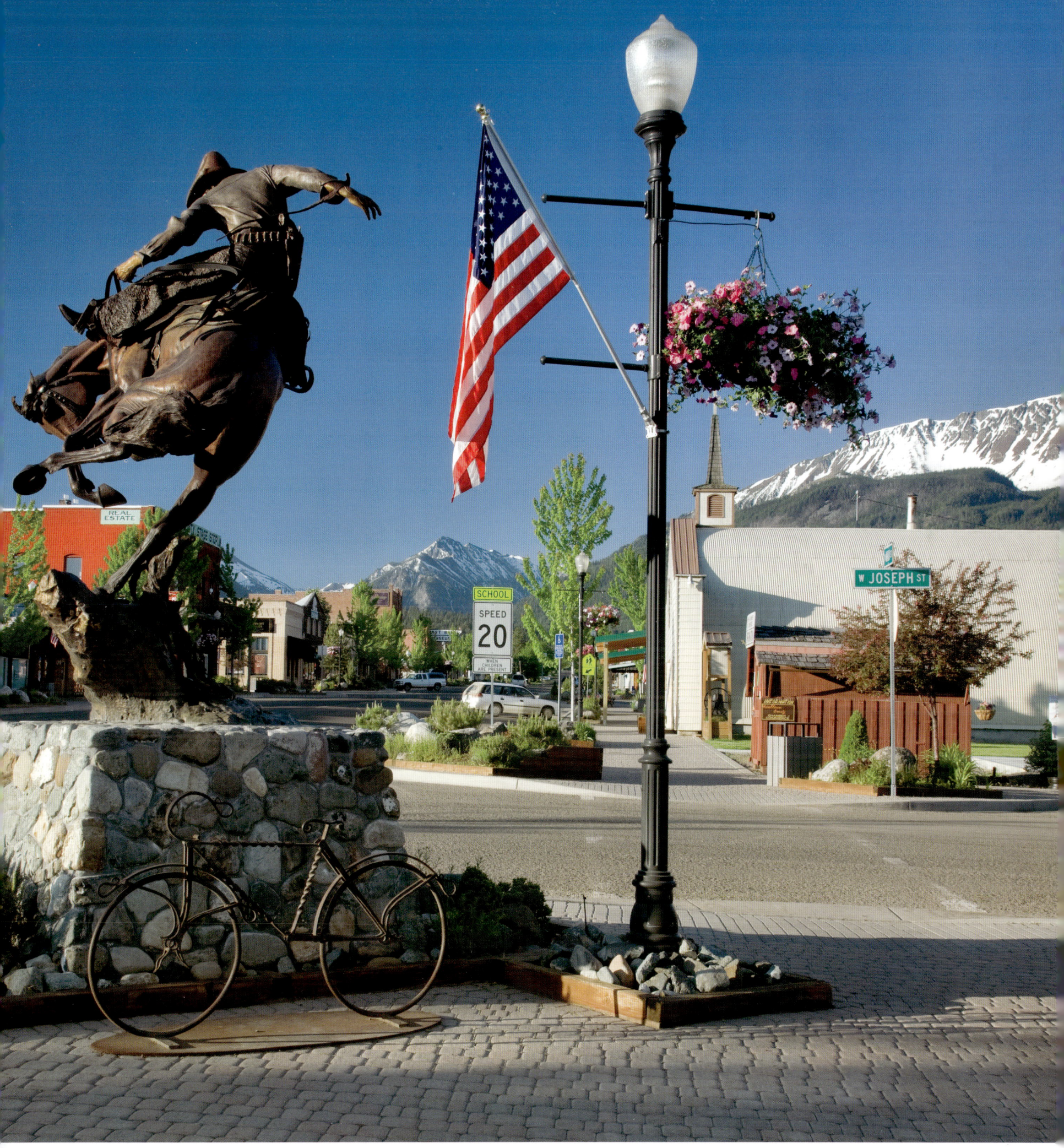

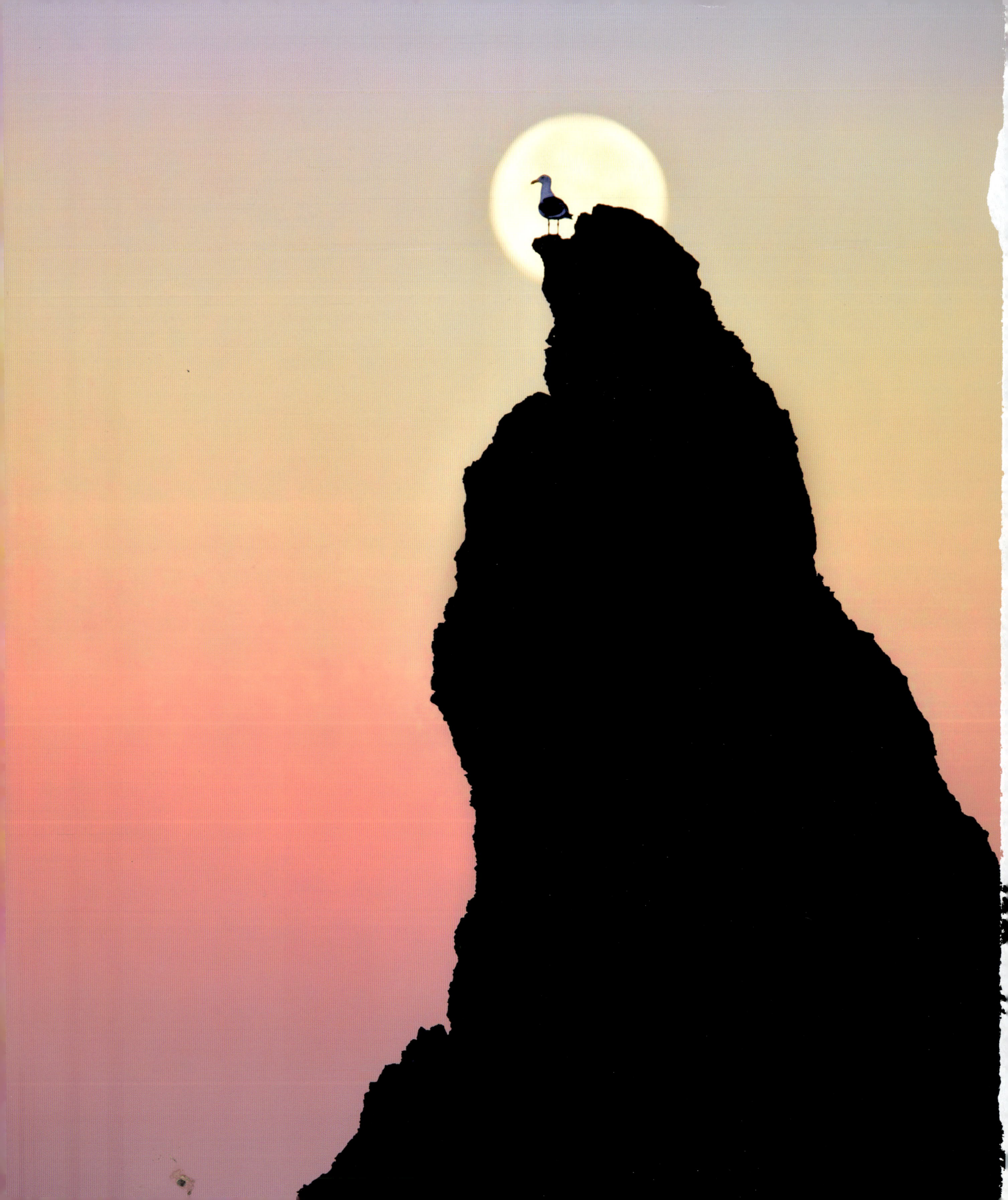